THE DEF LEPPARD STORY

by David Fricke

First published in Great Britain by Zomba Books, 165-167 High Road,
London NW10 2SG.

Cover and art direction by Andie Airfix, Satori
Designed by Cath Speight/Eian MacMeeking
Edited by Neil Jeffries/David Wingrove
Typeset by Opus
Printed by Eagle Colour Books Limited, Blantyre, Glasgow, Scotland
Additional photographs and illustrations courtesy of Robert Ellis,
Mike Rogers, Andy Smith, Phonogram, Alan Walter and Def Leppard

ISBN: 0 946391 55 6
Order No: OP46069

Exclusive distributors:

Book Sales Limited,
8/9 Frith Street,
London W1V 5TZ.

Music Sales Corporation
225 Park Avenue South,
New York, NY 10003, USA.

Music Sales Pty Limited,
120 Rothschild Avenue,
Roseberry, NSW 2018, Australia.

To the Music Trade only:
Music Sales Limited,
8/9 Frith Street,
London W1V 5TZ.

THE DEF LEPPARD STORY

by David Fricke

ANIMAL INSTINCT

ACKNOWLEDGEMENTS

Dedicated to Susan Klimley for her support, encouragement and patience

Special thanks to the members of Def Leppard – Joe Elliott, Steve Clark, Phil Collen, Rick Savage and Richard Allen – for their friendship and for their patience under interrogation. Also for their hospitality both in Holland and on tour. To Cliff Burnstein and Peter Mensch for their friendship and their help in completing this project. To Pete Willis for his honesty. To Andy Smith for his guided tours of Sheffield and to Keith Strong for his reminiscences and all the *Sheffield Star* clippings. To Sherry Ring Ginsberg for valuable assistance over the years and access to her press files. And to Kathleen Clark and her dedicated band of Leppard fans for the impressively detailed discography.

Thanks to Chris and Phil at Prism Processing for all the original colour processing and b/w prints.

Author

DAVID FRICKE is an Associate Editor of *Rolling Stone* magazine and USA correspondent for *Melody Maker*.

Lensman

ROSS HALFIN is a well-known photographer on the international rock circuit.

CHAPTER 1

[THE ACCIDENT]

"Flash bastard!"

Two men sat in their Alfa Romeo, waiting to make a left turn on to the A57 road to Sheffield, when they saw the shiny black 1984 Corvette Stingray zip by on the main road. They didn't see who was actually at the wheel, but they were certain this guy was some kind of jerk. Burning rubber like that in a fancy American sportscar that would have cost any decent working-class Englishman over a year's wages – whoever Mr. Corvette was, he deserved a good scare.

Rick Allen had no idea there was another car behind his new Corvette until the Alfa Romeo came roaring past him on a bridge. Rick had been out for a pleasant afternoon spin with his girlfriend, Miriam Barendsen, enjoying the lush green glow of the English countryside west of Sheffield on an unseasonably warm New Year's Eve. Rick had even opened up the Stingray's sunroof to soak up the sunshine and fresh air on the way back to Sheffield. Miriam was spending the Christmas holidays with Rick's family before she and the twenty-one-year-old drummer returned to Holland where he was in the middle of recording a new album with his band, Def Leppard. That afternoon, the two of them had nothing on their minds but the gorgeous weather, the promise of some jolly New Year's Eve festivities and the brand new year ahead of them.

The Alfa Romeo brought them out of their reverie – fast. Once the Alfa passed them, instead of letting the Stingray just eat his exhaust, the driver slowed up. Rick's temper started to get the better of him. He was out for a pleasure cruise, not a game of chicken. Rick tried to pass the Alfa a couple of times with no luck. This went on for almost four miles. Then Rick found an opening and pulled up alongside the Alfa. For a brief moment, Rick was window-to-window with the two punks, evil grins growing in twisted upward curves on their faces as they dangerously edged their Alfa closer to the Corvette, practically trying to push Rick and Miriam right off the road.

Rick was really mad now. He hit the accelerator and the Corvette took off at Indy 500 velocity. But with the sudden rush of speed and the disadvantage of driving an American left-hand drive vehicle on an English road, Rick didn't see the left-hand curve up ahead until it was too late. The Stingray whipped around the corner and hit a brick wall, taking a lot of the bricks with it as the car skidded along the wall, flipped over and finally landed on its roof. The Alfa Romeo took off like a shot. Police later questioned two men in connection with the accident, but they denied everything.

Miriam was trapped in the passenger seat. Rick, thrown free of the car, was in a field on the other side of the brick wall. Though he had landed on his head, a decade of playing rock & roll drums for a living had already exacted its quota of brain damage. But his left arm had been ripped off at the shoulder. Within two minutes of the accident, a nurse who lived nearby was tending to his injuries. Another nurse, who was passing by in her car, pulled over and bandaged his shoulder where the arm had been severed. The nurses, who later declined to be identified, also found the arm and packed it in a bucket of ice until the ambulance team arrived. Miriam, badly bruised, was helped out of the car and comforted at a nearby house.

Less than twenty minutes after the accident, Rick Allen was in the casualty ward of Royal Hallamshire Hospital in Sheffield, under heavy sedation. Later, though, he would recall being completely conscious in those first few minutes after the crash. Standing in that field on the precipice of total shock, suddenly realizing his left arm was no longer attached to his body, he screamed out to Miriam, "God, I'll never play the drums again!"

Rick aged 12 (centre) with his first band Smokey Blue.
OPPOSITE: Front page news, *Daily Star* 2 January, 1985.

The night before, Def Leppard bassist Rick Savage had woken up in the middle of a terrible dream. In this dream, he had been walking through an empty parking lot when a huge, ferocious dog jumped at him and clamped his jaws down on his left arm. Sav – as he was known to friends, drinking pals and the rest of Def Leppard – bolted upright in bed and felt a tingling sensation in his left arm, as if it was going numb. The next morning, he told his girlfriend, Joy Major, the sister of Rick's drum roadie Russell Major, about the dream but thought no more about it.

In the afternoon, Sav and Joy went out shopping for costumes in preparation for the annual New Year's Eve fancy dress ball at the South Seas, a popular Sheffield pub. Sav, Joy and Russell had just returned to Sav's house when the phone rang at 2:30. It was one of the band's managers, Peter Mensch. Mensch blurted out the bad news – Rick had severed his arm in a car crash that afternoon and was in intensive care at the hospital.

Sav hung up, sat down and cried while Joy and Russell, unaware of the call, were laughing it up in the kitchen. Afraid they might come out and see him, Sav tiptoed upstairs to his bedroom, still crying. When Russell finally came up and asked what was wrong, Sav told him. Then he had to go down and break the news to Joy. Within half an hour, Rick's mother and father, Geoff and Kathleen Allen, had come over from the hospital, which was only walking distance from Sav's house. Everyone sat around the dining room table, dumbfounded. Those who were not crying just sat in numbed silence.

"It was an unbelievable feeling, an emptiness," Sav says, still with considerable pain. "I've never been close to anybody that died or had something horrible happen to them before. It was a feeling I'd never experienced.

"The fact that it was New Year's Eve made it worse. It's always a time, especially around my house, where people forget whatever troubles they've got. They have a drink and the world's at peace for at least twelve hours. It was a new year, 1985, and I was thinking about future years, that Rick would never be the same again. How the hell can you celebrate New Year again, even in 1995, without thinking about this? It would always be a reminder to him."

Singer Joe Elliott was at his home in London that afternoon. His parents and grandmother were down from Sheffield for the holidays and they were all leisurely parked in front of the television when Mensch called at about four o'clock. The nearest thing to a tragedy he had ever experienced in his twenty-four years had been the death of his pet cat Tiggy in 1979. When he hung up, Joe sat on the kitchen stove and cried. His father walked up behind him, put his hand on Joe's shoulders and handed him a

MIRACLE OP FOR ROCK STAR

ummer Rick . . . his car crashed

Torn-off arm sewn back

By LYNNE GREENWOOD

MILLIONAIRE rock drummer Rick Allen has had his left arm torn off in an horrific car crash.

But doctors stitched it back in a miracle of micro-surgery.

And last night a hospital spokesman said: " We are hopeful we will be able to save it."

Rick, 21, whose British group Def Leppard are superstars in America, is described as "critical but stable" after the delicate four-hour operation.

The accident happened on New Year's Eve.

Rick was thrown out of his black Chevrolet Stingray when it le a winding moorland road near h home city of Sheffield and ove turned several times.

The arm was torn off at th shoulder.

Rick's Dutch fiancee, 22-year-o Miriam Barendsen, suffered hea injuries and had to be cut free fro the wreckage.

Rick—and the arm—were take 10 miles to Sheffield's Royal Hallan shire Hospital where the operatio

Turn to Page Two

Leppard Rick off the danger list

BUT SURGERY FAILS TO SAVE HIS ARM

THE WRECK of Rick Allen's Corvette, from which he was thrown, minus arm. Pic: Sheffield Newspapers

The wreck as photographed by Sheffield Newspapers (cutting from *Sounds*).

glass of whiskey.

"I swallowed it in one go and wiped my face. My granny is half deaf, so she couldn't figure out what I was crying about. She was too embarrassed to actually look at me. My mother just sat there and my dad . . . actually, I can't remember what my dad was saying, just things like 'Nothing you can do about it here, just wait and see.' "

That, for the time being, was all anyone could do. Joe then rang Sav in Sheffield, each sharing tears and sympathy. Joe also called Def Leppard guitarists Steve Clark and Phil Collen, who had been celebrating Christmas in Paris where they both had apartments. "I really wanted the whole lot of us to be in one room, just to be able to talk, I guess. We're always together, working, recording, touring, and you begin to take it for granted. This was one time I wanted us to be together, and it was impossible." That night, while Steve and Phil drowned their sorrows in drink in Paris, Joe Elliott celebrated New Year's Eve by playing a game of snooker with his dad, singing *Auld Lang Syne* at midnight and drinking a quiet toast to Rick with his family. "We wished him the best and hoped he'd pull through it."

While Mensch and the other Leppards kept British Telecom working overtime, a surgical team at Hallamshire Hospital led by microvascular expert Robert Page sewed Rick's arm back on in a delicate four hour operation. Rick was still under sedation when Sav and Russell visited him at the hospital on New Year's Day. Sav was pleasantly surprised by the color in Rick's left hand. "I thought great, the blood is going through. It's working."

Joe drove up from London on January 2 to visit Rick on his way back to Wisseloord Studios in Holland where the rest of Def Leppard were scheduled to resume recording, if possible. Along with Sav, Joy, and Rick's older brother and ex-Leppard road manager Robert, who had been keeping a bedside vigil and acting as *de facto* press liaison since the accident, Joe went into hospital via the laundry door to dodge the local reporters and photographers at the front step. Upstairs, he was greeted by Rick's parents and Miriam, sporting two kingsize black eyes and a badly swollen face.

Joe had done his best to avoid going to the hospital, not out of lack of concern for Rick, but because of what he was afraid he would see. Yet even his worst fears did not prepare him for the sight he saw. Rick was lying there with a few miles worth of bandage wrapped around his reattached arm. His eyelids periodically flickered open, the eyes momentarily gazing back at Joe as if in anger. Joe was convinced that Rick, although unconscious and unaware that Joe was even in the room, didn't want to see him.

Then Robert asked Joe if he wanted to feel Rick's left hand. "It's warm, have a feel," Robert said. Joe started to feel queasy, his knees began to buckle and he felt tears welling up in his eyes. Ashamed of himself, he apologized to Robert, went into the toilet and started to cry.

"I hated every minute of being there. I just didn't want to see him in that state. I'd seen this guy as a rippling, young, muscle-packed drummer that made John Bonham sound like rubbish. I don't mean any disrespect to Bonham or Led Zeppelin. But to me, this guy was the best rock drummer in the world. And in that bed, I was seeing a body that would never work the same again. I felt so bad for him, because I knew how much playing the drums meant to him."

On January 3, Def Leppard – minus their drummer – reconvened at Wisseloord Studios in Hilversum, Holland to resume work on their fourth album. The mood both at the studio and at the hotel in nearby Ood Loosdrecht was bleak, but the band had decided to continue recording in spite of Rick's condition. Indeed, they voted to continue, largely, because of it. "Most of Rick's parts at that time had been done," Joe argues, "so apart from the mental anxiety for the first week that we were obviously going to suffer, there was nothing physical to stop us from carrying on.

"But we also knew that if Rick had been conscious, if he'd been in any state to say anything about it, he would have said 'Get on with it.' We had to do it for him."

Two days later, during a late night session at the studio, the band received a fresh shipment of bad news. Rick's reattached arm had become infected and Dr. Page's surgical team, very reluctantly, had taken his left arm off again, this time permanently. "When we heard about the arm coming back off, everybody cried," Sav says grimly. "Finally, we decided, for both his sake and ours, that we had to go back to work. It strengthened our resolve. Because we knew he wouldn't want us to sit around crying over him. He wanted us to go in there and do it right."

To add to the misery, Def Leppard received an avalanche of phone calls at Wisseloord inquiring about the new opening for a drummer. Joe talked to a few of the ghouls personally, using the appropriate venom. Then, according to Phil Collen, someone came up with great, if somewhat improbable, idea. "We thought it would be real neat if Rick could answer the phone when one of those assholes called. That would have been brilliant, put him straight on the phone. That would have put 'em right."

For Def Leppard, Rick Allen's auto accident was both a beginning and an end. For Rick, it was the end of rock & roll drumming as he'd always known it. Ever since he'd joined his first semi-pro local band, Smokey Blue, at the age of 12, Rick had slammed the skins and kicked the beat with a muscular ferocity far out of proportion to his tender age and diminutive size. He was that rare combination in hard-

Def Leppard put their necks on the line with 'Mutt' Lange (second from right).

rock drumming – a mean hitter with a keen sense of timing. Unlike a lot of heavy metal show-offs who are often better at looking rough than playing tough, Rick Allen always let his thunder rip right on top of the beat, not on either side of it.

The accident meant that, at 21, he was entering adulthood with a handicap that could cost him his drumming, the only job he'd ever known. He was embarking on a long road to physical recovery and musical rehabilitation fraught with as many dangerous curves as the A57. It would be more than eighteen months before he would play before an audience again.

New Year's Eve 1984 was, for the rest of the band as well as Rick, the beginning of a two-and-a-half year grind that severely tested their patience as players and their solidarity as a group. Until Rick's Corvette hit that brick wall, Def Leppard had been a very talented, hard-working but unquestionably lucky group, blessed by nearly every good fortune rock & roll had to offer. They had emerged from the belching smokestacks and quiet working-class hearths of Sheffield, England with baby-faced good looks and a classic teenage determination to beat lifelong prison terms in the city's factories and warehouses. Within five years, Def Leppard had sold close to eight million records worldwide, at least six million of those in America alone. During the summer of 1983, the group's third album, the mega-platinum *Pyromania*, played second fiddle on the U.S. charts only to Michael Jackson's *Thriller*.

Def Leppard had also played on most of the world's biggest rock concert stages and become the idols of millions of headbangers and adoring teenage fillies. They were also quite wealthy; Rick's shiny black Corvette Stingray was ample evidence of the luxuries they could now afford.

In short, Def Leppard – whose average age was only 17 when they released their debut EP in early 1979 – had grown to manhood in a wonderland of rock & roll unreality. They paid for their success with plenty of sweat, on stage and off, but the rewards were unlike anything their parents had ever dreamed of back in Sheffield. Now, with Rick's life in the balance and his future as a drummer in question, their projected fourth album in complete disarray and the rock & roll world set to chase other heroes in their absence, Def Leppard were suddenly confronted with a serious crisis of confidence in themselves and their music. Literally overnight, they were confronted with life's harshest realities – death and failure – armed only with the glittering fantasies of pop stardom.

Largely because of their hardy working-class origins, Def Leppard –

like Rick Allen – beat the reaper. They persevered and ultimately succeeded, a little more weathered but better for the wear. Rick would drum again, the band would tour, and that fourth album, the prophetically titled *Hysteria*, would finally be released to a worldwide chorus of teenage hurrahs in the summer of 1987 – only two years overdue. The animal instinct for survival that led Joe Elliott, Rick Savage, Steve Clark and Rick Allen, along with original guitarist Pete Willis, to devote long afternoons and evenings writing their own songs and rehearsing them in a dilapidated spoon factory warehouse for two years was the same animal instinct that kept them going after Rick's accident. Def Leppard were formed in late 1977 as an alternative to the dead end nine-to-five life that awaited them in Sheffield's factories. And Def Leppard stuck together amid disaster and doubt nearly ten years later because they had no intention of ever going back to it.

Def Leppard earned their spots, so to speak, during a peculiar era in English pop. Beatlemania, psychedelia and glitter-rock were all ancient history by the time the young Leppards-to-be first picked up their instruments. Britain's Top 40 station, Radio One, and the weekly television show *Top of the Pops* peddled a saccharin diet of glitzy but superficial pop. The Beatles had waived the rules, but at the time T.Rex, the Bay City Rollers and Slade ruled the waves. So what's a poor boy gonna do 'cept sing in a rock & roll band?

The Leppards turned to heavy metal for their kicks. The bastard offspring of a three-way consummation between English blues-rock, the Cream/Jimi Hendrix power trio roar and the drug-fuelled Tolkienesque fantasies of psychedelia ("If there's a bustle in your hedgerow/Don't be alarmed now/It's just a spring clean for the May Queen" – *Stairway to Heaven*), heavy metal was all grit, grunt and hair, the only music still repulsive to parents until punk-rock came along. (And punk-rock, for all of its claims to working-class legitimacy, was basically an art-school vision of the empire in ruins.) Judas Priest, Deep Purple, Led Zeppelin, Thin Lizzy and UFO became the Leppards' daily soundtrack. By 1980, Joe Elliott had gone through four copies of Kiss' *Destroyer*.

Most of their early songs were direct emulations of their heroes. *Getcha Rocks Off* and *The Overture* on the group's 1979 EP bore the trademarks of Thin Lizzy and Rush respectively. The original twin guitar sound of Steve Clark and Pete Willis was modelled on the dual scream of Lizzy's Brian Robertson and Scott Gorham. But that nagging yeah-yeah-yeah of the glitz kids on the radio day in and day out had also left its mark. Def Leppard didn't just write riffs; they wrote songs with carefully contrived choruses that didn't just make a lot of macho barking noises in front of that twelve-string scream. The band developed a solid wall of vocal harmony that immediately impressed future co-manager Cliff Burnstein the first time he heard the *Getcha Rocks Off* EP. This was a streetwise metal band with pop potential and Burnstein believed that potential would be most fully realized in America.

The group's first two LPs, *On Through the Night* and *High 'n' Dry*, sold well Stateside, but *Pyromania*, released in February, 1983, was the big payoff. Without lightening up on the beat or turning down the guitars – now split between Clark and sharp Cockney axeslinger Phil Collen – Def Leppard released an album that satisfied a desperate mainstream FM radio hunger for songs and singers. Yet at the same time they were transcending the lumbering macho cliches of heavy metal, Leppard also dared to improve on the conservative pop values of FM and Top 40 radio. Egged on by producer Robert John "Mutt" Lange, a notorious perfectionist, they strove for quality in a field dominated by mediocrity and stomped the competition something fierce. On the Great Scoreboard of Rock History, *Pyromania* may not have eclipsed *Sgt. Pepper's Lonely Hearts Club Band*, *Who's Next* or *Physical Graffiti*, but it was *the* hard rock platter of that summer of '83.

Clouds were gathering on the horizon, though, as far back as 1980. British fans who championed the band as "the guv'nors" of the country's second generation of heavy metal killers accused Def Leppard of selling out to Yankee interests. The wave of cheers turned to a rain of beer cans by the time Leppard appeared at the 1980 Reading Festival. There was also the small matter of tax. The notorious inequity of British tax laws has caused many top pop artists to choose living abroad in lieu of paying up to ninety five per cent of their income in taxes. The success of *Pyromania*, ironically, forced Def Leppard to spend nearly all of the next three years living out of a suitcase. Still, that all seemed like small potatoes after Rick hit that brick wall on the A57.

There are few other rock bands around the world with tales of glory and horror equal to Def Leppard's. But in a pop world where too many artists simply "give the people what they want," Def Leppard are a band that succeeded beyond their wildest dreams simply by playing their best hunches. They were hard-rock fans who played music and wrote songs that *they* liked. They were also smart enough to take advice from pros like Mutt Lange when it counted the most.

Most rock biographies are about superstar artists and groups who have been set (or, indeed, have set themselves) on a lofty pedestal far apart from the crowd. Def Leppard *were* the crowd, kids who originally came from the other side of the stage. This is the classic saga of rock & roll schoolboys made good and an object lesson in how to succeed in music in spite of all the ways you can fail. From the beginning, Def Leppard had talent, desire and stamina. More than anything, though, they had good instincts. And in rock & roll, instinct is everything.

Joe on stage at Crookes: note imitation leather strides!

CHAPTER 2

CATS IN THE CRADLE

Deaf Leopard (sic) played their first gig in 1975 at Sheffield City Hall. Thin Lizzy, then on the verge of breaking big in England, opened the show with a red-hot set. But Leopard were unbeatable. According to a review of the show written by fifteen-year-old Joe Elliott, the group was delayed at Sheffield airport by fog. They took the stage fifteen minutes late, sweat dripping from their hair, running through their pancake makeup and mascara. Yet at this special homecoming show after their recent sell-out world tour, Deaf Leopard sent the screaming Sheffield crowd into heavy metal heaven, playing their biggest hits with the twenty kiloton power and mega-guitar glory that had made them Seventies superstars.

That review was never published. A poster for the show, designed with great care by Joe, disappeared into a file kept by Pete Farmery, an art teacher at King Edward VII School in Sheffield. Farmery had assigned his students to design a vivid poster. Joe's poster featured huge orange block lettering on a black background. The grade Joe received for his Deaf Leopard poster has been lost in the whirling duststorms of time. But Farmery, without realizing it, was encouraging young Joseph Elliott to pursue his rock & roll fantasies. Like all Deaf Leopard gigs, the Sheffield City Hall triumph was a figment of Joe's imagination, a pretend world full of fictitious superstar rock groups acting out his own pop star dreams. Farmery's assignments, and his understanding, would be Joe's first step in turning those dreams into reality.

"He was a real good guy," Joe says fondly. "He'd smoke his pipe and spend half our lessons just sitting around, talking about things. He used to think conversation was an art, so we'd talk about almost anything. The girls would talk about makeup, the other guys would talk about soccer."

Joe would talk about the Ian Hunter-Mick Ronson show he'd seen at Sheffield City Hall the night before, or a recent local Sparks gig. Joe Elliott, born August 1, 1959, made up his mind at an early date that he would never grow up to be a brain surgeon or a Government Minister. He was by no means stupid. He passed his exams with minimal studying. And the soaring career of Deaf Leopard, Joe's own rock & roll creation, in art and English class (Leopard concerts usually got rave reviews on homework and term papers) showed that he had considerable talent.

But all he wanted to do was rock &

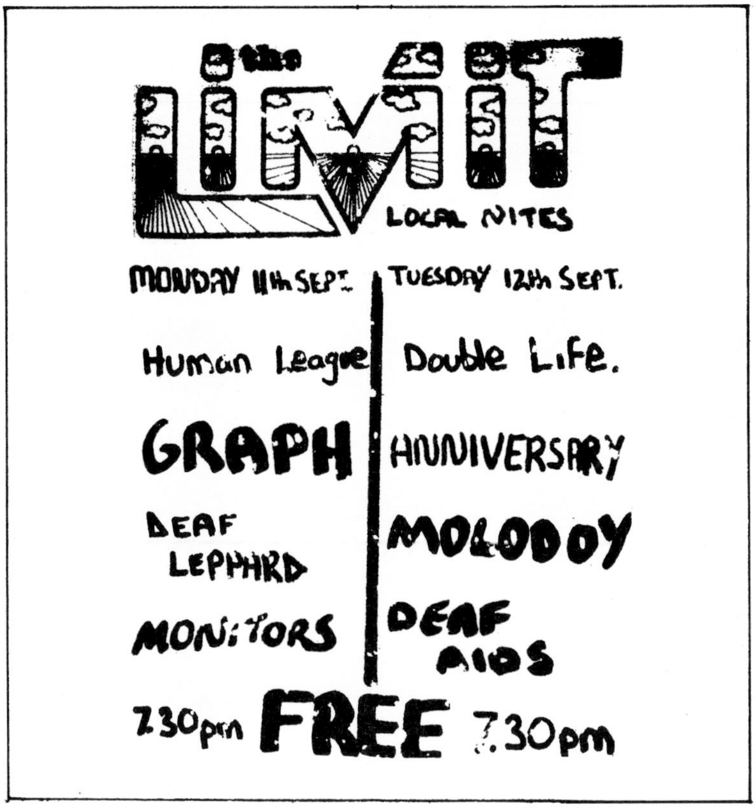

Leppard must wait

review

Def Leppard
Sheffield City Polytechnic

ACCORDING to Artery, Leppard are "positively the worst group ever to have graced this city with its presence."

That view, which was reported in an alternative publication, shows a certain bias towards bands that have been electronically tested.

Leppard are more your Thin Lizzy (well, they squeezed in Emerald and Bob Seger's Rosalie). But, dominantly, they're original material, heavy rock with more than just a touch of melody.

Time is on their side. With a drummer who looks as though he's about ready to sit O-levels, they have plenty to learn. While there's no doubting their musicianship, they have some swotting up to do on stagecraft, though that will grow as they play more concerts.

Cries of "rip-off" from drunker sections of a mainly favourable audience were unfair. Leppard aren't that derivative. Blooding a new number showed that they're still creating.

If they want to be tomorrow's band today, they could be disappointed. By the seat of singer Joe Elliott's shiny pants they're young enough to wait until the day after.

Keith Strong

roll. There would be plenty of time for adult responsibility and nine-to-five misery when schooldays came to a grinding halt and it came time to join the spiritless, embattled Sheffield workforce. There was a time when Sheffield was known the world over for its fine cutlery. If your knife or fork was stamped "Made in Sheffield", you were eating with class. By the 1970s, though, the city's steel industry was in the vise-like grip of economic recession. The machine shops and factories, that had traditionally been the next stop after leaving school for generations of Sheffield's youth, faced a bleak future. If you didn't get one of those precious dead-end sweatshop jobs, you'd probably end up with no job at all.

Joe believed rock & roll somehow, someway, was his ticket out of nowheresville. Writing about imaginary rock band Deaf Leopard and the slightly less legendary Blind Tigers, another phantom band of rock & roll killers, was only one demonstration of his belief that music would eventually set him free. Joe also had a passion for record collecting, specializing in groups that most of his classmates either despised or had never heard of. His upstairs bedroom in the two-storey brick terrace house at 61 Crookes Road was a monument to the unsung achievements of obscure hard rock bands like Budgie, Stray and Trapeze.

Paramount among Elliott raves, though, were the brilliant English glam-punk band Mott The Hoople and its chief singer-songwriter Ian Hunter. He collected every Mott and Hunter-related record he could get his hands on and memorized passages from Hunter's mid-Seventies autobiography, *Diary of a Rock & Roll Star*. When Joe started writing song lyrics, they were heavily influenced by Hunter's own unique mix of hard-bitten street lingo, rock & roll road life and funhouse Dylanesque imagery.

On Sundays, Joe and a neighborhood pal named Andy Smith would go to Sheffield Top Rank for local appearances by touring U.K. bands. During the week, the Top Rank was a discotheque catering, in Smith's words, "to posey over-twenty-fives." Sundays, however, were reserved for rock under the banner "Improvisations." At the Top Rank, Joe and Andy rocked their Sundays away to bands like Judas Priest, AC/DC and the post-Hunter version of Mott.

The Mott show, Andy recalls, was part of a "pyjama jump" series periodically held at the Top Rank. At "pyjama jumps", you could only be admitted if you were dressed in a nightgown of the opposite sex. This was, of course, a great excuse for getting outrageously dressed up and outrageously drunk. Smith actually has in his possession photos of Joe from that Mott-pyjama night decked out in a ladies' nightgown and heavy makeup, looking like a cross between Kiss and a transvestite grandma.

Between shows at the Top Rank, Joe and Andy hung out in the Wapentake, a basement pub underneath the Grosvenor House Hotel in downtown Sheffield. Local hard rock bands often played there, but the principal attractions were a DJ who shared Joe's tastes in British hard rock and a jukebox stocked with lots of Mott the Hoople. The Wapentake was quite a pit. Peeling wallpaper and graffiti scrawled across any available bare surface dominated the decor. "You didn't dare touch the walls or the seats, it was so filthy," Andy Smith claims. You could get high just walking through the front door because of all the marijuana smoke curling up to the ceiling. "It was a dirty hole," Andy swears, "and we loved it."

Watching bands, buying records and worshipping at the foot of the Wapentake jukebox were just preparation for Joe's great leap forward. Joe Elliott was determined to be a rock star. He certainly had all the right qualifications. He had a name for his band – Deaf Leopard. He looked pretty good, with long straight hair, a muscular frame with long lean legs and a ruggedly handsome face highlighted by striking eyes almost Oriental in shape. Aside from limited experience playing guitar and drumming at local jam sessions, Joe had no musical experience to speak of. But he had plenty of ambition. All he needed was four other guys to help make his dream come true.

Unbeknown to Joe, Rick Savage was dreaming the same dreams in another brick terrace house at 59 Forres Road, only five minutes' walk from Crookes Road. The son of a typesetter at the *Sheffield Star* newspaper, Sav was born December 2, 1960, the youngest of three boys. His oldest brother John was a junior draftsman-turned-chef. The second eldest, Brian, was a talented clarinet and piano player who was away at college most of the time studying science. Sav, in turn, had his choice of careers. He was either going to become a rock & roller or a world famous soccer player.

John Savage helped out with the rock & roll part. When Sav was ten, John showed him how to play Rod Stewart's *Maggie May* on an old acoustic guitar. "I didn't know a D from an A," Sav admits, "but the songsheet had these chord boxes that told you where to put your fingers. Within the evening, I'd learned the whole song. I was strumming away and singing miles out of key." When he was twelve, Sav was the envy of his schoolmates because he'd learned to play Don McLean's *American Pie* all the way through.

But most of Sav's early years revolved around soccer. In his last year of junior school, when he was ten, Sav was selected for an all-star boy's team, Sheffield Schools, to play teams from other English cities. During the three years that Sav played with Sheffield Schools, the team was unbeaten.

His performance with Sheffield Schools did not go unnoticed by scouts from the city's two professional soccer teams, Sheffield United and Sheffield Wednesday. Scouts from both teams approached Sav and his parents about enrolling the boy in apprentice team programs, the first step in a young soccer prodigy's rise to professional status. Sav, then fourteen, was faced with a serious dilemma. As a pro soccer fan, he was a devoted Sheffield Wednesday supporter. Except Sheffield Wednesday were at the bottom of the league. His father advised Sav to go with Sheffield United, a much better team with championship prospects.

Against his better instincts, Sav elected to sign on with Sheffield United. He felt out of place with both his junior teammates and the pros, whom he'd never rooted for anyway. He did not play to the best of his ability and, three months before he was due to leave Tapton Comprehensive School, Sav was dropped from the team.

"I had a chance to join a lot of other clubs, but that two years changed my mind about soccer. I was introduced at an early age to the backstage aspect of it and I wasn't impressed with the way the game was handled. It wasn't how I expected it to be. Some of the people weren't very nice. The people you see on television, the stars, weren't the hardened professionals you think they are.

"Also," he adds, "there might have been the fear of being rejected again."

At the same time his interest in a professional soccer career started to wane, Sav's interest in music picked up. Like most English kids his age, he grew up on a mixed diet of Sixties classics and Top Forty glitter-pop. Sav's early favourites included Sweet, Slade, T.Rex, pop thrush Kate Bush (the first single he ever bought was *Wuthering Heights*) and his older brother John's old Who singles. Together with a Tapton schoolmate, Tony Kenning, Sav started to think about forming a band. Sav and Tony would frequently sit around the dinner table at Tony's house and discuss "The Plan".

Gear was a problem. Tony drummed on a hatbox before persuading his father, a well-to-do salesman, to lend him money for a real drum kit (Tony paid him back with money earned on a paper round). Sav ordered an electric guitar from his mother's shopping catalog. Two schoolchums, guitarist Peter Doubleday and singer Nicholas McKay, rounded out Sav and Tony's living room combo.

"We managed to get two songs down," according to Sav. "One of them was *White Queen* by Queen. We didn't have a bass player, but we didn't really know what we needed a bass player for. We could hear the guitars, the drums and the cymbals. If there was anything we could afford to lack, it was a bass."

Word got around Tapton about Sav and Tony's as-yet-unnamed combo. Pete Willis, a year ahead of Sav in Tapton, was one of the students who inquired about jam session possibilities. Pete got his chance at a weekday gathering of the Tapton youth club. Sav and Tony set up to play a few numbers and Pete, together with a bass-playing friend of his named Paul Hampshire, joined in. That was the humble beginning of Atomic Mass.

Technically, Pete Willis, born February 16, 1960, was a much better player than Sav. Self-taught, he was mesmerized at the age of eight by a video on television of Jimi Hendrix playing *Voodoo Chile*. He tried building his own guitar out of plywood, using ketchup bottle tops for control knobs. It didn't have any strings, but that was okay because at first he just used it to pose in the mirror with. At twelve, he finally got a proper electric guitar, playing it through the family record player.

Pete and his buddy Paul Hampshire had rather advanced tastes in music compared to Sav and Tony. Although

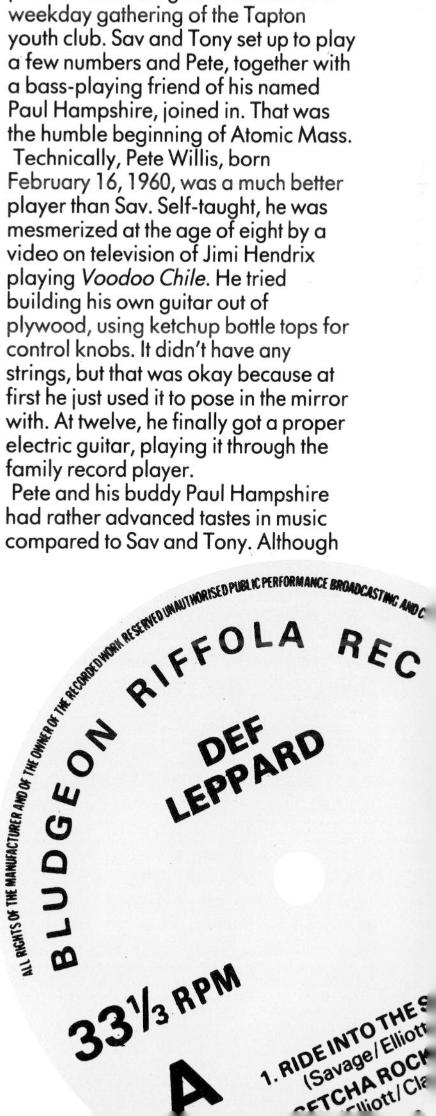

As seen in the *Sheffield Star* 5 October, 1978 – the first ever press feature.

they liked a lot of the same hard rock bands, Pete and Paul would often jam out Santana and Pink Floyd-style in Pete's living room at night until his parents complained about the noise. With Sav and Tony, Pete now had a chance to crank it up with a real band.

Atomic Mass did not play any paying jobs. Their only proper performance was at Tapton in the school gym. A teacher heard the lads jamming around and suggested they put on a show. Pete Willis says about a dozen people turned up to see the band, which at that point included a singer, Paul Holland, and a bass player named Andy Nicholas who took over from Hampshire.

Neither Sav or Pete realized it at the time, but Joe Elliott saw that show. "I remember one of the PA stacks broke down. And during one Queen song, Sav sat down on the stage to play. It was really funny." Joe recalls the Atomic Mass set list that night also included Led Zeppelin's *Whole Lotta Love* and *Boris the Spider* by The Who.

"We weren't writing any stuff of our own," Sav says of the Mass. "We did a few Deep Purple songs, some Queen tracks, and maybe a Slade song or two. Then it got to the stage where we thought about getting serious about this band thing. It was getting close to the time when we would be leaving school."

Sav, Pete and Tony agreed to stay together after finishing school in the summer of 1977. Following a short tenure stacking cans of beans on supermarket shelves, Pete got a job with the British Oxygen Company as a junior draftsman. Sav and Tony both became trainee technicians at British Rail in the telecommunications department. But leaving school meant that they couldn't use Tapton for rehearsals. Tony was designated to hunt for a rehearsal room where the three of them could make all the racket they wanted after hours with no complaints from parents or neighbors.

"I'd spend dinnertimes and evenings walking around old factories," Tony says. "I'd plead with the landlords, asking them if they had any space they could spare. I was also asking other bands, too, if they knew of any rooms in Sheffield. I got a few names and addresses and checked them all out. Finally, I managed to get one."

In September, Tony found a space in a spoon factory on Bramall Lane, a block away from the Sheffield United playing field (an irony hardly lost on Sav). The room, two and a half floors up and accessible only by a rickety outdoor stairway, was part of an old brick ironworks complex, typical of the steel and metalworks factories that rose up on the Northern English countryside during the Industrial Revolution. The place was tiny and dirty, but it was cheap. Tony got the room for £5 a week (about $8).

Things were getting serious. Sav agreed to take up the bass, leaving Pete to handle all guitar duties. The three also concurred that they needed a singer, badly. Which was perfect, because around the block from Sav's house was a would-be singer who needed a band.

"I knew this guy, Joe Elliott," Pete explains. "I'd seen him one or two times at a youth club, Columbus, in an area of Sheffield called Crosspool. His friend Craig was a friend of mine. Craig must have told Joe that I had an amplifier that I was interested in selling. So Joe turned up at my parents' house one day and said 'I hear you've got an amplifier. I just bought a guitar and I was wondering if you'd be interested in selling that amplifier.'

"I thought 'This guy's got cheek. He's got to be a good front man.' You could see it in him straightaway. So I said 'Well, do you fancy having a crack at singing for my band?' "

Joe remembers it differently. He claims that he missed his evening bus home from work one night. He started walking and happened to run into Willis, whom he vaguely knew on the street. They had a "starting a band" discussion and carried on from there.

In any case, the same month that Tony scored the rehearsal space, Sav, Tony and Pete "auditioned" Joe up in Joe's combination bedroom-and-record-museum. The audition consisted of asking Joe if he was willing to chip in a few pounds a week for rehearsal room rent and to hire a decent PA system. No problem, said Joe, whose income as a storekeeper for Osborn-Mushet Tools in Sheffield barely kept him in records and drink. He was in. (As for the PA, Joe was better than his word. He would later take out a bank loan in his own name for three hundred pounds to buy a PA, at twenty-five pounds interest.)

"His father gave us a funny look when we trouped into Joe's house," Sav laughs. "Joe ushered us up to his

Spoon factory rehearsal rooms 1977-79, minus bottles of sour milk.

bedroom and we talked for ages and ages, playing records. By the end of the night, it was signed, sealed and delivered. He was the new singer. We'd never even heard him sing a note. But it was his attitude and his ideas about being in a band. We thought 'God, this guy really means business.'"

"A lot of the band's success later on was due to Joe's pushiness," Tony asserts. "He was the one with real ambition, more than anybody else. When we first met him, he already had a name for the band and posters made up with the band's name on them – all this before he was even in a band."

Joe had wasted no time in turning the discussion to his favourite topic, Deaf Leopard. He told the other three about his schooldays designing tickets and posters for Deaf Leopard concerts and writing reviews of Leopard's imaginary sell-out gigs. Then he pulled out one of his Leopard posters for their inspection. It consisted of a photocopy of an American policeman with his nightstick drawn and a shakey drawing of a leopard with an earring. Pete Willis says the leopard "actually looked more like a moggy (house cat), nothing like a proud leopard."

"It was really two-bob, real silly-looking," Sav agrees. "But he had the posters, he had the idea and he had the name. After a while, it started to sound pretty good to me. And Pete and Tony didn't seem to mind.

After a few weeks, there was some grumbling about the spelling of Deaf Leopard. It was the high season for punk-rock in England and bands like the Flying Lizards and the Boomtown Rats (featuring future Live Aid impressario Bob Geldof) were all the rage. Deaf Leopard was keen to get out and play, but not to a pack of pasty-faced, spikey-topped chainsaw-carrying troublemakers. Joe says it was Tony Kenning's idea to change the spelling of the name. Tony can't remember. Everybody insists that the resemblance of the new spelling – Def Leppard – to Led Zeppelin was strictly unintentional. Whatever, it sounded good, looked good and eventually even Pete Willis, who thought the whole idea was "daft," came to like it.

Formal rehearsals did not commence immediately. It took several weeks to make the spoon factory room relatively inhabitable. The band decorated the room with Peter Gabriel and Ian Hunter-Mick Ronson posters (an Elliott touch) and used empty wooden boxes and battered old sofas for sitting on. They tacked moulded old carpets on the wooden floor so the guitars, drums and amps would not get scratched up.

Andy Smith, who by virtue of his keen

an

Week 4

15

16

U.F.O : Ci

+ Dial hou

17 Wednesday

Penthouse

£13

Porterhouse

with Bitter S

~~Canc~~

Crowle Comm

£45. (call

20 Saturday

Rotherh

21 Sunday

interest in music and friendship with Joe became a roadie and van driver for Leppard, says his strongest memory of Bramall Lane is the smell of sour milk. There was an old sink in the room, but it was so crusted with rust that no one dared to drink the water. Instead, an electric kettle was brought in for making tea and coffee. Someone usually bought a pint of milk for the tea and coffee and, invariably, it would never get used up. The milk would be left in its container behind an amp or a chair where it was forgotten – until it went sour.

Band meetings were held in the Sheldon Hotel pub on Denby Street, two blocks from the rehearsal room. The place catered mostly to steel workers and Sheffield United fans who argued about the day's football action on their way home. On many evenings, Def Leppard commandeered a table and, over pints of ale, worked out song lists, discussed gig possibilities and talked out future plans, like someday selling out Sheffield City Hall.

That day was still far off. At Joe Elliott's first official rehearsal with Def Leppard in late November of '77, he sang an infamous, out-of-key version of Led Zeppelin's *Stairway to Heaven* on a microphone borrowed from former Atomic Mass singer Paul Holland. Joe had to sing the song an octave lower because he couldn't reach Robert Plant's high notes on the record. The band also had a crack at David Bowie's *Suffragette City* and *Jailbreak* and *Emerald* by Thin Lizzy.

Despite that rather unpromising start, Def Leppard plunged headfirst into original songwriting. Joe, as the singer, agreed to write his own lyrics. He was only too happy to get a chance to emulate his hero Ian Hunter. What he came back with was pretty dreadful.

"He came to me one day and said he'd written lyrics," says Sav. "They were very everyday sort of lyrics, just what Hunter might have written when he was Joe's age. 'I remember travelling on the bus to Rotherham. . .' That sort of thing. They were alright, but not the sort of thing we wanted. I asked him if he could make them a bit more abstract,a bit more special. He said 'Like what?' I gave him a few examples, like Led Zeppelin. Joe came back the next day with all these new lyrics."

The song was called *Misty Dreamer.* The rest of Leppard were extremely impressed. Sav suggested an idea for a quiet bridge in the song and by the time they were finished with it, they had their own seven-minute *Stairway to Heaven.* By the time Leppard recorded its debut album, most of the song had been scrapped and Sav's quiet part turned into the basis for *Sorrow Is a Woman* but *Misty Dreamer*, for all of its rickety naivety, was Def Leppard's first complete original song. They rehearsed the number ten times a night, along with *Jailbreak* and *Suffragette City.*

By the time Christmas '77 rolled around, the four-piece Leppard felt confident enough to play for their friends. They invited a handful of pals down to Bramall Lane for a holiday party and performance. The Leppards put colored paper over the lights in the room and rounded up some flashy stage wear.

"We played five songs with about six people sitting around us," Joe chortles as he describes Def Leppard's first "live" show. "We even got an encore."

Still, something was missing. Pete was a good rhythm player, particularly adept at tight chorded riffs (he wrote most of Leppard's early *War Child*, noticeably modelled on Black Sabbath's *Paranoid*,)but he was not a strong lead soloist. Besides, one of the Leppards' favourite bands at the time, Thin Lizzy, had one of the tightest twin-axe teams in the British Isles, Brian Robertson and Scott Gorham. Their two guitars curled around each other in harmonic caress one minute, breaking into dynamite dogfights the next, accelerating the hard rock of songs like *Jailbreak* and *The Boys Are Back in Town* with their dramatic guitar showdowns.

That was the guitar sound Def Leppard craved. Coincidentally, Pete Willis was spending his Wednesdays at Stannington College on the north side of Sheffield, where he attended college-level classes as part of his training with the British Oxygen Company. One particular Wednesday, Pete was reading a guitar effects manual in the school library when a teenager about his age with light-red hair spotted the book, came up to him and asked "Do you play?" Pete said yes and told him about his band, Def Leppard.

The red-haired fellow was also a guitar player, named Steve Clark. Steve asked Pete if his band needed a second guitarist and Pete cooly suggested that Steve maybe stop by Bramall Lane during Leppard's next rehearsal. A few nights later, Steve ran into Pete and Joe at a Judas Priest show at Sheffield City Hall. In the bar, the three talked about music and equipment, Pete and Steve getting into a friendly game of one-upmanship, taunting each other with the spectacular array of guitar gear they each had, when in fact neither had much besides the cheapest essentials.

Before they split up that night, Pete and Joe repeated their invitation to pop down to the spoon factory for a get-acquainted jam.

Pete and Joe did not realize it at the time, but Steve Clark was the second guitarist Def Leppard were looking for. A native of the Hillsborough section of northern Sheffield, born April 23, 1960, Steve was turned on to music at an early age by his parents, who had a collection of early rock & roll records that included classic sides by the Shadows and guitarist Duane Eddy. One Christmas eleven-year-old Steve petitioned his parents for a guitar. His father Barry, a freelance cab driver, said he could have one only if he took guitar lessons.

For a year, Steve studied classical guitar with a local music teacher, patiently learning Bach and Vivaldi pieces at the same time he was trying to copy Led Zeppelin records. By the time he ran into Pete Willis at Stannington, he'd left his classical studies behind. Still, he'd assimilated his lessons well, becoming adept at slick intricate soloing between fuzzed-up barrages of hammer-and-anvil chords. He was able to play Led Zeppelin's *Stairway to Heaven* note

ABOVE: Original EP cover artwork (printed black on white).
BELOW: At Crookes Workingmens Club, Sheffield, June 1979.

for note as well as Thin Lizzy's *Don't Believe a Word* and *Anthem* by the Sensational Alex Harvey Band (SAHB guitarist Zal Cleminson was a major Clark influence). With Pete Willis laying down a hard riff foundation under Steve's alternating rhythm assault and sharp articulate lead breaks, Def Leppard could have a pretty snazzy two-pronged guitar attack.

Steve Clark fulfilled his promise in spades when he turned up at Bramall Lane on January 29, 1978. He wasn't too impressed with the "real grotty shithole" Def Leppard called a rehearsal room, but it was better than nothing. After plugging in, he suggested the five of them have a go at Lynyrd Skynyrd's popular guitar freakout *Free Bird*. Clark then proceeded to dazzle the other Leppards with his ability to play not only the song itself but the lengthy solo passage at the end as well. Now they were five.

"We also played him the two songs we had written," says Sav. "That really impressed him. All the bands he'd played with before hadn't even tried to write songs. Steve also had a lot of songwriting ideas of his own, so this was a way to give him a shot."

It wasn't long before Steve proved how invaluable he was to Def Leppard's future. Sav will never forget the day the Leppards, minus Steve, convened for rehearsal one night after work. The playing usually started at 6pm, but by 6:15, 6:30, Steve was still unaccounted for.

"Suddenly, we heard these footsteps on the cobblestones outside in the courtyard of the spoon factory. Then the footsteps came up the stairs. The door burst open and Steve raced across the room. He picked up his guitar where he'd left it the day before and started playing this riff that he later said had come to him on the bus on the way down. It was a brilliant riff, but he didn't say anything to anybody when he first came in, in case he forgot it. He just ran across the room, picked up his guitar and started playing this riff. That riff became the basis for *Wasted*.

"But he had more than just the riff. He'd put chords after it for the bridge and he had an idea for the middle section. He walked off that bus with an instant song. Fucking brilliant."

With Steve in the band and Joe gaining confidence as a lyricist, Def Leppard's songwriting accelerated at remarkable speed, considering they had yet to perform live (the Christmas party "show" not withstanding). Over half the songs that would later appear on the group's independent EP and debut album were written within the first six months of Steve's arrival, along with a few numbers that went unreleased like the full-throttle stomp *Glad I'm Alive* and the Zep-like epic *World Beyond the Sky*. *Overture*, a seven-minute mini-opera modelled on the complex power-rock suites of the Canadian trio Rush, was written in one night.

The Leppards were not exactly working under optimum conditions, however. The skimpy six foot doorway leading into the rehearsal room meant the band had to carefully measure all amps and PA gear before purchase, to make sure they could get it all through the door. To move the equipment in meant carrying it two hundred yards from the street across the factory courtyard and then up a total of forty-one steps. In the evening, the stairway was particularly treacherous; it was lit by a single lightbulb, which also happened to be the only one in the entire courtyard.

Day jobs put added strain on the Leppard rehearsal regimen. Steve had it especially tough since his job as a lathe operator at GEC Traction, a company that produced parts for electric train motors, included nightwork. He'd do one week of days, then one week of nights, which meant the band either rehearsed at very strange hours or without Steve at all. "It really fucked up rehearsal schedules," Steve admits, "but the rest of the guys persevered with it."

Curious to see how they sounded, Def Leppard frequently taped rehearsals

DEF LEPPARD's EP, which has been getting played on Radio One and has resulted in hundreds of inquiries, has almost sold out of its original pressing. There are a few copies still available for £1.00 plus a 12½ stamp from Revolution Records, The Gallery, Sheffield. It's likely that a further pressing of the EP will be undertaken shortly and may receive widespread distribution through one of the independents.

ABOVE: Small ad in *Sounds* April 1979.

Joe "Zeff" Elliott

Steve Clark

Pete Willis

Rick Savage

Frank Noon

Side One

RIDE INTO THE SUN
Savage / Elliott

GETCHA ROCKS OFF
Savage / Elliott
Clark / Willis

Side Two

THE OVERTURE
Savage / E
Clark / Wi

Recorded at Fairview Studios Hull Nov. 1978

Pete Willis – guitar (lead)
Steve Clark – guitar (lead)
Joe Elliott – lead vocals
Rick Savage – bass guitar & vocals
Frank Noon – drums

Engineered by Roy Neave & Keith Herd
Produced by Def Leppard
Art work by Dave Jeffery
Photography by John Wood

33 ⅓ r.p.m.

Thanks to
Tony Kenning
Paul Ainsbury
Kevin Clark
Ian Flint
Russ Major
Craig Robertshaw
Andy Smith
Keith Strong
Pete Titterton
Dave Walker
Gary Ward
Rent-a-Crowd

Frank Noon – courtesy of "The Next Band"

on a cassette recorder placed in the middle of the room. If the drums were too loud, they moved the tape machine closer to the guitar amps or the PA speakers. The quality of the recordings, naturally, was abysmal. At least it gave Leppard an idea of how far they were progressing as players and songwriters. They had yet to face the ultimate test, though. After nine months of concentrated writing and rigorous rehearsing, Def Leppard still had not played in front of a real audience. And Steve Clark was getting fed up. Real bands played real gigs for real people.

At a UFO gig in Sheffield, Steve told Joe in no uncertain terms that he was quitting the band, that he was bored with rehearsing. On a group vacation in June 1978, Steve repeated his threat to the entire band. "Steve left the band about eight times during these rehearsals," Joe claims. "He always got drunk and said 'I want to play in a band that gigs, I'm fed up with rehearsing.'

"But this time I panicked, because I knew if Steve left, it would be the end of the band."

Some time before that, Joe and his pal Andy Smith had made the acquaintance of a local Sheffield record freak nicknamed Bootleg Bill. A nice guy without much else going for him, Bill heard about Joe's new band and offered to help out, maybe book'em a date or two. With Steve ready to jump ship any day, Joe asked Bootleg Bill if he could round up a gig for Def Leppard, pronto. Amazingly, Bill delivered. He booked a show for them at Westfield School, located in a suburban area of Sheffield. There was no money in it (a teacher later paid the band £5 out of his own pocket) and Leppard only had three days to rehearse. Still, it was a gig.

On the surface of it, Def Leppard's public debut at 9pm, July 18, 1978 was a modest affair. They smuggled beer into the school in Tony Kenning's drum kit. The show was held in a small auditorium for a crowd of about one hundred and fifty schoolkids, mostly fourteen- and fifteen-year-old girls, and the band's dressing room was a classroom. It took three trips in Andy Smith's father's car to get all of Leppard's equipment – including a borrowed PA – from Bramall Lane to Westfield, a forty minute drive each way. And the opening number was a disaster.

"What happened was that just as we were about to go on, we realized we hadn't tuned the guitars," Joe explains. "So we had to get one of the guys helping us – I think it was Russell Major – to bring Steve's Marshall amp into the dressing room. We tuned up on that. But when Russell set it up again on stage, he left the switch on standby.

"Steve plugged in and walked to the front of the stage, looking brilliant in his tight jeans and long blond hair. All ready to go into the first song, *World Beyond the Sky*, he did this windmill arm motion, just like Pete Townshend, for the big opening chord – and nothing happened. No power. Everybody in the audience was laughing. After a few seconds, we started all over again.

Steve wasn't the only Leppard with problems. Halfway through one song, Joe forgot the lyrics and began singing about carpet slippers, belting out the first thing that came into his head.

Leppard in top spot at Dial House

YOUNG Sheffield heavy-weight hopefuls Def Leppard top a Dial House S.C. bill this week with rock'n'roll band the Rockets as special guests.

Fronted by singer Joe Elliott, the heavy rock five-piece have a date tomorrow at the Far Lane club, where they previously played as support to top Sheffield outfit Bitter Suite.

Despite Steve's technical difficulty and Joe's memory lapse, the Westfield show was a memorable beginning. All but one of the songs they played during the fifty-minute set were originals; they saved Thin Lizzy's *Jailbreak* for the encore. The audience demanded one too. Andy Smith recalls that a number of schoolgirls in attendance fell in love with Joe, who dazzled the dolls in his tight white jumpsuit (on which his mother had embroidered the name "Zeff," short for Joseph, above the breast pocket).

After the show, the Leppards plucked roses from a small garden outside the auditorium to give to their girlfriends. Someone took a photo of everyone together, the girls clutching their roses in celebration.

By the time Joe Elliott finally got home that night, his mom and dad were already in bed. "I was sneaking past their bedroom. Unfortunately, our floorboards creak and I woke them up. My dad came out and said 'How did it go, lad?' And I just went crazy. 'Oh, it was great! They were cheering for us, just like a real band. They all clapped and came down to the front of the stage, just like they do on TV on *Top of the Pops*.'

"He was real happy for me, too. From then on, I had their blessing to go out and play rock & roll."

Stardom was slow in coming after Westfield. Def Leppard didn't play another live show until August 26, five weeks later. Bootleg Bill scored a booking for the band as part of an outdoor festival in the accurately named Pitsmoor, a working class neighborhood in south Sheffield. The organizers set up a PA system in a field overlooking a depressing cluster of industrial buildings, using an outlet in a neighboring house for a power supply. All the gear was connected to a single long extension cable with four sockets in it. There was no lighting – and no stage. When the sun set in the middle of Leppard's set, Andy Smith, Russell Major and Ian Flint, a friend of Joe and Andy's, turned on their car headlights to illuminate the stage. The festival was cut short later in the evening when an elderly woman in one of the houses adjoining the field called the police to complain about the noise. The headline band, a local jazz combo, was yanked off in mid-set.

The band's next engagement seemed a little more promising. George Webster, who managed a club in central Sheffield called The Limit, had initiated a series of two-day festivals highlighting local talent. The Leppards, who frequented the Limit, bugged Webster to give them a shot. He finally caved in and added them to a September 11-12 local talent bill. The newspaper ad for the shows that ran in the *Sheffield Star* marked the first occasion Def Leppard's name appeared in print.

There was no money in the Limit gig – admission was free – and the line-up was iffy to say the least. Headlining on Leppard's night, September 11, was a new Sheffield electronic-pop group called the Human League, who coincidentally rented a rehearsal space across the courtyard from Leppard in the Bramall Lane foundry. A couple of other weirdo bands, Ton Trick and Graph (a drummerless proto-synth-rock trio), rounded out the evening. The show was reviewed favourably in the national music magazine *Record Mirror*, with the notable exception of Leppard's set. "Deaf Leopard (sic) were HM as HM always was and always will be," carped writer Chris Westwood. "Crosses, macho poses, bludgeon riffola that even the Sabs abandoned years ago and – ironically, me thought – the only band to screw the audience for an encore." Joe says that is English sarcasm, that in fact Leppard had screwed the Limit crowd by *playing* an encore when, in Westwood's opinion, they didn't deserve it. The reason Leppard did an encore was because the audience, stocked with a contingent of band friends and workmates dubbed Rent-A-Crowd, insisted.

Rent-A-Crowd came in handy when it came to coaxing pub owners to book Leppard. At one show in Barnsley, Rent-A-Crowd turned out in such force that the bar ran out of beer. Leppard kept Rent-A-Crowd busy that fall; the band picked up five dates after the Limit festival, including a return engagement at the Limit where they were billed as "The Young Kings of Rock."

Leppard's ample supply of pals made the nuts and bolts of roadwork much easier too. Joe was the only member of the band with a driver's license. Friends willingly helped when it came to hauling equipment around, especially Andy Smith who became Leppard's regular driver. And from day one Def Leppard never set up their own gear. Andy, Russell Major and Rent-A-Crowd helped with that. "We had a mutual thing," Joe explains, "where if we made any money, we always bought them beer. Even if it was five pounds, we paid for the beer..

In return, Def Leppard made a conscious attempt to dress like stars even if they weren't. Instead of going on stage in jeans and T-shirts, they always wore flashy scarves and silk blouses. "We were Steve Tyler dressers," Joe notes proudly. "We had a different attitude from most bands around us. It wasn't a superstar thing. We just decided it was important to look good, to look like an important band. And all our friends were ready to help. They wanted to be cool too, hanging out with a band and all."

In September, Sav's father Ken, approached a features writer and music critic for the *Sheffield Star* named Keith Strong about the possibility of checking out his son's new band. Keith agreed, but did so without much enthusiasm. He was frequently pestered to go see local no-hopers. Nevertheless, he set up a rendezvous with the Leppards at the Sheldon Hotel pub. Joe chewed his ear off over a pint or two, after which they led him up to the spoon factory room.

"They led me up a dangerous old stairway to a cramped workshop and did their stuff," Strong relates. "I've been a music fan since the mid-1950s. To me, the Sheffield scene had turned

weird and electronic. But Leppard were out and out rock, and bloody good. A little derivative, but mostly original. I was already sick of synthesizers played by non-musicians and Leppard were a refreshing change, even though they were considered old-hat. *Overture* was one of the numbers they played. It owed something to other bands, but they made it definitely their own. I felt renewed by them, musically, and I became an avid supporter.

Strong's story, headlined "Leppard's big chance to make the music stick," appeared in his Thursday "Hot Licks" column in the October 5 *Star*. "For such tender years", he wrote, "the five-piece are revealing a rare maturity in their writing and playing as they punch out heavy rock originals with more than a nod to melody." Joe, unsurprisingly supplied the quotes. "What are we? We think we're original. Possibly UFO/Rush/Styx without keyboards. Bits of songs can compare with others, but what don't?"

Strong signed off on an upbeat note. "So they're Def Leppard, which they admit is a daft name. 'But it sticks in the mind.' (Joe). Now they're out to prove that their music will, too." Strong claims that after the piece appeared, the Leppards asked him to manage them. He politely declined.

But Strong's next Leppard write-up, "Leppard Loses Skins," had nothing to do with music. "Young Sheffield rock heroes Def Leppard are drummer-less. . . are in urgent need of a replacement."

"Urgent" was putting it lightly. With only eight live performances to their credit, Def Leppard audaciously decided to make a record. Punk bands were making independent singles and EPs left and right, completely bypassing the time-honored tradition of getting on bended knee at a record company's door pleading for a contract. Why couldn't a heavy rock band do it? For one thing, a heavy rock band could not do it without a drummer and a week before Leppard's scheduled recording session at a small studio in nearby

Hull, the band voted to fire Tony Kenning.

There was nothing wrong with his drumming. Joe maintains that while Tony was sometimes slack during rehearsals, "he always gave two hundred per cent." Tony, however, was becoming less and less reliable. "I think his girlfriend at the time had a lot to do with it." Sav suggests. "She didn't like him messing around with the band. He was always a quiet sort of person anyway. He never had anything to do with the writing. Maybe he felt left out. I don't think his heart was in it like the rest of us."

Tony concedes that his girlfriend, Ann Brownbridge, complained that he spent too much time with the band and not enough with her. His parents were also in the midst of a divorce. He missed rehearsals, he insists, because of a very bad cold. "But at the time, Def Leppard thought missing a couple of rehearsals was unforgivable."

On November 17, at the South Seas pub, Joe, Sav, Pete and Steve agreed that Tony had to go. Sav was less enthusiastic about the idea than Joe; Tony was an old schoolmate, they'd first played rock & roll together. Joe, with typical bravado, assumed the duty of informing Tony of his early retirement. The next evening at the Wapentake, Joe and Tony met over dinner. "He said I wasn't putting enough into the band," Tony recalls. "I said I was thinking of leaving anyway. And it was true at the time. I didn't really want to leave, but I was feeling low. Also they'd all made up their minds that the band was the only thing they wanted to do. I was still a bit unsure."

That was it. Def Leppard scrambled to find a drummer for the next week's recording session and Tony Kenning went on to work as a technical officer at British Telecom. He also formed his own band, Cairo, a pop-rock quartet which released an independent single in 1984, *Eight Bells* b/w *Inside Out* on their own Pyramid label. And as of mid-'85, Cairo were rehearsing in a room in the old spoon factory complex, although the rates had gone up considerably, from £5 a week to £122 a month.

In a panic over the upcoming recording session, Joe called Frank Noon, the drummer with a Sheffield-based trio called the Next Band, asking if he could pinch-hit for Tony. Noon was an obvious choice. He was an acquaintance of the Leppards and the Next Band had been the chief inspiration for the recording idea. They had recorded their own independent EP, cutting it on the cheap and selling it at gigs.

One night previously at the Wapentake, Joe had cornered Frank and pressed him for information about the EP. Where did they record it? How much did it cost? Frank recommended the inexpensive little recording concern, Fairview Studio in Hull, where the Next Band had recorded their record, *Four by Three*, in September '78. Joe, in return for the info, helped sell a few Next Band EPs around Sheffield.

With barely a week's notice Frank Noon agreed to sit in for the session. Choosing material was no problem. Def Leppard had a wealth of originals rehearsed and ready to go. *Overture* captured everything that set Leppard apart from regulation British hard-rock – harmonies, intricate guitar arrangements, ambitious melodic structures. *Getcha Rocks Off* was a speedy invitation to party hearty, a natural headbanger's anthem. To lead off the EP, Def Leppard elected to go with *Ride Into the Sun*, a Savage-Elliott number stocked with solid commercial hooks. That would be the bait for radio DJs, if they ever got around to playing the record. The song selection also ensured that guitar solo duties were doled out evenly. *Ride Into the Sun* was Pete Willis' showcase; Steve Clark handled *Getcha Rocks Off*. They both shared the spotlight in *Overture*. "That way," Steve says, "we could both be stars for about thirty seconds."

The Fairview sessions took place on November 25 and 26, a Saturday and Sunday. Andy Smith arranged for cheapo accommodation at a bed'n'breakfast place near the studio. Def Leppard arrived at Fairview – an hour's drive from Sheffield – on Saturday morning, set up their equipment and tested sound balances with house engineers Roy Neave and Keith Herd. It took four takes to get the backing track of *Ride Into the Sun* down because Frank kept switching the tempo around the wrong way during the unusual seven-beat finish. Leppard then whipped through the basic for *Getcha Rocks Off* in one hot take, although Pete Willis momentarily went into the wrong key at the end (quite audible on the record).

Overture was also a one-take triumph. The rest of Saturday was taken up with guitar overdubs and Joe's vocals on *Ride Into the Sun* and *Getcha Rocks Off*. After much celebrating drinking and assorted merriment that night, Joe returned to Fairview Sunday afternoon to tackle his *Overture* vocals. It took six takes to get right Joe's big scream in the final thumping climax.

"I remember the engineer saying 'Now you mustn't be embarrassed to scream.' I said 'I'm not, I'm real good at screaming.' And I let one loose –

"WAAAAAAAH!' It was perfect." By 3pm, Joe was finished singing. Five hours later, the EP was mixed. It cost exactly £148.50.

"We listened to it in the car all the way back to Sheffield," Joe says fondly. "We were driving over a bridge and I said 'Ah, there's a wrong note there.' But it was a real good record. It really represented what we were. And somebody was watching over us when we made it. Apart from the four takes to get *Ride Into the Sun*, everything went perfectly. We never went out of tune. Steve was even using a borrowed guitar. He didn't want to use his Ibanez Les Paul Copy. He got a Gibson from John Lockton of the Next Band.

"And here we were, in these two little cars, drums piled up in the back of one, guitars in the other, listening to our first record."

Getting it onto vinyl and into record stores, they realized, would take more than £148.50. Joe covered the session costs by borrowing the money from his parents. But it would take another £450 to press up a thousand copies. Picture sleeves would be another £65. Joe raised the pressing money from a woman at Osborn-Mushet, Janie Taylor, who charged a ludicrous twenty-five percent interest on the loan. An amateur artist in the Osborn-Mushet development office, Dave Jeffrey, designed the sleeve, which was a clever ripoff of the HMV dog-and-Victrola logo. Jeffrey simply substituted a growling leopard for the dog and added discrete little dollar signs to the border design.

That turned out to be wishful thinking. The pressing costs, Janie Taylor's twenty-five percent interest and the fact that about a hundred copies were given free to Rent-A-Crowd and mailed to press and radio – using a lot of Next Band contacts – meant that Def Leppard's profit from the first pressing of *The Def Leppard EP* amounted to only £60. It was a nice production for the price, though. The first couple of hundred copies even included a lyric sheet with autographed (but not terribly flattering) ink sketches of the four band members.

In the meantime, Def Leppard still had a drum chair to fill. Some time during the week between Tony Kenning's dismissal and the recording of the EP, Joe asked Frank Noon if he would consider joining Def Leppard permanently. Noon declined, remaining faithful to the Next Band. But Keith Strong's "Leopard Loses Skins" item in the *Star* did not go unnoticed. A fifteen-year-old *wunderkind*, Richard Allen, somehow contacted one of the Leppards – no one can actually recall how – and arranged a meeting at the Limit club

PRICE LIST
COD 27 P
CHIPS 13 P
FISH & CHIPS 40 P
ROE 14 P
FISH CAKES 10
STEAK & KIDNEY PIE 24 P
SAUSAGES 6 P
FRIED TO
PEAS 8 P & 11
CURRY SAUCE
2

with (a) Joe and Steve, or (b) Steve and Pete, or (c) Pete and Joe, depending on who you talk to. Rick says it was (a), Joe says it was (b) Sav says it was (c).

In any event, Rick and two Leppards of undetermined identity had a nice chinwag in the men's toilet at the Limit the week before the band went to Fairview Studio to record. Rick had never seen Def Leppard play, but he'd read Strong's writeups in the *Star* and fancied having a crack at playing with an ambitious, all-original rock band.

"It was the first time I'd met people that were getting their money together and putting it back into the band, buying new gear. The bands I was in before, all they were into was taking the money for themselves, just making beer money."

In fact, Rick, who was born Richard John Cyril Allen on November 1, 1963, had pocketed quite a bit of beer money for someone of his tender years. For that matter, Rick had more professional musical experience than all of the other Leppards combined. As a toddler, Rick was already beating the hell out of his grandmother's old Salvation Army tambourine. Using a biscuit tin, some string, cellophane tape, a couple of sticks and a bit of imagination, he constructed a drum and marched around the Allen home in the Dronfield area of Sheffield like a pint-sized soldier boy. He was eleven when his parents Geoff and Kathleen finally caved in to his pleading and bought Rick a blue sparkle Del-Ray drum kit. Price: a princely £60.

After six months of drum lessons from a variety of local teachers (including one drummer, Kenny Slade, whose big claim to fame was a short tenure with Sheffield growler Joe Cocker), Rick formed his first combo, Smokey Blue, with neighborhood mates John Richardson and Trevor Dunford. He quickly graduated to a top-o'-the-line Pearl drum kit and started attacking Deep Purple and Black Sabbath covers with a semi-pro gang of hairies twice his age called Rampant ("Some crackin' names, aren't they?"). At thirteen, Rick was already a fixture on the pub and workingmen's club circuit with the Johnny Kalendar Band, a middle-aged sextet peddling the latest Top Forty hits. The repertoire was predictable and Rick's parents were not too keen on him hanging out in the local boozers with older musicians of dubious character. But the experience, Rick insists, was invaluable. And so was the money.

"For all I might knock it now, I was there, on stage. And the money was a little better. I was getting £10 a night – and I was still in school."

In school, Rick majored in hellraising. A holy terror when he put his mind to it, he was a tough fighter in spite of his size and, in one memorable bout at Holmesdale Infant School (an elementary school across the road from his house), Rick walloped the school bully so bad that he became a minor legend. Rick later enhanced his reputation by burning down the school fence one afternoon with the help of a few fellow conspirators. The police were called in, but Rick managed to get off with a slap on the wrist.

"I was a bit of a tearaway," he confesses. "And I loved bashing things. I think there was something trying to get out of me. But when I started playing drums, it calmed me down a bit."

As a Leppard, Rick would later cause more than his share of trouble. But at his audition, the day after Def Leppard returned from Fairview Studio, Rick wowed the band with his whiplash timing, riflecrack sound and his nifty Pearl all-chrome kit. Another drummer turned up for the audition, but he didn't stand a chance. After one number, he was swiftly dispatched into the night. According to Joe, Tony Kenning also turned up and made vague murmurs about getting his old job back. He was too late.

"We asked Rick if he knew *Emerald* by Thin Lizzy," says Sav. "We played that and suddenly the song sounded six times better than the way we usually played it. We were now in the company of a proper drummer. Even at fifteen, he was outstanding."

Steve was a little dubious when Rick took his shoes off and played his bass drum and hi-hat pedals in his bare feet. But all doubt evaporated from the spoon factory practice room when Rick blasted into *Getcha Rocks Off.*

"I could see the other lads were getting into it. Russell Major was on the other side of the room with a big beaming grin on his face that looked like he had a coathanger stuck in his mouth. Nobody officially said 'You're in,' but I knew it right away. It sounded so right. All they needed was someone to give that little bit extra, that fifth member who would pull the same weight they were." Def Leppard also got Rick's older brother Robert in the bargain. Ostensibly along as Rick's chaperone, Robert had some experience mixing sound for rock bands. He quickly became Def Leppard's sound man and *de facto* road manager.

The pieces were now all in place – the lineup, the sound, the songwriting. Def Leppard had passed the gig test at Westfield School with flying colors and now they had a record of their own, with three of their own songs pressed into the grooves. And it was on their own record label. This was heady stuff for a band barely a year old, with only half a dozen gigs under its belt. But what they lacked in experience, Def Leppard made up in determination. It was written all over them, from the smart rock star threads they wore on stage to the name of their fledgling record label. In smartass tribute to Chris Westwood's nasty review of their first Limit show, Def Leppard released their debut EP on Bludgeon Riffola Records.

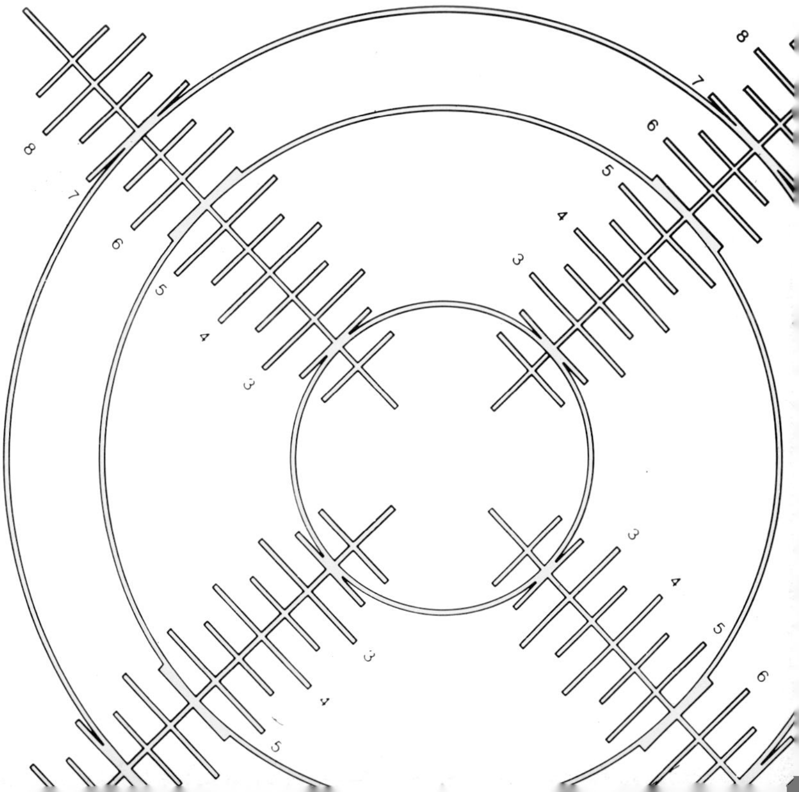

CHAPTER 3

TODAY SHEFFIELD, TOMORROW WOLVERHAMPTON

"All Cosmic Warriors must be cool unto the world and have long, curly hair, beard and tash (no other fuzz required) . . . Things that give Warriors a buzz and make life worth living are gangsters, cheese pie, Winston snouts, Ponty Mython, black stockings, being crazy, all things deep and purple, Rocky's horror, Vodka Martinis (as many as poshible-dribble), Rock and Tamla Motown, saxophones, old movies, keyboards, Dudes everywhere, laying down by still waters and, of course, having fun 99.9 percent of the time.

This then is the life-style of the Cosmic Warrior. It's life and life only . . . Beware of imitations . . ."

From *The Code of the Cosmic Warrior* by Andy Smith. Written in 1978 and pinned to the sidedoor of Def Leppard's first tour bus.

Nothing happens overnight in the music business. Lawyers can haggle over the fine points of a recording or publishing contract until their beards turn grey. International currency rates rise and fall while talent scouts engage in extended bidding wars over the Next Big Thing. An artist's manager and his record company president can run up hundreds, nay, thousands of dollars in lunch tabs bickering over promotion of the new single. Music itself changes overnight, bands can form and breakup within the space of a week, but the business of making, promoting and selling pop sounds can take forever.

Def Leppard was no exception. Joe Elliott's rock & roll dream was in incubation for years. Def Leppard spent nearly a year practising and re-practising the same half a dozen songs in their spoon factory rehearsal room before even venturing out to play for the public. Even after they had signed the Big Record Deal and toured America, their platinum reward was still three years in coming. It you form a band with the slightest intention of making music a career, you have to be in it for the long haul.

Def Leppard were in it for as long as it was going to take. Their day jobs were only a means to the greater end, a way to finance this noble adventure until the big payoff. Thus, it was with joyous stupefaction that at the end of 1979 Joe Elliott, Steve Clark, Rick Savage, Pete Willis and Rick Allen looked back on what they had accomplished that year. So did the entire British record industry. In twelve months, this band of Sheffield teenagers – average age,

Supporting Sammy Hagar at Hammersmith Odeon, 16 September, 1979.

eighteen – went from playing local pubs for chump change to touring with heavy metal godheads like AC/DC and Sammy Hagar. They sold over 15,000 copies nationwide of *The Def Leppard EP* by virtue of word of mouth, local radio play and press raves. The rock weekly *Sounds* crowned Leppard top cats in the New Wave of British Heavy Metal.

Seven months after the EP's release, Def Leppard were the cause of a record company *battle royale,* with several major English labels vying for their services. A month later, Leppard had the Big Record Deal and, by

> **Deaf Leopard were HM as HM always was and always will be. Crosses, macho poses, bludgeon riffola that even the Sabs abandoned years ago, and — ironically, methought — the only band to screw the audience for an encore.**

year's end, had recorded a debut album. Like every other year before and after it, 1979 was twelve months, fifty-two weeks and 365 days long (leap years withstanding). But Def Leppard, simply by working hard and capitalizing on unforeseen successes, shoehorned a lifetime of dues-paying into those months, weeks and days. In a business where time is money and record companies, managers and lawyers often waste a lot of both, Def Leppard literally happened overnight.

Joe Elliott kept a diary of sorts during 1979 in a blue pocket-sized datebook from Osborn-Mushet Tools. As the spokesman, booking agent and driver for the band, Joe kept pages and pages' worth of addresses and phone numbers for, among other things, band members, roadies, Rent A-Crowd members, media contacts and record stores selling the EP. The datebook's last two pages, a miniature map of the London subway system, were covered with examples of Joe's signature in assorted variations; he'd been practising his autograph.

But the interesting stuff was the calendar entries. Each show Def Leppard played that year was logged on the appropriate date, with relevant details like how much they were paid. And those dates, more than anything else in Joe's extensive archive of Leppard memorabilia, tell the story of that amazing year. Rarely in rock & roll has so much happened to ones so young in so short a time.

Def Leppard's "overnight" success actually got off to a slow start. Two shows on January 9 and 10 – a return engagement at one of the Limit's free local band fests and a gig with local band Bitter Suite at the Dialhouse Club – were cancelled. But Joe's datebook started to fill up a couple of weeks later . . .

JANUARY 24 – Dialhouse Club. This was a rescheduled date with Bitter

Suite. After Leppard's set, Joe and Steve zipped down to Sheffield City Hall to catch UFO, who were playing in town that night. Joe: "This is a place about two hundred yards from where Steve's parents live. Bitter Suite were a really good cover band. They did Lizzy, Hendrix, Boston and Foreigner covers. Where every other cover band played *Tie a Yellow Ribbon Around the Old Oak Tree,* they did *Purple Haze.*"

JANUARY 25 – Penthouse, Sheffield £13.
JANUARY 27 – Crowle Community Centre (a whopping £45). Joe: "A cousin of mine, Keith, set that one up for us. They had a volume meter in the place; if you went over 96db, this red light went on and the power went off. I put putty inside the alarm so it wouldn't go off during the show. We were so loud during the soundcheck that the power went off after the first chord."
JANUARY 28 – Dickens, Rotherham £20 Joe: "Russell Major, our drum roadie, missed this one because he got snowed in. It was a long drive for us, twenty-five miles, to the gig, all for £20. On some shows like that, after expenses, we were often £5 in the hole at the end of the night."

FEBRUARY 8 – Wapentake, Sheffield £15. Def Leppard's debut appearance at Joe's favourite heavy metal pub.
FEBRUARY 28 – Sheffield Polytechnic £40.
MARCH 3 – Oscar's, Liverpool £40. Def Leppard's first major show outside Sheffield. The audience, to the band's dismay, was a gang of local bikers in greasy jeans and weather-worn black leather jackets. Throughout Leppard's set, the bikers did a bizarre dance in which they spread their feet apart, rubbed both hands on their thighs, thrust their fists up in the air in a "fuck you" gesture and then jerked off with invisible penises. Watching this evil little pantomime, Steve Clark was convinced this was the bikers' own quaint way of saying they hated Def Leppard and were going to kill them after the show. In fact, the bikers liked Def Leppard. Apparently, they always did this dance if they were having a good time.

Joe Elliott assumed the responsibility of spreading the word about Def Leppard's maiden record release. Using a list of press and radio contacts compiled from his own collection of rock magazines with additions from the Next Band's mailing list, Joe mailed copies of *The Def Leppard EP* to all of the major music papers – *Sounds, Melody Maker, Record Mirror, New Musical Express* – and to pop radio outlets like Radio Hallam, the commercial pop station in Sheffield, and BBC's Radio One in London, the national pop station. When Radio One jock, John Peel, made a live appearance at Sheffield University, Joe handed him a copy in person.

Peel was no heavy metal maniac. The high radio priest of Britain's underground music community, Peel had been instrumental in the popularization of classic English hippy bands like Hawkwind, Caravan, Family and Pink Floyd in the late Sixties and early Seventies. When the Sex Pistols fired the punk-rock shot heard 'round the world, Peel became the principal Establishment media voice of punk and its assorted offshoots. He was especially partial to young bands with independent records, encouraging their separatist stance with frequent airplay and specially-recorded sessions for his program.

Joe was aware of Peel's bias against heavy metal. He also knew that Peel would at least be impressed by Def Leppard's initiative, recording an EP on their own. He walked up to Peel that night and boldly announced "I'm Joe Elliott and I'm with a local band called Def Leppard. We've made a record. Would you like to give it a listen?" Peel said "I'd love to" and told Joe to write his name and phone number on it.

The next day, Joe's phone rang. He

N SHEFFIELD AV
98KZEW
THE ZOO
DEF LEPPARD
WBAB
102.3

picked it up and the voice on the other end said in a low droll DJ tone "This is John Peel. I listened to your record and I really liked it. I'm going to play it tonight at 10:30." True to his word, Peel played the record at 10:30 that evening. It was the first time Def Leppard were ever heard on British national radio. The airplay, plugs from Keith Strong in the *Star* and the band's stepped-up gigging helped Leppard sell off their first thousand copies of the EP. Leppard usually moved ten or twenty EPs at every show. Joe also visited local record stores to see about selling them over the counter. At Virgin Records in Sheffield, the manager demanded twenty-five pence for every copy sold (Joe passed on the deal). The owner of another store, the Record Collector, struck a more friendly deal. He told Joe that if the band wanted to sell the EP for £1 each, he would just buy the records outright and sell them as a favour.

Peter Martin, who ran a hip little Sheffield record boutique called Revolution Records, made a similar arrangement with Joe. Joe was already a regular customer at Revolution, a favorite hangout for rock & roll kids and record collectors in the area. The store, located on the second storey of an outdoor precinct in the downtown shopping district, had a bright sign with the words "Revolution Records" written in bright white psychedelic script against a deep purple background. In good weather, Martin frequently put speakers on the balcony outside his store and blasted the latest sounds for kids hanging out in the precinct below. Joe could usually be found in Revolution during any weather, buying the bootleg albums Martin discreetly kept under the counter.

A Scotsman by birth, Martin had already seen Def Leppard play. He had been the sax player in the jazz band which headlined the festival-in-the-field the previous August. This record, though, showed that Leppard had come a long way since then. When Joe came over to Revolution after work one day to check on sales of the EP, Martin asked him if Def Leppard had management.

"I said no," Joe remembers. "Then he said that he'd played the record for a guy who worked for Arista Records and that this Arista guy also thought the record was really good. 'I'd really like to help you out, do something for you,' he said. And of course, I said 'Yeah, wow, brilliant!' "

Poor old Bootleg Bill, who had proffered his services for free, was out of the picture. Martin and his pal at Arista, a promotion man named Frank Stuart-Brown, formed a company, MSB, and quickly signed Def Leppard to a three-year management contract. Someone in the band, Joe can't recall who, took the contract to a lawyer to make sure MSB was not taking Leppard to the cleaners. But the deal got a clean bill of health. MSB would get fifteen per cent of Leppard's gross earnings in return for booking gigs, arranging for studio time, getting a record deal, etc. etc. Neither Martin or Stuart-Brown had ever managed a rock band before.

"But I knew the promotional side of the record business and Peter knew the retail side. It was a perfect arrangement," claims Stuart-Brown, who started out in the industry as a junior sales representative for the giant WEA Records combine. "And I knew there was no way this band could fail. What hit me was the fact they were all teenagers, and they were playing heavy metal. They weren't playing punk. That decided it for me. I figured there was no way this band could fail because if they were only seventeen and eighteen years old, then there must be thousands of other heavy metal kids around the country just like them."

It was a rocky marriage from the beginning. Def Leppard wanted to get out there and play. Frank Stuart-Brown had a different plan. "My first instinct was not to even put the band out. To be big, I felt, you've got to be seen big. If you're seen in poxy little clubs all around the place, you'll always be judged as a small band. When the time was right, I wanted to just hire some choreographers, put them in a hall somewhere and work the balls off of them."

Joe was miffed because he'd been booking the gigs. Not many, to be

sure, and not exactly for dynamite bucks. But he enjoyed the responsibility and resented losing it. But Stuart-Brown did have a nose for promotion. One night, Stuart-Brown was wining and dining BBC DJ Andy Peebles and his producer Jeff Griffin on a junket to see Simple Minds in Manchester. On the way to the show, Griffin, a well-known hard rock advocate, listened intently, dissecting the sound: "Harmonies are good, it's strange to hear them play heavy metal."

No more was said about the tape that evening until Stuart-Brown dropped Peebles and Griffin back at their hotel. Jeff Griffin turned around as he got out of the car and said 'Give me a couple of copies of the record. We'll get it played.'" After that, Peebles played *Ride into the Sun* and *Getcha Rocks Off* at least twice a week on his early weeknight slot for nearly three months.

MARCH 16 – Harwood Miner's Welfare Club £70. This was Def Leppard's biggest payday to date.

MARCH 17 – Wombwell Reform Club £20 ("and what we want at the door"). Both club and band benefited from this arrangement. The clubowner paid Leppard a flat fee of £20, plus any admission fee they wanted to charge at the door. This way, the more friends Leppard coaxed to the show, the more money they'd make. And the more money the club would take in at the bar.

MARCH 19 – Wosborough Dale Workingmen's Club £50.

APRIL 19 – Middlewood Club.

APRIL 23 – Wosborough Dale Workingmen's Club £55. A slight increase from Leppard's last visit.

APRIL 28-29 – Fairview Studio, Hull. Frank Stuart-Brown says his daytime employers, Arista Records, were interested in hearing more Leppard material. So he and Peter Martin booked a weekend of studio time at Fairview; Stuart-Brown claimed the money back through his Arista expense account. Def Leppard cut seven new songs during the session, including *Wasted, Sorrow is a Woman, When the Walls Came Tumbling Down* and *Answer to the Master,* which would eventually be recut for the group's debut album. Live staples that never made it to official vinyl were *See the Light*, a heavy Thin Lizzy-Status Quo boogie number called *Heat Street* and the brute rocker *Glad I'm Alive,* Leppard's usual set opener. In 1985, long after Leppard had severed relations with him, Stuart-

I thought vodka was a tonic until I discovered. . .

Brown tried to capitalize on the band's *Pyromania* success and issued the demos in disastrously remixed form as an album, *First Strike.* The band successfully applied for a legal injunction against the release and had all copies of the record yanked off the market.

MAY 2– Dialhouse, Sheffield (door takings)

JUNE 5 – Crookes Workingmen's Club.

One of the music journalists included in the initial mailing of *The Def Leppard EP* was a young penman at *Sounds,* Geoff Barton. In the fall of '78, Joe wrote a letter to Barton about Leppard's music and the success of their first few shows, inviting Barton to sample the goods personally. Barton wrote a nice letter back, thanking Joe for his invite and wishing Def Leppard the best of luck. "It's very encouraging to hear of a new, young outfit into (as you say) heavy/pomp rock . . . lotsa luck with the future and keep in touch." Joe duly sent him a cassette tape of the EP upon completion and repeated his invitation to see Leppard live. Finally, on June 5, Barton relented. Together with *Sounds* photographer Ross Halfin, he journeyed up from London to Sheffield to see Def Leppard perform at Crookes Workingmen's Club, a members-only establishment only a short walk from Joe's house on Crookes Road.

A heavy metal fan disenfranchised by the wholesale press embrace of punk, Barton was just the man to spread the word about Def Leppard in the British music press. He maintained unswerving allegiance to the great grandaddies of English metal – Zeppelin, Purple, Lizzy – and had taken it upon himself to hype the rising breed of young HM groups being overlooked in the media's race to find the new Sex Pistols. In an early June issue of *Sounds,* Barton unveiled what he dubbed the New Wave of British Heavy Metal, a motley assortment of aspiring high-volume Visigoths including Angel Witch, Saxon, Samson (whose major distinguishing feature was a drummer who wore a black leather rapist's mask) and future chart kings Iron Maiden, who like Leppard had also recorded an independent EP in late '78.

The headquarters of this Big Rock uprising, according to Barton, was a heavy metal disco in London called the Soundhouse, run by DJ Neal Kay. At his weekly sessions in a London pub, Kay mixed current hits and sacred metal classics on the turntable with demo tapes by new local HM outfits. Indeed, Iron Maiden titled their EP *The Soundhouse Tapes* in Kay's honor. But when Barton got to Sheffield, he quickly discovered that there was more to his New Wave of British Heavy Metal than he thought. The noise was also alive and well in the provinces.

Crookes Workingmen's Club was not the ideal venue for Barton to see Leppard live. It was a vestige of old British imperial macho, a haven for working class men after their eight hours in the steel factories and coalpits ringing Sheffield. Each member had his own seat for life; if a visitor, newcomer or even another club member sat in someone's designated seat, he got the evil eye from other members all evening, or until he moved. Stocked with poker machines and plenty of bars, the workingmen's club was the hub of social life for the over-35 s.

Only a few dozen kids attended Def Leppard's June 5 performance there, most of them sons of the members. (Attendance was particularly low because Status Quo were playing Sheffield City Hall the same evening). Fans were eyed suspiciously by old-timers who checked membership cards at the door. And no one knew what to make of Barton and Halfin. Blown away by Leppard's stage power and musical proficiency, not to mention several shots of whiskey (only twenty-five pence a glass), Barton stood at the foot of the stage, shaking his hair in a wild headbanging frenzy with Halfin snapping photos at his side. Kids and old-timers alike stared in amazement at the two daft out-of-towners. After the show, Barton interviewed the band in the backstage dressing room while Halfin pissed in the sink. "That was my first experience of the rock & roll lifestyle," laughs Joe. Joe later invited Barton and Halfin back to his house for tea, sandwiches and more chatter.

"I think there must be a new generation of heavy metal fans, people who must be a bit pissed off with listening to bands that were formed over twelve years ago like Zeppelin and Black Sabbath," he told Barton. "The Sabs really burst onto the scene in the early Seventies didn't they, so how many of today's fourteen or fifteen-year-old rock fans can remember that? How old would they have been then? They want somebody young."

The whole band was bursting with *chutzpah* that night. "If we had the backing, I'm sure we could go out and be quite successful," Rick Allen declared. "If we get to support UFO or Priest or Sabbath, I reckon we could scare any of them off," Rick Savage said casually. "Van Halen came across riding on top of a vast publicity thing," Joe chimed in. "I daresay if we had the publicity, we could do as well if not better than them."

The publicity was not long in coming. Barton's June 16 *Sounds* feature (complete with Halfin photos of Joe in mid-leap in tight black pseudo-leather pants, Steve Clark attacking his Ibanez model Les Paul at full throttle and Joe digging into a fistful of fish 'n' chips at a local takeout restaurant) intersected nicely with a BBC Radio One studio session recorded on June 7 and broadcast the week of June 18. A session for Piccadily Radio in Manchester on June 13 – with Steve handling all lead and rhythm chores because Pete could not get off from work to make the session – was aired a week later. By then, any record company talent scout as yet unaware of Def Leppard was on the horn to MSB headquarters. "The phone,"

Phil unwinds post-gig backstage '83.

Frank Stuart-Brown says, "didn't stop ringing after that."

JUNE 12 – Sheffield University. Def Leppard performed as part of an all-day festival with ten other area bands. The Leppards went on eighth.
JUNE 18 – High Green Liberal Club, Packhouse Lane, Sheffield £85. Another record paycheck.
JUNE 25 – Leeds University, Leeds £60.
JUNE 26 – Crookes Workingmen's Club, Sheffield.
JUNE 30 – Manchester University, Manchester £75. Rescheduled from June 23.
JULY 7 – Porterhouse, Retford. £80.
JULY 23 – Wombwell Reform Club.
JULY 26 – Porterhouse, Retford. At Peter Martin and Frank Stuart-Brown's invitation, talent scouts from eleven major English record companies and booking agencies attended the show to see what the Leppard excitement was all about. "It was so hot in there, you could part the atmosphere," says Rick Allen. "There is nothing worse than the smell of hot bodies and this was one of those places. They had this mirrored wall behind the stage and it had all this condensation on it, water running down the wall. Russ was behind me, literally pouring water over my head to keep me cool."

JULY 27 – Rock Garden, Middlesbrough. Two record company representatives stopped by to see the band. One of them was David Bates from Phonogram, one of the original eleven from the night before, back for a second look.

David Bates was a junior A&R man at Phonogram Records in London when he received Frank Stuart-Brown's invitation to see Def Leppard perform at the Porterhouse in Retford. Three years before, his first assignment had been to check out a band of foul-mouthed spiky heads called the Sex Pistols. But his taste ran more along the lines of Leppard's; he'd been raised on a steady diet of British hard rock like Free and Led Zeppelin. He had even lived in Sheffield for four years, during which time he had worked as a DJ at, of all places, the Wapentake.

Bates was well aware of Leppard and their growing reputation long before he talked with Stuart-Brown. *Sounds* was plugging the band heavily in the wake of Geoff Barton's June feature and Bates was tight with Soundhouse DJ Neal Kay, a major Leppard supporter. A couple of Phonogram promotion men had kept Bates up to date on sales of the band's independent EP. Bates also had a significant advantage over most of his peers in British A&R. He was, at the time, only twenty-three – not much older than the acts he was supposed to sign.

But when he saw Def Leppard at the Porterhouse, he practically felt like an old man. "I was stunned by their age," says Bates, who later became head of Phonogram A&R. "Rick was only fifteen. Everybody else was seventeen, eighteen. I couldn't get over the fact that these guys were so young, doing what they were doing. It was like coming to terms with the fact that people younger than yourself were doing something that you would have liked to have done at that age, and doing it so amazingly well."

Later, when he talked with the Leppards, he was struck by their intense study of the music they were playing. "They would talk about albums they heard, their favorite tracks, favorite guitar solos. They were true fans. And apart from being true fans, they were now getting actively involved in it. When they eventually went on tour with people like Judas Priest, they were very nervous. These people were their heroes. They were so in awe of what was going on around them. But when they went out on stage, they gave it their all."

Bates was very excited about Def Leppard – about their sound, their songwriting ability, their enthusiasm on stage. He believed Phonogram was the right label for Leppard. The company already had a long history of breaking English hard rock acts via their subsidiary imprint Vertigo (Black Sabbath, Thin Lizzy, the Sensational Alex Harvey Band).

But Bates had to jockey for position like everybody else. Frank Stuart-Brown claims that after the Porterhouse gig, contract bidding heated up quickly. Chrysalis and WEA immediately put big bucks on the table, although not as big as he and Martin were asking for. They demanded £50,000 up front; the record company would also have to pick up all recording costs, recoupable from future royalties but not from the advance, which was the standard practice. Stuart-Brown wanted £50,000 to last, to cover salaries, tour costs and other promotional activities until the royalties started coming in.

The A&R men who saw Def Leppard at the Porterhouse and the Middlesbrough Rock Garden the next night were unquestionably impressed, although some more than others. Joe Elliott recalls WEA's Dave Dee (formerly of the twee Sixties British group Dave Dee, Dozy, Beaky, Mick and Tich) giving him advice on how to move around stage more. "Well, there was this big pillar in the middle of the Porterhouse stage. And all night, I was doing this Tommy Steele number, swinging around the pillar with the microphone stand. And he says 'You don't move enough.' I told him there was nowhere to bleeding move!"

Phonogram also agreed to front recording costs, no mean investment in itself. But a key factor in the label's interest was an A&R executive named Cliff Burnstein, headquartered in the Chicago office of Phonogram's corporate counterpart in America, Mercury Records.

Burnstein had an unusually discerning ear when it came to heavy metal. He had signed one of the company's biggest hard rock sellers, the Canadian trio Rush, and he was loaded with contacts both in commercial FM radio and in the highly influential heavy metal underground. He not only could tell what radio would play, but what fans would buy – which is not always the same thing. Burnstein scored a copy of *The Def Leppard EP* not long after its release and sensed a winner. He believed Def Leppard had a future in England with Phonogram. He also believed Def Leppard had a bigger future in America with Mercury. Burnstein made plain to his U.K. counterparts that Def Leppard were a band worth signing.

Lawyer John Kennedy, then the legal and business affairs manager at Phonogram U.K., was responsible for all contract negotiations for the label. He dug right in to hard bargaining with Pete Martin and Frank Stuart-Brown. Despite their relative inexperience as managers, Kennedy says, they were not pushovers when it came to dealing on Leppard's behalf.

"They were pushing for a firm long term commitment to the band. They didn't want just one EP or even one album. They were asking for three albums firm, and a lot of discussions took place as to how long that commitment would be."

Stuart-Brown begs to differ. "Phonogram wanted one album with an option to go into a second. My idea was that most bands break big with their third album. I wanted them to do well with two albums, then renegotiate – 'Okay, this band is going to break big, give us more.'" Stuart-Brown did not realize at the time how the future would bear him out, although he would not be around to reap the reward.

The contract eventually agreed upon provided Def Leppard with a healthy royalty on record sales. The band would receive ten percent during the first two-year period, with increments up to eleven and then twelve percent. The royalty was based on one hundred percent of sales, too. "Record companies usually allow ten percent for marketing purposes, but that's just a ripoff. We insisted on the full one hundred percent."

Only two weeks passed between the Retford Porterhouse show and the signing of Def Leppard's contract with Phonogram. On Sunday, August 5, 1979, the five members of Def Leppard assembled at Rick Allen's house to sign the deal. Because Rick was underage, his father Geoff signed an additional clause in the contract which

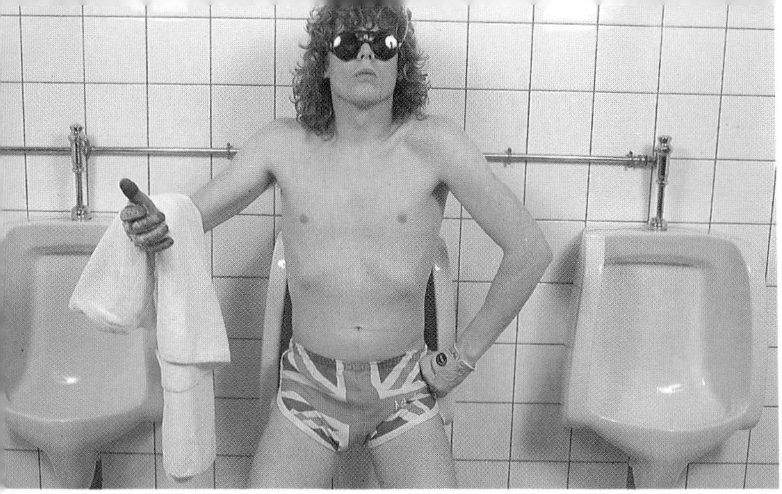

basically said he was satisfied with the document.

Ironically, the day before, August 4, Joe Elliott treated himself to a trip to Knebworth to see the band that helped invent heavy metal, Led Zeppelin, perform at an open-air festival. Within a year, Led Zeppelin would break up and Def Leppard would be riding high with their first album, tearing it up in the States. The torch was being passed.

AUGUST 10 – Mayfair, Newcastle £200. Another record payday. Sav had tonsilitis when the band played this show; he did not sing backup vocals that evening. Joe also got into a serious scrap with Pete Martin. Rick Allen drank an entire bottle of wine that night and threw up inside the equipment van. Martin told Andy Smith, "You're the roadie, you clean it up." Andy refused and Joe stuck up for him. Martin, who possessed a fierce Scottish temper, became very angry and pushed Joe up against a wall and threatened to flatten him. This was the beginning of the end of Def Leppard's relationship with MSB.

AUGUST 17 – Village Newport, Shrophire £125, plus fifty percent of the door. On the way back to Sheffield, the band decided to crash somewhere for the night rather than face another long overnight drive home. They were turned away from two boarding houses. At a third, they asked the landlady for two double rooms in their clipped Yorkshire accents. The landlady very graciously went behind the bar and poured two double *rums*. When she asked if they wanted anything in them, Sav quipped "Yeah, two beds and a carpet might be nice."

AUGUST 30 – Fusion, Chesterfield.
AUGUST 31 – 76 Club, Burton-on-Trent.
SEPTEMBER 1 – Sheffield. In his datebook, Joe wrote "Do not tell anyone." This probably was for a live Sheffield radio broadcast. Steve broke four guitar strings during the broadcast.
SEPTEMBER 5 – Swan Hotel, Bolton. This was an autograph session. A DJ going by the name of Prince John, who staged hard rock radio sessions at the Swan Hotel, asked Def Leppard if they would come down and make a personal appearance, sign some EPs, etc. On his way to Bolton, Joe got a speeding ticket for doing 45mph in a 30 zone.
SEPTEMBER 6– Norbeck Hotel, Blackpool.
SEPTEMBER 7– Lafayette Club, Wolverhampton £125, plus fifty percent of the door . Cliff Burnstein flew from America to see Def Leppard perform for the first time. Joe, practising splits in the dressing room, ripped his stage pants right up the back of his crotch before showtime. He did the whole show facing the audience so they wouldn't see his bare ass. (Joe refused to wear underpants on stage.)
SEPTEMBER 8 – Pavillion, West Runton £100.
SAMMY HAGAR TOUR Stuart-Brown's major score at the time was the support slot on a four-date U.K. tour with American heavy metal shouter Sammy Hagar. The Leppards were paid a hundred and fifty pounds a night.
SEPTEMBER 13 – Newcastle Mayfair. Def Leppard had already headlined here on their own.
SEPTEMBER 14 – Manchester Free Trade Hall.
SEPTEMBER 15 – Birmingham Odeon.
SEPTEMBER 16 – Hammersmith Odeon, London. Def Leppard's first performance in London. "They dispelled any of my too-much too-soon doubts by putting on a splendid display, resplendent in their new stage costumes – singer Joe Elliott wearing a kind of leopard waistcoat printed in paw marks in recognition of the band's delightful misspelt name. They abandoned their Thin Lizzy covers ... and presented a stunning set of originals with *Sorrow Is A Woman*, *Wasted* (great lyrics about a bottle of wine and pills and a marvellous chant line of "Wastid") and the new number *Rock Brigade* particular highlights ... The spearhead of the New Wave of British Heavy Metal, these boys have a great future ahead of them. Watch them go, watch them rise, catch them wherever you can ... Keep your cool, you Leppards, you will become the success story of the decade. No rash prediction." Geoff Barton, *Sounds*.

Events continued to move more swiftly. Shortly after Def Leppard signed the Phonogram deal, Rick Allen stopped going to school. The band's accelerating gig schedule prohibited daily attendance and Rick's parents fretted about his education even though his immediate future with the band was assured. As a compromise, they arranged for Rick to visit a tutor two days a week; the hitch was that the tutor was all the way up in Edinburgh, Scotland. A difference in the length of the school year in Scotland would have permitted Rick to graduate early.

Five go to the toilet.

But after two lessons in Edinburgh, Rick stopped going, bored with the classwork and exhausted by the commuting. There was no more talk of school after that.

Earlier in the year, after the initial thousand copies of *The Def Leppard EP* sold out, Frank Stuart-Brown arranged for additional pressings. They came without picture sleeves, bore yellow labels in place of the original dark red ones and had a new catalogue number, MSB 001.

The EPs, meanwhile, continued to sell briskly. Phonogram's initial move on Leppard's behalf was, in fact, to repress the EP *again*, this time on the Vertigo label. They didn't bother with a picture sleeve and, for some unexplained reason, reversed the track order on Side One, giving *Getcha Rocks Off* the leadoff spot. The company also arranged for the band's first official photo session. In the worst possible taste, the photographer had the band members dress up in leopard print shirts and pose in front of a stuffed leopard.

Phonogram's next step was to arrange for the recording of a new single. Def Leppard were given a choice of producers – ex-Animal and Slade svengali Chas Chandler, pop eccentric Roy Wood of Move/Wizzard/ELO fame and Nick Tauber, whose name the Leppards recognized from old Thin Lizzy records, including the Irish band's early Seventies breakthrough hit *Whiskey in the Jar.* They selected Tauber – and came to regret the decision.

Four songs – *Wasted, Rock Brigade, Hello America* and *Glad I'm Alive* – were recorded at Olympic Studios in London in mid-September. Tauber claims he was under orders from Phonogram's A&R chief at the time, Rodger Bain, to tone down the guitar solos and accentuate the songhooks. In other words, to deliver a hit record.

Flying high. . .

He also says that he had the impression that the four songs were meant for a seven-inch EP; that meant keeping the tunes short and punchy.

Only two songs, *Wasted* and *Hello America*, were issued and the single did chart. But the band sounded stiff and Tauber's production dulled the razor-cut of Pete Willis and Steve Clark's guitars. According to Tauber, the recording budget was less than extravagant, somewhere between two and three thousand pounds. Responds Joe, "We did the three songs on the EP in fifteen hours for a hundred and fifty pounds and got better results than he did.

"He didn't push us on performance," Joe complains, admitting his vocals on the single were less than thrilling. "I was drinking milk during the session. I didn't know that it coats your throat. Tauber should have known enough to tell me." Joe also complains that Tauber's only show of authority during the week-long recording session was throwing Pete Willis out of the studio for farting.

Tauber has kinder words for Leppard. "They were very patient and very willing to learn. They weren't pigheaded. They wanted to be a great metal band and they made that clear. But they were very keen to learn about studio technique." And he concedes that the blame for *Wasted*'s failure to capture the band's stage bite was entirely his.

"The whole thing was too dead. The sound wasn't big enough, not live enough. There wasn't enough power and rawness. And that wasn't the boys' fault. It was mine."

Stateside at Mercury Records, Cliff Burnstein listened to the Tauber tapes and cringed. "I told the English company that under no circumstances would the U.S. label put those tracks out. I also advised them not to put them out in England. At least they cut it down to a single. (David Bates also made sure the Tauber tracks would not be included on Leppard's debut album).

"But I refused to issue the record in America. I told them 'If we put this out here, we'll kill the band stone dead before we've even started.'"

SEPTEMBER 28 – Leicester Polytechnic, Leicester.
SEPTEMBER 29 – Nottingham Boat Club, Nottingham.
OCTOBER 2 – Imperial College, London. This was Def Leppard's first headlining show in London. Because there was no dressing room at the hall, the band switched into their stage clothes behind the PA speaker stacks.
OCTOBER 4 – Civic Hall, Wolverhampton. Although headliners Slade constructed a ten foot stage

extension for the show, they would not allow Joe to go out on it during Def Leppard's opening set. That left a total of three inches between Rick's bass drum and the edge of the stage. Joe had to sing to one side of Rick's kit. To add to the misery, Rick left his wallet in a Wimpy hamburger bar, with £60 in it.

OCTOBER 5 – Rock Gardens, Middlesbrough.
OCTOBER 6 – Norwich University.
AC/DC TOUR
OCTOBER 25-26 – Mayfair, Newcastle. The first night of the show was cancelled because of a fire in the hall. Chairs went up in flames and the smoke damage was so bad cleanup crews were unable to make the place ready in time for the gig.
OCTOBER 27-28 – Apollo, Glasgow. The Leppards went out drinking with AC/DC singer Bon Scott after one of the shows. Scott, a native Glaswegian, took the boys to a bar in one of the roughest parts of the city. "Bon was really good to us on that tour," says Rick Allen. "He would come into the dressing room every night and wish us luck before we went on."
OCTOBER 29-30 – Apollo, Manchester.
NOVEMBER 1-4 – Hammersmith Odeon, London. On the second night, Rick Allen celebrated his sixteenth birthday.
NOVEMBER 5-6 – Empire, Liverpool.
NOVEMBER 8 – Bingley Hall, Stafford. Def Leppard played to nearly 8000 people at this show, their largest audience to date. At one point during the evening, AC/DC manager Peter Mensch told the band he was interested in handling them and offered to buy out their contract with Pete Martin and Frank Stuart-Brown. Unbeknown to the band, future Def Leppard producer Robert John "Mutt" Lange, who had just done AC/DC's *Highway to Hell* album, was also in the audience.

Cliff Burnstein was therefore not the only Yank with an intense interest in Def Leppard. He had a conspirator, Peter Mensch, a London-based American manager who already handled AC/DC and the German heavy metal band Scorpions on behalf of major U.S. rock entrepreneurs Steven Leber and David Krebs. Sharing a mutual taste for selling the unorthodox in a business that catered to the obvious, Cliff and Peter had already been through a few rock & roll wars together. In 1978, they founded Blank Records, an alternative music label distributed by Mercury in the U.S. It was Peter's first major industry job (although he had been working the promo phones at Elektra Records for a few months after leaving the University of Chicago); for Cliff, it was an opportunity to market promising new bands, square pegs that didn't fit into the boring round holes cut out by commercial radio and the mainstream press.

Blank was a short-lived utopia; the label released only two albums (one was the underground classic *The Modern Dance* by Cleveland pop dadaists Pere Ubu). But it was the beginning of a beautiful friendship. When Blank folded in '79, Cliff recommended Peter for a position at the Leber-Krebs organization, where he started out as Aerosmith's tour accountant before taking on management responsibilities for Leber-Kreb's main overseas acts, AC/DC and Scorpions.

The Burnstein-Mensch program for world heavy metal conquest was now underway. With Peter in England, where hard-based rock was undergoing a major renaissance, Cliff had a hot line to action central. If there were any young bands of merit aching for a record deal, Peter would know about it. In turn, Cliff could improve his young signees' chances for longevity by arranging for Peter to ink them to Leber-Krebs for management. Cliff had the record company side under control; Peter monitored studio progress and tour activity. Although they officially worked for different parent organizations, Cliff Burnstein and Peter Mensch were a rock & roll business team to be reckoned with.

Pete Martin and Frank Stuart-Brown would quickly find out how unbeatable Burnstein and Mensch were. At Def Leppard's September 7 show at the Lafayette Club in Wolverhampton, both Cliff and Peter were in attendance, the latter at Cliff's insistence. Cliff, as a representative of Leppard's U.S. label, handled the backstage schmooze ritual, reassuring

. . .in Brussels

the band after a rather mediocre set that they were ready for America. "I said to them 'Hey, it wasn't a great show, but you're doing fine. Unconsciously, you're doing everything right for America.' I don't think they believed me."

Management etiquette required that Peter remain in the audience. "I acted like I was there to see the promoter. I didn't want it to look like I was this American vulture pinching someone else's act." Actually, Peter already had a directive from Cliff to ease Pete Martin and Frank Stuart-Brown out of the Def Leppard picture. Although Martin and Stuart-Brown had a good record deal to their credit, Cliff did not feel these rookies had the experience and savvy to take Leppard all the way worldwide. "Essentially, Cliff said 'Peter, blow them out.'" Peter says he found out later there were bets throughout the English music industry on how long it would take him to get Def Leppard to fire Pete Martin and Frank Stuart-Brown.

The beginning of the end was the October-November English tour with AC/DC. "Pete and Frank were so proud of how they'd gotten us on this tour," says Joe, "not realizing this had all been previously set up by Cliff and Peter. They were basically following this dangling carrot from Burnstein and Mensch." Peter acknowledges that Def Leppard in fact paid £5000 to be on that tour (it is an accepted practice in England for new bands to pay headliners for the privilege of doing a major tour), although he says that AC/DC's crew transported Def Leppard's gear as a bonus.

Peter Mensch says Rick Allen set the ball in motion. "I was getting friendly with the group during the tour. Then Rick came up to me and asked me to do him a favor. He wanted me to hang out in the Leppard dressing room and make believe I was interested in them, to make their managers work harder." At the same time, Peter was having chats with Leppard road manager Robert Allen about management. Finally, the day of the Stafford Bingley Hall show, Peter proposed to the Leppard over hamburgers back at the hotel. "We discussed producers for the album and said 'Here's my number. But you have to get rid of your managers first.'"

Steve Clark opposed the move. "I remember him saying 'Well, they've gotten us this far, why can't they get us any further?'" recalls Joe. "We were sitting in a pub over pints of lager and I said to him 'These guys are better, this is the move we need. This is going to break us out of what Budgie are, to being what Zeppelin are.'"

"Steve had mixed feelings about our managers," adds Sav, "especially Pete Martin. He was a good drinking partner, a Scot, a bit on Steve's wavelength. He'd always have a beer and whiskey with Pete Martin – and then another beer and whiskey."

In the end, it was a unanimous decision. Steve reluctantly agreed to go along with the switch to Mensch, although Joe suspects Steve's theory is "that if I'm ever wrong, he can always turn around and say 'I told you so.'"

Joe cannot recall the exact circumstances under which Martin and Stuart-Brown were served their termination notice. Stuart-Brown says the bad news came a week before the Bingley Hall show, at the Manchester Apollo. Joe sticks with Bingley Hall, claiming that the band told Martin first. "I don't know how it happened, but I distinctly remember Pete Martin saying 'Well, I can't blame you and as far as I'm concerned, that's it. We'll tear up the contract and you can go.' Next thing, we hear a few days later from Pete Martin that Frank Stuart-Brown totally opposes Pete's theory about letting us go."

Legally, Stuart-Brown had every right to hold Leppard to their obligations. The group signed a three-year management deal with MSB, a deal that was less than a year old. Lawyers for both sides immediately went into action (Def Leppard retained Peter Mensch's English attorney). When the dust settled in March 1980, MSB had received a small royalty percentage on Def Leppard's first two albums, along with five percent of the band's publishing overseas.

All on this page: European tour November '83.

Peter Mensch could not officially sign Def Leppard to Leber and Kreb's Contemporary Communications Corporation until the litigation with MSB was concluded. Nevertheless, he quickly undertook concert booking and recording arrangements in the U.K. for the group, with Cliff Burnstein overseeing the band's affairs Stateside. In February 1980, Cliff resigned his A&R post at Mercury and started working at the Leber-Krebs office in New York. Def Leppard's Leber-Krebs deal went into effect April 1 – April Fool's Day.

Pete Martin left the music business altogether; as of the summer of 1985, he was selling advertising space for the *Sheffield Star*. His wife continued to run Revolution Records in Sheffield for a time, but business declined and the store closed. Stuart-Brown now divides his time between work in the home computer field and managing new hard rock bands. At the end of 1982, he signed a band called Wolf to Chrysalis. Peter Mensch even gave the group a slot on a British tour with Scorpions free of charge. Stuart-Brown says he and Pete Martin stay in touch, listen to audition tapes together and sometimes talk about going back into the rock management business together.

Def Leppard recorded the bulk of its debut album in only one day. *Rock Brigade, Hello America, It Don't Matter, Getcha Rocks Off, When the Walls Came Tumbling Down* – these were songs the band had been rehearsing and performing for nearly

two years. They couldn't get them any tighter. In less than twenty-four hours at Startling Studios, a converted mansion in Ascot owned by ex-Beatle Ringo Starr, Def Leppard recorded nearly a dozen backing tracks. They were, however, financially committed to a month's worth of studio time at Startling, which they felt obliged to use up. A month's worth of overdubs and remixes later, *On Through the Night* sounded like the life had been boiled out of it. "It was like painting a picture," Steve Clark says, "without knowing when to stop."

The man with the brush was Tom Allom, a producer with major successes by guitarist Pat Travers and Judas Priest to his name. Pete Willis was a big fan of Allom's work with Travers and the rest of the Leppards were longtime Priest freaks, so Allom seemed to be a good choice after the Nick Tauber disaster. He was also good at getting a live sound out of the band. On their first day at Startling, Def Leppard set up their equipment and tried to cut a backing track for *Wasted.* After four run-throughs, they dejectedly called it quits. But the next day, Leppard went in there and cranked out ten backing tracks with a ferocity that, for the first time in a studio, matched their stage rage. Nine of them ended up on the album.

Allom's only problem was knowing when to say "enough." "The whole backing for the songs – bass, drums, rhythm guitars – were all done in that one day," Joe says. "But then we used up a good two weeks just doing overdubs. We could have done that entire album in a week. If we had, I'd probably like it a lot better now."

There was a lot to like about it then. Whatever its shortcomings in retrospect, *On Through the Night* vividly documented Def Leppard's shoot-from-the-hip guitars, Queen-aphonic harmonies and three-minutes pop song savvy. With youth comes ambition and *Overture* was full of it, to be sure. But the song's breakneck middle and heavy guitar-choir climax bespoke of Leppard's precocious vitality just as eloquently as the torpedo rockers *Rock Brigade* and *Wasted* which detonated Sides One and Two respectively.

Hello America, released as a single in February 1980, three weeks before the album, was vastly improved from the Tauber version, pumped up by Rick Allen's awesome teenage horsepower and brightened by sheetmetal vocal harmonies. *It Don't Matter* remains one of the hottest rockers in Leppard's songbook, a driving UFO-esque workout. Even songs like *Sorrow Is a Woman* and *It Could Be You,* overloaded with unnecessary rhythmic changes and overcomplicated riffs, demonstrated the band's diligent attention to hooks and choruses, the songbait with which they intended to net an audience far beyond the borders of Headbangerland.

In the Rock Epic Department, roadie and aspiring lyricist Andy Smith checked in with an ambitious end-of-the-world scenario for *When the Walls Came Tumbling Down*, applying the Biblical image of Jericho's crumbling edifice to a post-Hiroshima landscape ("The city's heart no longer beats/No pity have I left to lend/A sinner sits reciting Dylan/It's now that I welcome the end"). Smith, a rabid fan of English folk-rock group the Strawbs, was beside himself with delight when Allom brought in Strawbs vocalist Dave Cousins to recite the Orson Welles-style intro to *Walls. . . .*

Yet there was no lack of laughs in Def Leppard's metal-pop attack either. *Hello America* was nothing less than Joe Elliott's version of the Beach Boys in spandex and fuzztone, singing "I'm takin' me a trip/I'm going down to Califor-ni-yaay!/Yeah I'm going to try Hollywood and San Pedro Bay yeah yeah" – with he-man delight. In truth, Joe had no idea there even was a San Pedro Bay when he wrote the words. He simply picked up an atlas and used the first California city he saw with an "a" sound at the end.

The only noticeable gaff on the album was the phony applause tagged on to the end of *Getcha Rocks Off* (billed on the album as simply *Rocks Off)* In spite of Allom's overattention to detail and Leppard's own studio naivety, *On Through the Night* was the best possible album Def Leppard could have made at the time. Upon release, the record quickly sold 30,000 copies in Britain and polevaulted into the Top Twenty.

The dawning of 1980 found Def Leppard back on the road, heading out on a gruelling two-month tour of clubs and universities – by Joe's count, forty-five shows in forty-seven days. On opening night in Aberdeen, Scotland, the heat from the band's new stage lighting was so intense that Joe ran off stage after the set and threw up. A reviewer who saw the show was about as enthusiastic. "Having just seen the Clash, I didn't particularly want to come to this gig," he wrote. He went on to dub Pete Willis "Pete Wells" and got all the song titles wrong (*Answer to the Master* became *And So to the Master*).

The Leppards received a terrible shock midway through the tour. On February 19, Bon Scott, their hard-drinking, good natured pal from AC/DC, was found dead in London in the back seat of a friend's car after an all-night session with the bottle. The next evening, the band dedicated a song to his memory during their homecoming gig at the Top Rank in Sheffield.

To add insult to injury, Geoff Barton of *Sounds* journeyed up from London to review the show and interview the band. Barely seven months after he'd praised Def Leppard to the heavens, he now grumbled that they were softening up, turning into major label stooges. "Because we were now with a record company, Barton came up on a nice train, had a hotel and had been taken out for a salmon dinner before the gig," Joe explains, still somewhat miffed. "So he complained that I didn't pick him up at the train station and the gig didn't have the same atmosphere. And he slagged us for it. He apologized a year later, but it was too late for that." The press backlash against Def Leppard in England had officially begun.

Following *On Through the Night*'s U.K. release on March 14, Leppard embarked on their most ambitious trek yet – a headline tour of major British rock theaters, including some venues like the Glasgow and Manchester Apollos where they had previously opened for Sammy Hagar and AC/DC. An ostentatious pomp-rock band called Magnum got the official support slot, but the Leppards demonstrated their support for the new heavy metal scene from whence they'd sprung by adding a young local band to the bill at every stop.

Def Leppard still had a lot to learn about making a proper showbiz entrance. Backstage at the Manchester Apollo, the band was in the dressing room getting ready to go on – trousers still around the ankles, shoes untied – when they suddenly heard their intro tape, the opening recitation of *When the Walls Came Tumbling Down*, booming over the PA out in the hall. "We ran, practically naked down six flights of stairs, and literally went for it," laughs Joe. "The guitars were tuned, the roadies holding them at the ready and we got out there thinking 'We've done it, how cool.' Steve and I jumped out on stage and then Pete Willis came running out to make his big appearance. Except he tripped over the lighting rig. He went sliding on his stomach right to the front of the stage. His guitar stayed in one piece, but it was the most embarrassing entrance of his life."

One of the shows, at the New Theatre in Oxford, was recorded for a live EP; its release, however, was scrapped by Peter Mensch and Cliff Burnstein, much to the annoyance of Phonogram's David Bates. The Leppard's April 13 London appearance at the Lyceum received a surprisingly positive, and astute, review from *Melody Maker.* "There was a genuine feeling that Def Leppard were attempting to revive and update a flagging musical genre," wrote Allan Jones, hardly an HM connoisseur. *"When the Walls Came Tumbling Down* may lunge awkwardly in the direction of the apocalypse, but it's played with the force of, say, the Clash's *Safe European Home."*

The biggest high for Leppard on that tour was headlining at Sheffield City Hall. For Joe, in particular, it was his dream come true, five years after Deaf Leopard played that legendary imaginary show with Thin Lizzy. One night, back in the early spoon factory days, Joe and Pete Willis were walking past Sheffield City Hall after a late rehearsal; Joe stopped and scribbled on the wall "Def Leppard will play here in 1980." On April 10, they made good on that promise, with a beaming battalion of Leppard moms and dads in attendance.

But all was not well in Leppardsville. Success brought pressure and the wrong kind of temptations. Rick Allen, especially, was falling prey to bad influences and the abuse of leisure substances. After the Lyceum show, the Leppards convened at Peter Mensch's London apartment for a band meeting, a conflab which quickly turned into a point-the-finger-at-Rick session.

"They started getting on me because I was smoking grass too much with the crew," Rick says. "I used to get a dressing-down every month. I think sometimes they were really just taking out their frustrations on me.

"But I did have an attitude problem. Big mouth, speaking out of turn all the time. To me, the rest of the world was out of line and I was always right." His brother Robert, along with his regular road manager duties, tried to keep Rick in line, "but nobody had much control over me." Rick finally started to straighten up and fly right after he heard a rumor that the rest of the band planned to fire him.

Rick's attitude was not the only problem. Peter was also concerned about the band's often over-spirited drinking. He already had one alcohol-related death on his hands, that of Bon Scott. Then shortly after Scott's death, another Mensch client, ex-Scorpions guitarist Michael Schenker, was picked up drunk in London's Kings Road by police and tossed into the slammer. "I didn't want to see that happen with Leppard. I was the one who had to be the father figure. It was 'This is the voice of God speaking, you will follow me.'"

But "God" only had so much to say about it. There was trouble on the horizon even as Def Leppard boarded their maiden flight to America in May. After ten hours of flying and in-flight bar services, Pete Willis got completely pickled and had to be carried off the plane in Los Angeles.

CHAPT

4

[HELLO AMERICA]

There's this seedy heavy metal club called the Rainbow, right next to the Roxy in Los Angeles. The first night Def Leppard got to town, somehow a couple of them made it to the Rainbow, as if guided by radar. And I swear they were back with chicks that night. So I knew these guys could pull. And if they could pull, they could sell."

Cliff Burnstein

America was ripe for the taking. At the turn of the Eighties, heavy metal kids Stateside were still worshipping English bands old enough to be their parents. Led Zeppelin, Deep Purple, Judas Priest and Black Sabbath – with and without Ozzy Osbourne – still reigned supreme, sometimes (as with the defunct Zeppelin and Purple) *in absentia*. Most American groups were either mirror images of the olde English kings or churning out identikit platters based on the Boston-Foreigner-Journey platinum design of sweet stacked harmonies and harmonized guitar fuzz. There were notable exceptions, like Detroit guitar maniac Ted Nugent and Pasadena party boys Van Halen. But in America, heavy metal was in serious danger of wimping out. And the average age of English bands touring the U.S. was double that of the girls they usually picked up backstage. The girls, in particular, were relieved when into this crowd of dirty old men and ninety-eight pound weaklings came Def Leppard.

In order to conquer America, Leppard had to get their bearings straight – fast. When the band arrived in Los Angeles, they checked into the Chateau Marmont hotel in Hollywood. The day before the first show at Santa Monica Civic Auditorium with Pat Travers, road manager Robert Allen called Cliff. "He said to me "What time do we have to leave the hotel to make the gig? How many hours should we allot?' I asked him what time the soundcheck was and he said 5 p.m. I told him if he left by 4.30, he'd be there in plenty of time. He didn't understand. You see, the itinerary he had didn't say Los Angeles. It said Santa Monica. He thought Santa Monica was in another part of the state, when it's just part of L.A. I explained it to him and he was a little embarrassed." Fortunately, Cliff and Peter Mensch hired Rob Cooksey, an experienced English road manager whose clients included Deep Purple and Ritchie Blackmore's Rainbow, to travel with Leppard for the first few weeks and show Robert the ropes.

Driving out of New York, June '83.

Shopping was a lesson in itself. "Pete and Sav went out to buy cameras and these guys didn't know anything," Cliff chuckles. "They got ripped off right away. They overpaid, they got no receipts and they had faulty merchandise." But the success of Leppard's visit to the Rainbow, where they were treated like rock royalty, was a good omen. Opening night with Pat Travers was another.

"I was shitting myself," Rick Allen admits. "I had a brand new drum kit, never seen it before, and it was all out of tune. It had been specially ordered and arrived the day of the show." Travers' drummer Tommy Aldridge, one of Rick's idols, helped him set it up right and tune it in time for Leppard's curtain call.

"Within two songs, there were kids shouting for *Wasted*," Joe marvels. "Only four or five of them, of course. But there were 2500 other people there that had never heard of us and they accepted us as well. Nobody booed. There was always a reaction and it was ninety-nine percent positive." The band opened with *Hello America*. "Surprise, surprise," laughs Sav. "But we could not believe the reaction. Sure, we'd come from England where we were very popular and you couldn't pick up a music paper without reading something about us. But this was America, where we thought nobody would know anything about us. And these people not only knew the songs, they were going mad for them. We thought 'Hey, this is it, this is fantasic.' It was better than England – and we were known in England." When the Travers-Leppard package pulled into Portland, Oregon two weeks later, the Leppard bandwagon was really rolling. An audience of 11,000 ignited matches and cigarette lighters as Leppard left the stage. "We went down better than Travers that night," Joe says proudly. "We were very big in Portland apparently.

"The album had only come out in March, yet it was the end of May and we were going down an absolute storm. From then on, we believed in the actual truth of it all. Before that, our attitude was 'Yeah, we can do it' because we had nothing else to believe in but to work in a factory. But all of a sudden, we were *there* – at the bottom of the ladder, granted, but after that kind of reaction we knew we could definitely build on this. We were going down better in America than we were in England where people knew who we were."

Leppard's sex appeal was immediately apparent. Heavy metal, as a rule, is boy music, played by males for other males about such crucial male concerns as sex, living dangerously, getting high and fighting mythical dragons. As a top act in the so-called New Wave of British Heavy Metal, Def Leppard was firmly in that established tradition. They were reviewed, praised and marketed in the same way their influences had been ten years before. From the very beginning in America, however, Def Leppard attracted a substantially large female audience that usually shied away from the aggressive macho tensions of heavy metal. These weren't biker molls either, motorcycle Irenes and black leather Bettys. Many of them were young attractive women drawn to the Leppards by their baby-faced good looks and the hard driving sound of their music.

"We started noticing that there was a growing number of females hanging around at the gigs," Sav explains. "It wasn't something we noticed on stage. But it became very apparent when we came off stage. It was amazing how many females there were, not just backstage, but around the hub of the concert itself. Easily fifty-fifty, whereas in England our shows were always ninety percent male.

"At the beginning, it was just something we'd remark on. Then after a while, it became amazing, that there were actually teenage females who liked heavy rock music."

"There are no female groupies in England," Joe continues. "There's not very many female fans. In England, normally it's the guys who wait out back for an autograph. You very rarely get panties thrown at you in England, unless you're Spandau Ballet.

"We didn't get our first panties thrown at us until the *Pyromania* tour," he adds, laughing, "but there were lots of girls on that first U.S. tour."

"Blimey, I went mad!," Rick exclaims. "I went nuts over there, women left, right and center. It was great being the support band because you had time to stand at the side of the stage and pick out all the best birds. I ended up getting a few undesirable diseases," he admits, "but I had a good laugh over it."

"We all had our individual fans," Joe says, "maybe only two or three in each city, but it was a start. They were very, very young too. They were all our age."

Joe remembers one trio of girls who turned up in San Antonio, shouting "Elliott!" throughout the show in a deliberately silly accent. "It was obviously some kind of in-joke between them. But I always knew who it was when I heard my name out there." Joe was disappointed when Leppard passed through San Antonio on the *Pyromania* tour and the "Elliott!" girls didn't turn up. "Then when we finished the *Pyromania* tour in Hawaii, I was talking to some guys from the press and suddenly I hear this 'Elliott!' I couldn't believe it. I turned around and it was one of these three girls. She was married, had moved from Texas, the whole thing. It was very strange."

After two weeks opening for Pat Travers, Def Leppard did time with Judas Priest in Texas. Unfortunately, Leppard's gear, which was being shipped from Portland, Oregon down to Houston for the first date with Priest, mysteriously went AWOL. Robert Allen and Russell Major rounded up some emergency equipment from a local music shop but the drums didn't stay together very well and the drum riser at the hall vibrated up and down every time Rick hit a beat. All during Leppard's set, the kit skittered back and forth across the riser, with the bass drum going one way and the cymbal stands going another. Russell tried to keep things together for Rick while Steve and Pete tried to make as much noise as they could through their rented amps.

By set's end, however, Rick had had enough. "Russ was coming on stage for the fiftieth time, pulling drums and mikes together, and I thought 'That's it, I don't care whose drum kit this is. It's going off stage – now!" Because Leppard's gear was set up so close to the front stage, when Rick kicked his kit over the riser, most of it went straight into the photographer's pit. The bass drum nearly knocked Joe into the pit with it. "Oh, dear, I got a good lecture that night," Rick says humbly. "It was very unprofessional what I did."

The Leppards' comparatively tender ages made it hard for some people to tell whether they were actual musicians or just fans trying to con their way into the gig. At one show during the Texas swing with Priest, Joe and Rick left their laminated stage passes back at the hotel. The security guard at the hall refused to let them back; Joe's protestations of "But I'm in the band" and then "I'll have your bloody job for this" were to no avail.

"Joe always used to leave his backstage pass on the tour bus," Rick notes. "He'd take it off and hang it on a hook in the bus. The driver would drive back to the hotel for a little sleep after dropping us off, so Joe'd be walking around without his pass, getting pulled up every five minutes by some goon from security."

Age was also a problem when it came to after-hours drinking back at the hotel. At sixteen, Rick was barely eligible to drive in most states, much less enjoy his favourite poison. In some states, Joe was the only one old enough to get a drink. Rick usually borrowed his older brother's driver's license to con sceptical bartenders. "There's a number on English driver's licenses," Rick explains, "your birthday in code and I'd tell these guys that the number would mean one thing or another, and a lot of 'em used to buy it. Also, English licenses don't have photos on them, so that made it easier." When Rick's ruse didn't work, his brother or Russell Major would sneak a few beers up to his room.

Drinking was also a problem with Pete Willis, but in a wholly different way. The plane flight from England boded ill for Pete's welfare Stateside and, subsequently, that of the entire band. Cliff Burnstein says that the first

DEF LEPPAR
65
SASKATCHEWAN
MONTANA
WYOMING
COLORADO
65
NEBRASKA
KANSAS
TEXAS
OKLAHOMA

.S.A. TOUR 1981.
Lake
Superior
Lake Michigan
Huron
Erie

time David Krebs of the Leber-Krebs organization saw Def Leppard perform was at a July festival gig with Ted Nugent at an outdoor raceway near Atlanta.

"They had to carry Willis off after the set. He was lucky he didn't die out there. It was a forty-foot-high stage and he would stand way up front, lean over the edge and zoom back. The guy was totally out of control. After seeing that, Krebs made up his mind that Def Leppard would never make it, that we were wasting our time."

At the heart of Pete's increasing reliance on alcohol was a touchy insecurity about his height and an innate shyness that became evident when he was dry. "The thing was that when Pete was drunk, he was brilliant on stage," Joe points out. "He'd do all the shapes that he couldn't do when he was sober. When he went on straight, he played great but he was very shy. He used to go and hide behind the amps between songs while I'd be talking to the audience."

Pete confesses that he did periodically suffer from stagefright. "I know it's daft to do. If things are going bad, you can only make them better if you try to jump about and take people's attention away from the problems. But sometimes you can't.

"Then there'd be nights when I'd be running all over the place and Joe would come off stage ranting and raving, 'Get out of my way, you're always in my way.' Oh, sorry, Joe, sorry about steppin' on your stage, man."

The growing friction between Pete and the rest of the band was already causing sparks to fly. On several occasions, Steve – who roomed with Pete on the road – knocked on Joe and Sav's door, clutching his toothbrush and a blanket, growling "I'm not sleeping with that bastard anymore." According to Joe, Pete also had a habit of using up all the bathtowels in the room, which made Steve understandably angry. "It got to a point," says Joe, "where Steve used to laugh about it because he'd gone past the stage of anger."

But the group's unexpected success in America overshadowed any bad trips between band members during that first tour. Joe Elliott was taking on-air phone calls from fans at a Chicago radio station when Ted Nugent's mother called up. "My boy's been telling me all about you guys," she told an astonished Joe. "He says you're real good and he sent me a copy of your record. I checked it out and I think you've got some real good stuff on it." Later, when Leppard got the opening slot on a tour with Nugent, he always gave Leppard a namecheck during his set: "How'd you guys like Def Leppard?" The band was thrilled just to get the tribute, not to mention the ovation that often followed.

Fan mail was coming in by the bagloads. Cliff Burnstein had convinced the boys to fill out questionnaires for *16* magazine, lots of "what's your favorite color" and "what kind of girls do you like to date" questions. Leppard hated filling them out. It was pretty demeaning stuff for a band that prided itself on the quality of its records and stage show. But it enabled "the five foxy rockers," as *16* so delicately put it, to reach a female audience that usually stayed away from heavy metal bands. The answers were quite enlightening as well.

Joe, for example, "is very fond of football, fish'n'chips, golf, cars and girls, not necessarily in that order!" (*16* editors are extremely fond of exclamation points). Steve Clark, on the other hand, "has oh-so-touchable blond ringlets and bright blue eyes" while Rick Savage's idea of a dream date is "a rock concert and steak dinner with an outgoing girl!" And, yes, it's true, Pete Willis likes eggs for breakfast and Rick Allen is "crazy about rock & roll, junk food, the color red and girls who write him letters." Gripping stuff, huh?

Financially, the 1980 U.S. tour was nothing to write home about. On most dates, Def Leppard were paid an average flat fee of $1000. Sometimes there was an extra $500 if the show sold out. At one outdoor festival with Nugent and the Scorpions, Leppard were paid a princely $33,000. But touring costs totalled over $10,000 weekly, only about $1500 of which went to salaries for Leppard, Robert Allen and the four man crew. There was nearly $5000 a week for transportation and $1575 for hotels. Expenses for the first six weeks of the ten week tour alone totalled over $91,000 leaving the band $51,000 in the red.

Still, record sales and radio action were heating up on Leppard in the wake of their tour. In the radio tipsheet *Friday Morning Quarterback*, *On Through the Night* was racking up major airplay points. In its first week of release, it came in second only to Genesis in *FMQB*'s airplay index. Thirty-eight stations across the country were playing the album, some reporting Top Twenty sales in their respective markets. At its peak, *On Through the Night* made it to Number 51 on *Billboard*'s Top 200 album chart, a highly respectable debut for a band that didn't even have a record contract twelve months before.

Even more surprising was the response to *On Through the Night* and Def Leppard's live show from the Yankee music press, particularly from mainstream publications. Show biz bible *Variety* reviewed Leppard's American debut with Pat Travers in Santa Monica with unexpected favour. "Def Leppard drew a respectable response from the near-capacity house with its own version of hard-driving but melodic rock. Group has all the requisite elements well in hand for this type of approach, including a 'long live rock' anthem or two which suggest the early potency of Foghat . . . Rick Savage is an aggressively active bassist who provides a solid underpinning for the twin guitar assaults of Steve Clark and Pete Willis."

People magazine, noting the band's potential sex appeal, described Leppard as "the world's first cuddly metal band" while generously noting the band's "verve and enthusiasm" on *On Through the Night.*

Not everyone was kind. *The Boston Phoenix*, in a cynical roundup of current heavy metal kings, compared Def Leppard's album to, of all things, *Never Mind the Bollocks, Here's the Sex Pistols.* "There's no mistaking the headlong dive-into-the-fray of *Anarchy in the U.K.* for the mudfight of Def Leppard's *Rock Brigade* . . . the only thing these records share is volume." *Creem*, given its strong heavy rock constituency, was a lot more understanding in its capsule review of *On Througth the Night*, citing its "amplified zeal and spirited bravura" and noting that while "Leppard's tunes border on the derivative . . . this band frequently transcends the mundane through sheer musical energy and playing ability."

By the time Leppard made their New York debut on Joe's twenty-first birthday, opening for AC/DC at the Palladium, the band had noticeably improved on stage, according to Cliff Burnstein. "They were not the world's greatest live band at the time. They were competent, but from that very first show in Santa Monica to the Palladium in New York with AC/DC, they'd come a long way. There was a lot of pressure on them when they got to New York, but they made a real good impression on that night."

The Palladium show got off to a weird start. During soundcheck, the lighting rig almost collapsed, dropping six feet without warning before coming to a halt just above Rick's head. "It frightened everybody to death," Rick says, "because when those things drop, they show no mercy."

But the jolt Leppard got that afternoon did wonders for them that night. The *New York Times*, hardly your typical heavy metal fanzine, raved about the band's set. Critic Robert Palmer wrote that "compared to AC/DC, the group positively sparkled . . . the playing is crisp and tight, the tempos are varied, the rhythm section rocks instead of lumbering along like a dinosaur, and macho excess, both vocal and instrumental, kept to a minimum. The music certainly isn't profound, but it isn't meant to be. It *is* rock-and-roll, and it's likeable."

It had been, in Steve Clark's words, "a rollercoaster year." Def Leppard went from playing clubs and opening for AC/DC and Sammy Hagar in the fall of 1979 to recording a debut album, headlining their own U.K. concert tour, touring America hockey arenas and nearly getting their album into the U.S. Top Fifty. "Just six months before, we were playing these little shitholes in the north of England," Steve remembers, still awed by it all. "And here we were third on the bill in front of all these people, playing with bands that were in our record collections." Not bad for five refugees from the Sheffield steel mills.

What goes up, naturally, must come

down and rollercoasters are no exception. Def Leppard returned to England in August to an unexpectedly chilly reception. They had gone from being home country heroes to traitors, selling out to the Yankee dollar, in three months.

"We knew it couldn't go on forever," says Steve. "We knew there was going to be some flak. But we didn't expect to get it so hard."

Tension had already been building in Sheffield, as far back as the Phonogram signing. "People in Sheffield thought we'd just been handed six-figures worth of money to do with what we liked," Joe notes. When Steve went into a local heavy metal hangout to have a drink, one guy came up to him and said "I don't think you deserve that contract" and punched him. Joe recalls shopping with his mother and having a kid walk right up and spit at him.

Success made things worse. Def Leppard had been local lads appearing weekly at tiny pubs like the Wapentake. But touring and studio work made them less and less available. The band's Sheffield following resented this inaccessibility, that Def Leppard no longer just existed for their neighbors and mates. Pubgoing in Sheffield, for the Leppards, was downright dangerous."

"The barmen would give us free drinks," Steve explains, "and then the girls would hang round us and the guys would get pissed off – 'What makes them so special and we're not?' I had a few punch-ups now and then, stuff like 'Fuck off, you American twats.' Their additude was basically 'Fuck you, you don't give a shit about us anymore.'

"They felt we'd used them to get something, to get a record deal, to go to America and that we didn't care about them anymore. But we didn't have a way to prove to them that it wasn't true.

Steve admits that returning to Sheffield after the U.S. tour felt very strange, as if a trap door had been shut behind him. He'd headlined in London, been to Europe and toured America. Now he and the other Leppards were back living with their moms and dads.

Any remaining jubilation over their American success was killed stone dead at the Reading Festival in late August. Originally founded in the Sixties as a showcase for top English blues, jazz and rock bands, the Reading Festival was almost entirely a heavy metal event by 1980. Iron Maiden, the Ian Gillan Band, Whitesnake, UFO and Budgie were among the metallic monsters booked for Reading that year and Peter Mensch, in what he thought was quite a brainwave, booked Leppard into the second-bill spot on the big Sunday night finale between Ozzy Osbourne and headliners Whitesnake. Theoretically, it was a good position for the band to show off the stage chops they'd picked up in the States.

Instead, Def Leppard practically got canned off the stage. Jealousy over their U.S. success and fears that they were lost to Britain forever turned the tide against Leppard with frightening speed. In addition, fate made a critical play. Just before Reading weekend, Ozzy Osbourne cancelled his appearance; former glam-pop sensations Slade were booked in his place. After topping the British charts throughout the mid-Seventies, Slade had gone into a deep commercial funk for a few years. At Reading, though, they were in the midst of a roaring comeback. And Slade ended up roaring all over Leppard that day at Reading. As Joe puts it, "Slade played all their hits. And we didn't have any."

'Pyro' Pete.

Def Leppard, in fact, played very well at Reading. BBC Radio aired five songs from the band's set on a post festival broadcast. But Leppard played that set amid a torrent of vegetables and beer cans. Already psyched up for Whitesnake's neo-Zeppelin thunder-rock, audience energy had been raised to a fever pitch by Slade. Def Leppard, caught in the middle, didn't stand a chance. It rained garbage through their entire set. Joe was hit in the balls by a full can of beer. Pete Willis received a huge chunk of dirt and grass in the face. When they finally left the stage, Def Leppard were, to all intents and purposes, finished in England.

"When the first tomato and beer can hit the stage, I knew this was it," Peter Mensch confesses. "Def Leppard were happening in America and they were coming back to England where four months before they were doing eighty five per cent in theaters. But to come back following Slade, combined with the fact that people thought we had sold out, that was it. We were gone."

Hurt and humbled by their Reading experience, Def Leppard took off for Europe, where they were booked on a brief Scorpions tour, before returning in October to Sheffield for extensive songwriting sessions. The band was able to move into a large warehouse space thanks to Rick Allen's mom. She worked as a secretary for the head of a local paper company, who was kind enough to let her son's band use a huge room in the company's Dronfield factory for next to nothing. There was a catch – Leppard had to agree to play a free gig at the Chesterfield Aquarius, a club that the paper boss apparently had some financial interest in.

But with that minor caveat, Def Leppard had unlimited access to the paper factory room, which was very important since the band was deeply in debt. According to Peter Mensch, *On Through the Night* had sold 200,000 copies in America up to that point, and an additional 40,000 copies in England. With about $75,000 in advances, plus tour support money and recording expenses from the first album, Def Leppard were nearly $175,000 in the hole to the record company.

Time is money as well. In securing the production services of hard rock studio superman Robert John "Mutt" Lange for their second album, Def Leppard made an investment that cost them nearly a year in rehearsal and studio time. Lange was scheduled to begin work with Leppard in October, 1980. But the extra innings that were mounting up in his production of Foreigner's *4* album forced Leppard to postpone recording for several months. Committed to Lange and convinced that he was the man to turn the embryonic crunch of *On Through the Night* into widescreen kerrang, the band resigned themselves to a cold hard winter of writing and rehearsing.

Leppard already had two numbers ready to go when they got down to business in the paper factory. *Lady Strange*, a battering-ram minor-chord rocker with Thin Lizzy/UFO overtones, was debuted on the spring British tour to fatten out the band's short set. Another song, tentatively titled *When the Rain Falls*, was written shortly before that same tour. After some reworking by Mutt Lange and the band, it would bow on the *High'n'Dry* album as *Let It Go*.

Without Mutt around to coach them in the mysterious art of hit songwriting, Leppard went about their work the best way they knew how – cooking up riffs and choruses, mixing and matching them until everything seemed to fit while Joe concentrated on lyrics and titles. They still paid rather direct homage to their original idols. *You Got Me Runnin'* opened with cannonball guitar chords right out of the AC/DC songbook. An instrumental fragment called *Switch 625* featured Steve and Pete's guitars roaring in tight harmonic formation à la Lizzy.

Yet the early demos which found their way to Cliff Burnstein's desk in New York were encouraging. One song in particular, *A Certain Heartache*, caught Cliff's ear. "Peter was a little embarrassed when he played it for me because it was a ballad. The demo had no chorus, but it had a great verse melody. I thought 'This could be a hit single for somebody.' Probably not Def Leppard, though. I thought we should shop it around to somebody like Bonnie Tyler." That song, with some pre-production surgery under Mutt Lange's direction, became the second album's breakthrough track, *Bringin' on the Heartbreak*.

Although the songwriting was going well, the group was getting restless waiting for Mutt. The October starting date had turned to November, then January. Joe became impatient and suggested a short December club tour to test the new material and get a little press, to at least show British metal fans that Def Leppard hadn't turned its back on them. The tour was originally just going to be the two shows at the Chesterfield Aquarius promised to the paper factory mogul. But over Steve and Pete's misgivings, it turned into a weeklong series of shows at some of their old club haunts like the Nottingham Boat Club and Retford Porterhouse.

"I didn't want to do the tour," Steve asserts. "It was a way to test the new songs, but it seemed silly, that we were trying to prove something to the kids. It would look like we'd already peaked and that we were trailing off, going back to the old clubs. I wanted to play in front of 3000 people again, not 300.

"He was right," Joe concedes. "It was my fault and it was one of the first big mistakes I'd ever made. Steve was totally against it and rightfully so. We got some good press from it, but it was a financial disaster and a waste of a week.".

Attendance was depressing. When Leppard played at the Nottingham Boat Club eleven months earlier, four hundred people were turned away at the door. This time, eighty-seven people showed up. Only one hundred and fifty fans came to Retford Porterhouse. In Dunstable, Leppard did good business, about eight hundred folks. But the show was a disaster. Joe only got halfway up the speaker stack during one of his climb-the-PA stunts when he fell off, straight on to his ass. Peter Willis' guitar also kept going on the fritz. Fortunately, two guitarists from a London-based glam-metal band called Girl, Gerry Laffy and Phil Collen, came to cheer the Leppards on. Phil helped Pete switch guitars during one number when Pete's roadie momentarily disappeared.

The band debuted four new songs at the show but without much success. Joe called out one number and when the band kicked in, Rick Allen started playing the wrong song. "We weren't familiar with all the titles yet," Joe says sheepishly. "We had to start that one again."

A little poorer and a lot wiser, Leppard went back to Sheffield to resume waiting. In March, they would finally start pre-production with Mutt Lange on *High'n'Dry* and by June the band would be back on the road, supporting Ritchie Blackmore's Rainbow in Europe. But for Def Leppard, still smarting from their Reading defeat, with nothing to show for the last six months but a disastrous club tour, those few months seemed like forever.

"The traumas and tribulations of recording *High'n'Dry* are covered in exhaustive detail in the next chapter. The end result, though was worth every bucket of blood. Def Leppard's second album was a significant improvement over the first in every category – songwriting, arranging, vocal performance and production. Coated with a deceptive commercial gloss, *High'n'Dry* glistened with silvery background singing and chrome-plated clusters of harmonic guitar. The massed choir of young Leppards in the clever middle break of *Let it Go* sounded like 10cc in triplicate while *Bringin' on the Heartbreak*, the former *A Certain Heartache*, swelled in the chorus with a youthful operatic vigour that would have turned Queen green with envy.

Joe's singing, under Mutt's tutelage, evolved from a sandpaper bark to a theatrical Ian Gillan-esque wail shooting up in stratospheric arcs while Steve and Pete sandwiched his mega-shriek with sharply executed aerial guitar ballets above the hard dropkick chords down below. Def Leppard had yet to assimilate their strong points into a single unified sound as they would two years later on *Pyromania*, but *High'n'Dry* was an impressive resume of their shotgun hard rock genius. For every artsy stab at epic metal like *Mirror, Mirror (Look Into My Eyes)*, there was Grade-A grunge like *High'n'Dry (Saturday Night)* or a locomotive killer like *Another Hit and Run*. The track *On Through the Night*, ironically, sounded like a leftover from the first album, although it was in fact a new song with an old title. Yet except for that minor wrinkle in their armor, Def Leppard beat their sophomore jinx with class, sass and a good solid kick in the ass on *High'n'Dry*.

So why was there so much initial resistance to the album when it was released in America? Cliff Burnstein confesses that the high degree of studio polish evident on *High'n'Dry* threw him for a loop at first. "It was very upsetting to me. It was so accomplished, whereas the first album had a certain roughness and spirit that I always liked. But in terms of what radio stations like, *High'n'Dry* should have been received much better than first album. In fact, it wasn't."

High'n'Dry sold a brisk 200,000 copies in its first couple of weeks Stateside. *Let It Go* was peddled to FM program directors as a key airplay candidate because of its uptempo rush and grabby chorus. It met with a damp reception, however, while *Bringin' on the Heartbreak* met with similar resistance, principally because it was a ballad, the last thing DJs expected from a band of heavy metal juveniles.

"I think a lot of people felt Def Leppard weren't going to make it," suggests Cliff. "They looked back at the first album and thought they'd been fooled a little bit by the eighteen-year-old shit, that the album hadn't gone gold or anything." Another drawback was Leppard's less-than-suitable '81 tour itinerary. The concert business was in one of its periodic slumps, with promoters hedging their bets on new acts in favor of easy sell-outs in arenas and outdoor stadiums. The best Leppard could do that late summer and fall was a month and a half supporting ex-Black Sabbath vocalist Ozzy Osbourne and then a couple of months co-headlining with a Florida boogie band called Blackfoot, which had a small following and a heavily-hyped connection with Dixie demigods Lynyrd Skynyrd (guitarist Ricky Medlocke played drums with an early Skynyrd line-up). For Leppard, playing arenas with Ozzy would be a gas as well as good promotion for the album. With Blackfoot, they'd be playing smaller halls for crowds half full of pseudo-Confederate yahoos.

The European prelude to the U.S. tour

got off to a bleak start as well. The first of Leppard's twenty-two dates with Ritchie Blackmore's Rainbow was scheduled for Essen, West Germany. The morning of the show, Joe was still in the studio with Mutt Lange in London, cutting last-minute vocals for the B-side of *Bringin' on the Heartbreak*, a hot little rocker called *Me and My Wine*. As the sun rose over the white cliffs of Dover, Joe caught a flight to Essen where he landed at 2pm. Leppard were on stage by 7pm.

Because the *High'n'Dry* sessions lasted right up to the tour deadline, the band never had a chance to adequately rehearse. Consequently, the Essen show was a disaster. Joe's voice was in shreds from the late-night recording and the rest of Leppard vainly tried to rehearse on the ferry ride to the European mainland. In Essen, Joe says candidly. "We were disgusting, We were really bad. We made the Rolling Stones sound like Supertramp. There was all this hype there about these hot-shot nineteen-year-olds – I was already twenty-one anyway – and we were awful. And we continued to be awful for the first week of that tour."

Blackmore, whose hot temper is legendary among roadies and ex-Rainbow members, got on quite well with Def Leppard. The two bands frequently played soccer on offdays, although Joe says after one game Blackmore disallowed a Leppard goal so his band could win. (If you're a headline act, you can get away with anything). Otherwise, the tour proceeded swimmingly until July 3 when Rainbow, Leppard and extra added attraction UFO arrived in Madrid for an outdoor show at the Estadio Roman Valero. Blackmore had a bugaboo about being on stage outdoors after midnight and the Spanish promoters refused to start the show during daylight hours. Subsequently, Leppard – being the youngest act on the bill – drew the short straw. They got on *after* Rainbow played. While thousands of Spaniards filed out of the arena following Rainbow's set, Leppard's crew scurried to set up their gear. By the time they started playing, Joe says, "we had about seven percent of the crowd left."

On July 13, Def Leppard set out on a short headlining tour of England before galloping off to the States. Attendance-wise the outing was a disaster, although *Sounds* blessed the band with a favourable if somewhat snide review – "However hard you scrutinize the new-found versatility, the arrogant practiced stagecraft or . . . the music itself, you'll detect little trace of the stars'n'stripes supposed to

have sprouted on the young face of the band . . . It was one long highlight, an orgy of sweat'n'dandruff." Peter Mensch says the tour was done strictly to prove to British audiences that Def Leppard had not sold out to America, despite sniping to the contrary. For the most part, the band preached to an empty congregation.

In America, at least, people were willing to listen. Despite the early lukewarm response to *High'n'Dry* by radio heavies, the band diligently hit local stations on almost every stop of the Ozzy and Blackfoot tours, doing on-air interviews and station promos at least every two days. Joe, the band's resident mouth, did most of them, although Steve, Sav and Rick were frequently pressed into service when there were two competing stations in the same city craving Leppard's presence.

The questions put to them by most DJs verged on the idiotic. "Who are your influences?" "How did you get the name of the band?" Some jocks confused the Leppards with old yellers like Kiss and Ted Nugent, coming on strong with the Hey, man, let's *rawk'n'roll* jive. It would take fifteen minutes for me to bring the conversation down to human level," says Joe, "away from this party animal nonsense. Certain people like Paul Stanley and Nikki Sixx do it real well. I couldn't do it."

Doing station promos was fun. One of Joe's favourite gags was borrowed from *Saturday Night Live* comedian Chevy Chase. "Hi, I'm Joe Elliott and you're not. And you're listening to..." At one station, Joe and Steve went through the usual "Hi, this is radio station blah-blah-blah." Then, in a nod to their first album, they said "And here's something to take you on through the night" and made a loud snorting noise as if they were sniffing cocaine. That promo never made it to air.

Sometimes their efforts went for naught. In one city during the Blackfoot tour, the band was riding in a van to the gig when a female DJ plugged the evening's show over the radio: "And tonight in town, we have Blackfoot and special guests Def Leppard, a three-piece band from Germany." "Well, we couldn't even get off the bus after that," Joe screams hysterically. "We were scraping each other out of the ashtray over that one. A lot of bands would have been insulted. But we couldn't stop laughing."

There were giggles aplenty during the Ozzy leg of the U.S. tour. At one hotel in the Midwest, Steve and lighting director Phay MacMahon thought it would be fun to present their own personal fireworks display from the

hotel balcony. "What we didn't realize," Steve explains sheepishly, "was that the grass was really dry from the heat. And the sparks from these fireworks, which were going off the balcony, proceeded to ignite the whole lawn below. I'm pissing myself with laughter while Phay is running around below trying to stamp out the flames with his foot. Eventually, the fire department was called."

On closing night in Daytona Beach, Def Leppard's tour bus got stuck in the sand when their driver and Ozzy's driver had a race and Leppard's driver pulled up too close to the beach. After the show, an end-of-tour blowout got out of hand when Joe and Ozzy drummer Tommy Aldridge (an old pal from his stint with Pat Travers on the 1980 tour) began throwing firecrackers from Aldridge's balcony down into the hotel swimming pool. The police, taking a dim view of this kind of entertainment, threatened to arrest the pair of them and nearly did. Joe managed to escape into an elevator, rode it down a couple of floors and sneaked into his room up the fire stairs.

Not so funny was the August 7 show in Providence, Rhode Island. Blaming poor ticket sales, the promoter informed both bands that he did not have the money to pay either of them. Backstage, while Joe was doing a quick interview, Ozzy's wife Sharon Osbourne walked up to the promoter and spat in his face, after which she kicked him in the balls. Twenty minutes after that, Don Arden, Sharon's father and Ozzy's manager at the time, looked the promoter straight in the eye and said "Listen, asshole, you're gonna pay my artist or I'm gonna break both your legs." "I think he paid," Joe says.

Aside from the fact that Def Leppard were obviously outdrawing Blackfoot in most cities as well as beating them in after-show merchandise sales, the fall Blackfoot tour was a low-key affair. In Norfolk, Virginia, burglars broke into the band's tour bus. The thieves made off with assorted T-shirts, trousers and sweaters, nine plane tickets to London, road manager Robert Allen's passport, a hair dryer and two cans of baked beans.

A carful of crazies in Atlanta, Georgia got their jollies when they spotted Rick Allen and Cliff Burnstein hitch-hiking into town from a local hospital where Rick received treatment after the show for a touch of clap. "We radioed for a cab at the hospital, but it never came," Cliff remembers. "So we thumbed it. Some wild kids picked us up and they went 'Hey, man, you're the drummer with Def Leppard.' These rednecks had driven two hundred miles to see

HAMER

the gig, in this car that was ready to fall apart at any minute. They will always remember that, having Rick Allen in the back of their car, hitch-hiking."

In Denver, Leppard and Blackfoot were booked for two shows at a club called the Rainbow on October 27. Joe estimates that of the 1200 people at each show, at least 1150 had come to see Leppard. Leppard played the opening set for the first show, per their deal with Blackfoot which always closed the show. For the second show, however, Blackfoot's manager – sensing the lack of interest in his band by the crowd – insisted that his boys do the opening honors, thereby avoiding getting blown off the stage by Leppard.

To make matters worse, Def Leppard were not travelling with headliner equipment and the lighting was at best adequate. "So we thought 'Okay, that's the way they want it? That's the way they're gonna get it." Def Leppard took the stage for the second show and blew the roof off the Rainbow. Joe claims it was one of the best shows the band has ever done. During *Getcha Rocks Off*, Joe leaped off the stage and ran up to the console in the back of the hall where Robert Allen was mixing the sound. Before Robert knew what had happened, Joe yanked his trousers down and dashed back to the stage in time to finish the song. When a female security guard, mistaking Joe for a rabid fan, refused to let him back on stage, Joe replied sharply "I'm the fucking singer."

A worrisome side effect of touring was the deteriorating relationship between Pete Willis and the rest of the band. Drinking was no longer the principal issue; it was whether Def Leppard itself could withstand the pressure of five young men on the verge of blowing their tops. While the band was on tour with Ozzy, Joe and Sav nearly came to blows over Willis. Sav believes that Joe sometimes overdid the disciplinarian act with Pete, often getting heavy with Pete when in fact lecturing him only made the situation worse. One night, Pete and Steve had one of their periodic blowups. Pete came over to Joe and Sav's room for a talk with Sav while Joe went down the hall to chat it out with Steve.

When Joe returned to go to sleep, Sav told him to get lost. "Fuck off!" he snapped. "You want to go to sleep? Go sleep with Steve. I'm sticking with Pete. He needs looking after."

"That's the only time I can remember having a real face-to-face argument with Joe," Sav claims. "Neither of us was going to give way."

Sav honestly believed the end was at hand when Steve went on a booze-a-thon during a few days' stopover in Seattle during the Blackfoot tour. "It was the only time I ever considered the possibility that the band was finished, actually dying. We were having problems with Pete. Rick was just getting over his attitude thing and I just couldn't see much life in us if Steve went over the edge. We were so close – the album was in the Top 40, people were telling us it was good. And this one evening, I just got the feeling that it was ending. This was as close as we were ever gonna get."

Two days later, Steve came down from his hotel room and apologized to the band. "Sorry, I've been like a bee. It was one of those things." He didn't touch a drop of liquor for the next three weeks.

A second *High'n'Dry* tour of Europe, this time with Judas Priest, extracted the last drop of road sweat out of Leppard. The group played eleven shows in eleven days. They would have played more except their passports were stolen in Amsterdam, forcing the cancellation of the final shows in Germany. There was no love lost with the fans there anyway. The Germans had not been impressed with Leppard's sloppy performances in June and the band was not that interested in prolonging the agony of touring. Def Leppard had been on the road non-stop for six months.

Pete Willis was the only member of the band who went home broke. For the European tour, each Leppard was paid a salary of two hundred and fifty English pounds. But in Amsterdam, Pete went ape-crazy with a fire extinguisher in the hallway outside his hotel room. There was six feet of white foam in the hallway and tiny little footprints leading to his room. It cost Pete £275 to pay for damage to the hallway floor and have the extinguisher refilled.

With 1982 around the corner, Def Leppard was now another year older, a whole lot wiser and a little bit sadder. After three months of recording and six months of touring, all they had to show for it was 300,000 in sales on *High'n'Dry*, a meagre 100,000 more than *On Through the Night*. The record was good and the shows were strong. They made new fans in every city they played. But the Big Break was still an album away. With Mutt Lange back behind the board for Album Number Three, it was going to be a long haul too. The next step in Def Leppard's career, as Cliff Burnstein puts it, "was another year of nothing going on."

Cowboy Joe from Mexico. Yee-haa! (1962)

CHAPTER 5

THE "MUTT" FACTOR

There are many different kinds of record producers – slick svengalis who call all the shots; benevolent uncles who cut it any way you like it; formula men who concentrate on maximum commercial potential at the expense of heart and soul; hot-dog philanthropists who put up all the money, take all credit and sit behind the console reading *Yacht World* magazine while the band slaves away on the other side of the glass.

Then there is Robert John "Mutt" Lange. He is none of the above and everything a modern rock band could ever ask for. He has infallible radio ears, killer commercial instincts and no small talent as a songwriter and singer. He doesn't just produce records; he midwifes them. He coaxes an album through its early songwriting gestation process, attends it through hard labor in the studio and then mothers it through the mixdown until it is finally ready to go out into the world on its own.

During the course of some projects, Lange is so intimately involved in the development of sound and songs that he literally becomes an additional member of the band he is working with, whether the band likes it or not. Despite a few rough moments here and there, Def Leppard have always liked it – a lot. Mutt was so indispensable during the recording of *High 'n' Dry* and *Pyromania* that when he initially declined to work on their fourth album, Leppard were uncertain whether they could even make a fourth album without him. As it eventually turned out, they couldn't.

By the same token, Mutt had a love affair going with Def Leppard before he ever stepped into a recording studio with them. "I had some involvement with them that they were not aware of at the time," he says. "Because they were signed to the same management as AC/DC, who I was working with, I used to hear tapes of their first album while they were making it. I was often at Peter Mensch's house and I'd hear *Hello America* and a few other tracks. I heard those vocal harmonies and thought 'Wow, an English band doing that stuff.' The album sounded a little clinical, though. *Hello America* sounded like they were listening to groups like Boston but didn't quite have the experience to use the harmonies and blend them in a rougher way.

"But I knew the potential was there. See, I prefer English rock bands. They write better riffs. All the classic riffs come from England and I could hear that those two guitarists could really write riffs. I'd also seen them when they supported AC/DC in England and they looked great. Since they had the looks and they had the riffs, I knew that with me as an extra member, so to speak, we could pull the songs together."

By the time Mutt agreed to work with Def Leppard on their second album, he was one of the most sought-after producers in the record industry. He was so sought-after that Def Leppard sat around twiddling their thumbs in Sheffield for six months waiting for him to finish off Foreigner's *4* album before they could commence work on *High 'n' Dry*. A native of South Africa, Mutt first came to the attention of the British record-buying public in the mid-Seventies with his production of a classy Birmingham sextet called City Boy. They specialized in an eccentric 10cc-style blend of highly commercial songwriting, intricate art-rock arranging and silvery harmonic singing, kind of like a landlocked north-of-England Beach Boys. City Boy were not exactly heavy, but for a while they were pretty hot. The 1977 single *5.7.0.5*, a Lange production, went Top Ten in the U.K.

It wasn't long before Mutt was going Top Ten worldwide. His A-1 job on AC/DC's 1979 crunch classic *Highway to Hell* (the band's last studio outing with the late Bon Scott) put him in the running for the title crown in the heavy metal production sweepstakes. A year later, *Back in Black* clinched it. Mutt had developed a special knack for giving the savage abrasive sound of macho thud-rock a rich studio resonance that, instead of making the brothers Young sound like Top Forty candyasses, made the rolling thunder of their atomic blues rock sound like it was exploding in a big concert arena inside your head. The result was accessible but not compromising, highly commercial yet almost surrealistic in its recreation of a Big Rock blowout right in your living room.

Def Leppard, then, were really a Mutt Lange dream band. They had the singing and they had the slam. They also had good song ideas, despite their tender years. And just as Leppard could benefit from Mutt's experience, Mutt believed he could achieve something very special – and very successful – with them in a recording studio.

The problem was how to reconcile their youthful impatience with his insistence on perfection. Mutt's slow, methodical way of working often brought out the worst in Leppard. At one point during the recording of *High 'n' Dry*, when progress seemed to be at its slowest, Robert Allen telephoned the studio to talk to his brother Rick. Joe Elliott, who had been up two days straight working with Mutt, took the message and, in his haze, forgot to give it to Rick.

"Later that day, I was in the bathroom, having a piss, when I saw Rick and told him that Robert had called and said so-and-so," Joe relates. "Rick said 'Oh, no, he didn't.' I told him that Robert had called, that I'd spoken to him myself. Rick just said 'Piss off, you asshole.' I turned around and said 'Don't talk to me like that.' So he said it again straight to my face – 'Piss off.' So I shook the drips off, zipped up, came out and we had this massive fight. We beat the shit out of each other for two minutes."

"But the funniest thing," Mutt continues, "was that afterwards Rick came back and very humbly said 'Joe, I'm sorry about what happened.' And Joe said okay. Rick stood there and, after a minute's silence, said 'Well, aren't you going to say you're sorry?' Joe said no and POW! It started all over again."

What frayed nerves and increased tensions during the *High 'n' Dry* sessions was the combined amount of time it took to (a) examine, edit and sometimes re-edit the songs to Mutt's satisfaction and (b) record them in Mutt's preferred way – piecemeal, instrument by instrument, sometimes note by note.

Mutt was not present at the band's 1980 songwriting sessions in Sheffield. Leppard had set up shop in the paper factory there with a Fostex deck and a Teac four-track recorder, laying down rough versions of the compiled material. A couple of those demo tapes made their way to London for Mutt's consideration. Then in March of '81, Leppard relocated to a rehearsal space in North London, down the street from a women's prison, ready to start pre-production. On the very first day, Mutt walked in looking like Robert Plant, according to Joe, sporting long wavy blond hair and wearing a heavy trenchcoat.

"He introduced himself and said 'Right, let's get started then. This song you do *When the Rain Falls* – play it faster.' So we played it for him, faster than usual. Then he said 'Play it slower.' Then it was faster. He asked me to sing a different melody, to change the meter. This went on and on. And eventually that song became *Let It Go*."

Mutt was quite happy with a number of the songs essentially as Leppard had written them. There were few significant changes made on *Another Hit and Run* or *No No No*. *High 'n' Dry (Saturday Night)*, on the other hand, was practically unrecognizable from the song Leppard brought down from Sheffield.

"I wanted one song on the album to have a kind of *Highway to Hell* feel –

Battery Studios, London – time out from recording *High'n'Dry*.

no bass to start with, coming up in stages," Mutt relates. "We got a groove going for the verse, and then tried to figure out where we wanted to go with it. We'd throw ideas around, these basic feels, sing them and then have the guitarists play them to make them sound a bit more credible. Once the verse was in shape, we worked on the chorus. It had to be a real anthemic sort of thing."

A similar overhaul was done on *A Certain Heartache*, the epic ballad that would become *Bringin' on the Heartbreak*. The song didn't have a chorus when Mutt first heard it. "It consisted of the jangley verse with a bit of the bridge in there somewhere. I think they had in mind a kind of *Stairway to Heaven* thing; Steve likes that long wrangled guitar jangle." With Mutt listening closely for the knockout punch, he and Leppard came up with the song's hard-hitting chorus and then orchestrated the bridge so it had more kick.

"That was the way it was usually done. We'd pull out the key riff, break it down and build it up again amongst ourselves. This is probably the best example of total democracy within a band. I really am an extra member. And it was the first band I'd ever been in where the democracy worked. The best idea always wins; it doesn't matter who it comes from."

Pre-production for *High 'n' Dry* only took about a month, but it was a month of solid work. "We really worked on the dynamics," Mutt claims. "They had the riffs, but they would start loud and then just get louder. That was one area where they were not experienced. So we'd break up a riff into parts, take it down as well as up.

"That was the one thing the band learned from that album – the dynamics of songwriting. Because the song structures were pretty much there already. They had learned their craft off bands like AC/DC before I'd met them. The style was similar, but Def Leppard's was more expansive in the sense that their songs had these little modal sections, which AC/DC would never have had.

"There was a possibility in those songs for an orchestral sound. With AC/DC, you'd just have Malcolm Young's guitar on one side and Angus' on the other. But with Def Leppard, the choruses in their songs deserved a real big sound, sort of like Queen, not just a straight guitar sound."

In retrospect, the actual time spent at Battery Studios (Mutt's studio of preference) cutting *High 'n' Dry* was only about two months. The band started in April and, according to Peter Mensch, the last overdub was

Robert John 'Mutt' Lange – producer cum sixth Leppard.

recorded on June 11, after which Mutt invested another couple of weeks for mixing. But the process of recording each instrument and vocal individuality, subdivided into sections, was a bit more arduous than Def Leppard were used to. Those two months, at times, seemed like years.

Strangely enough, since Mutt recorded Leppard an instrument at a time, he had them start by playing the songs together live in the studio, minus Joe's vocals. But the only thing he would keep from the take was Rick's drumming. To keep Rick from racing ahead or falling behind the beat, Mutt had him play to a mechanical click track. And because Joe was not singing, Mutt would count off a take over the intercom by saying "Okay, chorus, one-two-three-four . . ."

Sav's telepathic link with Rick's drumming would normally have meant laying bass tracks next. However, Mutt, Sav and engineer Mike Shipley had trouble getting a satisfactory bass sound. Since the album was being done piecemeal anyway, they eventually decided to go with the guitars next. This was particularly advantageous; rather than let the bass frequencies dictate how the guitars would sound in the lower registers, Mutt, Steve and Pete were now free to experiment to their hearts' content. They could create their own guitar space and work Sav's bass into it later.

To achieve that spatial Queen-like quality in the guitars, Mutt not only cut Steve Clark and Pete Willis' parts separately, he cut parts of their parts separately. "We wouldn't go for a guitar track all the way through the song," Mutt outlines. "We would get a guitar sound which would just suit the verse. We'd put that part down and layer it with more guitars until the verse had the right vibe.

"I would only layer as many guitars as

the part seemed to require," Mutt insists. But that would sometimes mean as many as six guitar tracks just to achieve that certain "Steve Clark scream" or "Pete Willis crunch." "It was usually in a lower register, to get a more ballsy effect. Jangley sounds would be double-tracked with dirty growls or super-clean strumming.

"It was pretty dicey going that route, I must admit. For a band like Leppard, the key thing in a situation like this was to retain the feel. The guitarists would get really tired, playing the same thing over and over again. They'd just forget where they were. And if you double-tracked a lot and didn't get it exactly in time, it could become mushy, which there was a bit of on *High 'n' Dry*.

"Nobody in the band was terribly experienced at this style of recording. But the songs and performances still had that special vibe."

Mutt claims that the principal reason he adopted this studio approach was because Def Leppard already had the song department well-covered. He didn't have to worry about creating the sensation of A Band Playing A Song Together because the songs already packed that wallop. "If you heard the pre-production tapes, it was THERE. It was just a sound thing. I didn't want an album that was just meathead from beginning to end.

"We could have pissed that album off literally in a couple of weeks and it would have been fine. But we wanted it to be more listenable. Most of the songs were pretty pure metal. But there were the odd numbers like *Bringin' on the Heartbreak* that I knew Leppard could crossover with, that they could reach a wider audience with and still have the balls."

The balls came from the tight deliberate pacing of the songs, even in racier entries like *Let it Go* and *Another Hit and Run*. Mutt believed that hard-rock guitarists – the English species in particular – didn't actually listen to the rest of the band when they were in full freakout. They concentrated on their own riffing, using that for their rhythm guide. "English guitarists," he says, "go for excitement, and excitement means not holding back. They go out on a limb and blitz."

With Leppard, he wanted to slow things down and tighten them up. *Let It Go*, which roared right out of the starting gate, was a lot slower than Leppard had first written it. Mutt also worked with Joe to insert more space in his vocals, like the "Cool woman . . ." interlude in the song. "Power," Mutt argues, "comes from space if you can get it right. I always thought the guys in AC/DC were masters of slow-rock. They could play in half-time and sound so much more powerful."

Leppard in half- or three-quarter-time meant Joe had more room to experiment with his singing, to dramatize his enunciation and belt out those notes that deserved it. The maturity of Leppard's songwriting on *High 'n' Dry*, seasoned with Mutt's wisdom and experience, opened up new possibilities for Joe, who often found himself gasping for breath on stage trying to keep up with the rest of the band as they stormed through *Rock Brigade* or *Wasted*. One way Mutt helped out was by changing the vocal melodies of some *High 'n' Dry* numbers as Joe was cutting his parts in order to emphasize certain vocal dynamics and maximize Joe's singing strengths.

"Dynamics – that's what Mutt really taught me," Joe says gratefully. "Not just in the vocals, but in everything Def Leppard did. He could make the guitar solos sing instead of just wail. A lot of things Mutt suggested didn't work. But more often than not, they did.

"He also taught me how to sing properly. I used to ramble all the time. In *Rock Brigade*, I didn't leave myself a gap so I could breathe. No wonder I was always running out of breath in the middle of a gig. Mutt showed me how to sing two words and then breath without losing my place. I'd never though about how to do that before. I'd done it all the wrong way around. I got into a band and *then* I learned how to sing. I wouldn't recommend it to anybody else though."

Their first semester at the Mutt Lange University of Hard Rock Hitmaking proved to be a great education for Def Leppard, but they were so absorbed in their studies that they nearly missed the summer tour recess. Having spent two months on recording, Mutt only had a couple of weeks to mix the entire album and the first couple of those went out the window when engineer Mike Shipley literally dropped out of the project.

"We were really tired," Mutt confesses. "We tried mixing the record for about two weeks and it just wasn't happening. Mike Shipley kept passing out. Not from drinking, but from exhaustion. He fainted a couple of times right on to the studio floor. One time, he went to the toilet. After a while, I went in to see how he was and he had fallen asleep on the floor." On top of that, Mutt was forced to switch studios in mid-mix.

He took up residence at London's Roundhouse Studios with a new engineer and knocked the whole LP off in six days, cranking out two tracks a day. "We couldn't do a lot of the things

that we would have wanted to do. We just tried to get a reasonable sound."

Mutt barely made his deadline – an omen of things to come. Indeed, Mutt and Joe polished off *Me and My Wine*, the B-side of *Bringin' on the Heartbreak* with only hours to spare. On the day Joe was scheduled to depart for the first European leg of the *High 'n' Dry* tour, he and Mutt were still cutting vocals in London at 7:30 in the morning. Six and a half hours later, Joe was on a 2:00 pm flight out of Manchester.

Pyromania was more of the same – a lot more. The ritual of song dissection, guitar architecture, vocal study and remix magic that had taken more than four months with *High 'n' Dry* would require an investment of nearly three times that for *Pyromania* – an entire year that Def Leppard, on the cusp of a major commercial breakout in the United States, could ill afford. The advent of MTV in America, the world's first twenty-four hour music video cable television channel, gave *High 'n' Dry* an extended shelf life when MTV slotted the "performance" video for *Bringin' on the Heartbreak* into heavy rotation in late 1981. At that time, the infant channel had a shockingly small library of existing videos to choose from. Major U.S. record companies, plagued by the lack of prime time outlets for pop music on the major networks, lagged far behind their European counterparts in the production of promotional videos. Anything English, then, was hot on MTV and Def Leppard were not only English, they were a good-looking hard rock band, an anomaly among MTV's initial glut of New Wave synth-pop poster boys.

"The *High 'n' Dry* album was already

history on the charts," says Cliff Burnstein. "But then MTV started playing *Bringin' on the Heartbreak*. Slowly but surely, we started getting sales reports on the record and it started selling about 5,000 copies a week, which was enough to get it back on the charts. This was a whole new ballgame. Before *Pyromania* came out, *High 'n' Dry* had gone gold."

That was not enough to keep the wolf away from the door, though. Complicating the picture was a nasty legal action between Leppard guardians Burnstein and Peter Mensch and the Leber-Krebs management organization. Peter, doing double management duty for Leppard and AC/DC, had been fired by the latter during the recording of their *For Those About to Rock* LP. He continued to work with Leber-Krebs on behalf of Leppard, guitarist Michael Schenker and Scorpions. But in January 1982, a disagreement over his and Cliff's financial arrangement with the company got ugly. According to Peter, Krebs held back payments he believed were due him. Then Krebs announced that he wanted to alter the terms of the Mensch-Burnstein contract.

Burnstein declared war, threatening to sue Leber-Krebs if the company did not cure its breach of contract. Krebs replied by firing Burnstein on April Fool's Day. Mensch resigned immediately. The unemployed duo then went to Leppard, Schenker and Scorpions and gave them a choice – work with us or stay with Leber-Krebs. Schenker and Scorpions elected to stay with the company. Leppard, without hesitation, told Cliff and Peter "Right, where do we sign?"

Unfortunately, Mensch and Burnstein now managed a band with essentially no income. The pair also had a major lawsuit on their hands. As the band's bank balance plunged into the red – to the tune of nearly $700,000 – Mensch borrowed money from his father and from Burnstein to keep the band fed during the recording of *Pyromania*. The band's merchandising firm, Brockum in New York, also fronted Def Leppard $100,000 to keep fiscal disaster at bay.

Thus it was crucial for Mutt and the band to get a quality record, at least three tracks deep in hit singles, out as soon as reasonably possible. Of course, they did nothing of the sort. *Pyromania* was loaded with hits. It became the model by which future hard-rock chart bands would be judged. But recording it seemed to take forever.

Forever started in January '82 in the Sheffield paper factory where Leppard had previously cooked up the

ABOVE and BELOW: Filmin' for *Foolin'* video.

songs for *High 'n' Dry*. This time, however, instead of writing songs that Mutt Lange would dismantle anyway, the band concentrated on developing parts of songs – knockout riffs, drop-dead choruses and soaring bridges which Mutt and Leppard could stitch together into song form later on. Mutt subsequently received co-writing credits on all ten *Pyromania* tracks.

"We gave Mutt songwriting credits because this time he actually helped us structure the songs," says Joe. "They weren't written songs that he changed. He sat down with us as a sixth member of the band and participated in the whole thing."

Several *Pyromania* songs have rather interesting histories. *Rock of Ages* was a song without a chorus until one day, during recording, Joe spotted an open hymnbook laying on a nearby organ. Right there in front of him was the old hymn *Rock of Ages* (Cleft for me, etc. etc.). He tried singing it over the melody. It sounded perfect. He tested it on Mutt, who said "Yeah!"

Too Late for Love had no words at all until Joe trotted out an old set of lyrics left over from an ancient Leppard stage number called *This Ship Sails Tonight*. *Ship* had been a staple of the band's disastrous pre *High 'n' Dry* winter club tour but had never made it to vinyl. Joe had used the words from *Ship* with another melody for about five shows, then ditched the lot. But they fitted nicely with *Too Late for Love*, which is where they stayed.

The basic riff for *Die Hard the Hunter* was written on the Leppard tour bus during the 1980 U.S. tour. Although commonly thought to be an Elliott salute to Mott the Hoople's Ian Hunter, Joe says the title was inspired by *The Deer Hunter*, the acclaimed 1978 film about the tragic physical and spiritual costs of America's military involvement in Vietnam. "I was going through a period when I wanted to write about something other than sex, drugs, women backstage and Jack Daniels. I wanted to deal with a serious subject that I didn't necessarily have to be a big expert on. I didn't want to write about the Falkland Islands war because that would have been too mercenary, cashing in on a current event. But I'd already written *Billy's Got a Gun* for the album, a kind of *Death Wish* scene, a real New York subway song about a guy that fell into bad company and turned into a troublemaker.

"I wanted to do something similar, but with a different setting. And I thought an interesting twist would be a song about a guy who comes home from war and can't adjust to civilization. Lo and behold, three months after the album was released, Sylvester Stallone came out with the first Rambo movie, *First Blood.*"

While Stallone was making *First Blood*, Leppard had been sweating blood at London's Park Gate Studios, where they laid the basic instrumental beds for *Pyromania*, and at Mutt's home away from home, Battery Studios. Mutt's finely tuned hearing and almost obsessive attentiveness to the slightest sonic detail not only made progress slow; it was hard for outsiders to detect any progress at all. After a late-night session, Mutt would often pop into Peter Mensch's house – a short drive from Battery – and play tapes of the evening's accomplishments. "Mutt would come in and say 'Listen to what we did tonight' – and three more words would be added to a vocal. It got to a point where I'd keep listening to these tapes and I couldn't tell what was there and what was missing."

After a while, even Mutt's ears began to deceive him. "We were going deaf," he confesses. "We were singing a semi-tone sharp, our ears would get tired and we couldn't hear the bass anymore. We watched Elton John on *Top of the Pops* one night and he sounded really out of tune."

A considerable chunk of the album itself, they soon discovered, was also out of tune. Unlike *High 'n' Dry*, where Sav's bass was the last instrument to be recorded, it was the first to be cut on *Pyromania*. That posed a unique problem. Wherever Sav's playing wavered in pitch, the guitars laid on top had to be retuned to match him. If Sav went sharp, every one of the guitars on top went with him. Not surprisingly, when it was time for Leppard to put down the backing vocals, they discovered to their horror that the guitars were a little out of tune. It was too late to redo them all, so they were put through a harmonizer (an electronic device that approximates a choral effect) to cover the bum notes.

Tempers flared on both sides of the console. Rick Allen remembers one agonizing day laying down four bars' worth of cymbal overdubs at Battery. "Mutt's voice would come over the intercom after every take, going 'The timing is brilliant, but the vibe isn't there' or 'The vibe's great, but you haven't quite got the feel.' I was thinking 'Hang on a minute, I'm only playing four bars.'

"I had done this one particular take and Mutt just sat in the control room listening to the tape, analyzing it for what seemed like ten minutes. I sat there in the studio, wondering what I was supposed to do. So I decided to try and attract his attention. I said 'Mutt? Why don't you play it to me and I'll have a listen, see what I think about it?' He turned around to me and said 'When I want your opinion, I'll ask for it.' Well, I had this handful of drumsticks and they went *flying* towards the control room window.

"He did apologize to me after that, though. He knew he was out of line for saying that."

Mutt's impatience, to be sure, was understandable. He started by setting up rhythm patterns on a Linndrum machine for Sav and the guitarists to play by. The patterns were just basic boom-chick-a-boom sounds; the big drum thunder could come later. Mutt figured if the instrumental tracks had mighty metal balls just with that Mickey Mouse Linndrum sound, then when a real bass drum or snare exploded in the right spots, the songs would have real fat.

Sav's bass was next. It only took testing of about fifty different amplifiers to get an acceptable bass sound. The Peavey amp Sav ended up with did a yeoman job for the entire album and then, fittingly, blew up at the end of the sessions.

Then came Steve Clark and Pete Willis' guitars. Something as simple as the key a particular song was in could have Mutt pulling his hair out. "Let's take *Billy's Got a Gun*. That big orchestral riff is in C, which is a really balls-less key. But the riff only sounded good in C, so we couldn't move it out of there. In order to get a good, cutting sound and still keep the bottom end nice and fat, we had to work on the sound in stages."

That meant, in some cases, working on only one guitar string at a time. "We'd get a powerful sound with a lot of attack on one string. Then we'd set up a clean harmony on a lower one. After that, we could cut the exact same riff on those strings with a more honky sound to get a solid mid-range. Then we'd do the same riff a third time to get a real booming sound down below. And that would be one guitar – three weeks later."

The Leppards would probably have all become complete basket cases if it had not been for the World Cup soccer championship games broadcast on television throughout the summer. Watching the games was very therapeutic, particularly for soccer fiends Joe and Sav. After a good late morning/early afternoon workout in the studio, the band gathered around the idiot box at 3 pm and watched the great feet of Europe and Latin America kick up a storm until 7 pm, when they adjourned for dinner before returning to the business at hand.

Leppard's nightly soccer vigils inadvertently had a lot to do with the later success of *Photograph*. According to Joe, the song had a great bridge, a good chorus and a limp verse riff. Steve Clark changed that.

"Steve was the only one not interested in the games," Joe points out. "He'd sit around with us if England was playing, but he couldn't be bothered if it was Uruguay vs. Argentina. One night, we were watching the game when the announcer suddenly got quiet and we heard this loud guitar blasting from the room next door. It sounded great, so we got up and ran over to see what was going on. Steve sat there beaming, saying 'I fixed it.' And that was it. *Photograph* was born."

As the songs began to take shape, it became apparent that the blood, tears, toil and sweat invested in *Pyromania* were paying off. *Rock of Ages* and *Rock! Rock! (Till You Drop)* were packed solid with classic arena rock kerrang, metallic to the very last crunch. *Photograph*, with its artful mix of macho strut and singalong swing, had "single" stamped all over it. *Billy's Got a Gun* and *Die Hard the Hunter* combined cinematic production with boot-in-the-groin power. In short, *Pyromania* was, as the song goes, "Action! Not Words."

To be sure, the combustible commerciality of the songs made it that much harder for Mutt and the band to say "enough's enough." Nothing could be left to chance. Ironically, their diligence cost them quite a bit of sound quality in the end. There were so many overdubs, so much winding and rewinding of tape, that the oxide started coming off the tape to the point where Mutt could

Fing(er)s aint what they used to be.

actually see through it. Rewinding the tape also meant a significant loss of high end in the final mixes.

More alarming was Joe's vocal condition. He recorded his vocal parts in no less than six studios, working on different lines on different days in different studios. After finishing only two songs, his voice was in shreds.

"Screaming things like *Stagefright* is not a natural way to sing. It would tear my throat up. I'd come in one day to sing normally and leave that evening sounding like Tom Waits."

"He didn't want to be beaten," Mutt says in admiration. "He wanted to carry on even when his throat was stripped raw. But you're not dealing with a guitar string you can change."

On Mutt's advice, Joe took voice lessons from his ex-wife Stevie Lange, a talented and well-known session singer. She taught him different ways of singing as well as the importance of vocal confidence. Upon his return, Joe knocked out the entire vocal to *Rock! Rock! (Till You Drop)* in two hours. "That was good for me," he insists, "because I could see that I could still do it."

But there was another problem which required a much more drastic solution. Pete Willis was still drinking heavily and his resulting actions were jeopardizing completion of the album. When the band was recording the background handclaps for *Rock of Ages*, Pete was so out of it that his hands kept missing each other.

Pete was not Def Leppard's only problem drinker. During the *Pyromania* sessions, Steve had taken some time off to see a psychiatrist about his drinking. But Pete's tippling had brought out a frustration and unhappiness that created friction within the group. As Cliff Burnstein explains, "Steve is a real gentle person. And if he's got problems, he's usually quick to admit them. He doesn't blame the world for them. With Pete, it was 'this sucks, that sucks, everything sucks.' He would externalize his problems, say they were caused by something else and make everybody miserable."

Pete had already distanced himself from the rest of the band, missing many of the pre-production sessions because of frequent trips to Sheffield for dental surgery. He was a founding member of the band and a solid rhythm guitarist. But he was becoming a liability.

The last straw came the morning Pete stumbled into the studio to record his solo for *Stagefright*. He was, in Mutt's words, "pissed as a skunk. I could smell it when he walked in. But he was trying not to act like he was drunk.

"I thought it was funny at first. When he tried to play his solo, I said 'Okay, Pete, here we go' and it was just plink-dah-plink-da-da-plink. He'd try it again – same vibe. He could hardly hit the string right. Finally, for his sake more than mine, I just chewed him out. I told him 'Go home and don't even show your face in the studio again until you really know your stuff.'"

Pete Willis never showed his face in a studio – or on stage – with Def Leppard again.

CHAPTER 6

[PYROMANIACS]

Sunday, July 11 1982 is a day Rick Savage will never forget. It was the day of the final World Cup soccer championship game. He missed the game on television, though, because that was also the day Pete Willis met the rest of the band face to face at Peter Mensch's house in London and was bluntly told that he was no longer a member of Def Leppard.

The day before, Joe Elliott had called Pete in Sheffield, where Pete was trying to dry out and recharge his batteries after the *Stagefright* incident, to inform him that his services as a Leppard were no longer required. Originally, the band wanted Peter Mensch to call Pete. He refused. "I said 'No, it's your band. You're big boys.'"

Joe was then chosen to be the bad news bearer because of his previous experience handing out pink slips to Tony Kenning, Pete Martin and Frank Stuart-Brown. It was a nasty job, but somebody had to do it. Joe at least had practice.

The conversation basically consisted of Joe telling Pete that he'd been warned repeatedly over the past two and a half years about his drinking and his attitude and that he'd finally run out of last chances. Pete said he wanted to come down to London and discuss the situation with the rest of the band. Joe told him there was nothing to discuss, but if he wanted to come down, they'd give him their verdict personally. Pete decided to confront the inevitable in person.

"He was nice about it," Pete says of Joe's phone call. "He said 'I'm really sorry, Pete, I didn't want to have to be the one to tell you this, but I got the job anyway.' After he said that, I knew what was coming next. I said I wanted to come down and talk about it. I didn't want to change their minds as much as to ask them why – although deep down, I knew why."

Drum roadie Russell Major was charged with driving the unhappy Pete down from Sheffield for the final confrontation. Joe recalls that during the meeting Pete offered to seek psychiatric help. Joe responded that it was too late for that. "I had to be adamant because I knew nobody else would stand up. I said 'It's finished, there's nothing to discuss.' After that, he went 'Well, to be quite honest with you, I'm slightly relieved about it.' And that was it."

"It had to be done, "Pete acknowledges sadly. "I didn't like it, but it was necessary. I don't hold any grudges at all about it. Actually, the

Dumb Blondes 1978.

guys were pretty nice about it, saying things like 'Don't think of it as an end. Think of it as the start of something new.' They said if I ever needed any help from them, to give 'em a shout.

"I did ask them if I could go and see a psychiatrist, as a last resort." But it was more than just screwing up in front of Mutt that sealed Pete's fate. It had been the incidents and aggravations that had accumulated since that first plane flight to America. "After I got over it, my face burning with rage, I calmed down a bit and said 'Okay, I suppose it's the best thing really.' "

Pete became a recluse upon his return to Sheffield. He stayed in his house with his girlfriend, uncertain what to do next. He'd just lost his job and there was no money coming in. *Pyromania* would not be released for another eight months and royalties from his songwriting credits on the record would take at least a year after that to come through.

Worse still, his mother Jean died of a heart attack shortly after Pete left the band. "I think it was something to do with me coming out of the band. She was always keeping scrapbooks and things like that." The shock of her death sent Pete back to the bottle again for a time.

A month after Leppard gave him his notice, Pete formed a new band made up of local Sheffield musicians; they practised in Leppard's old rehearsal room in the spoon factory. Pete was still contracted to Phonogram in England, so he submitted a demo tape of two originals, hard rockers in the Thin Lizzy-Judas Priest mould with solid commercial flourishes. The company's reply was "guitars are good, singer's got promise, your drummer's weak and you should go away and do some more work before you present any more tapes." In other words, get lost. The band broke up a few months later.

"I didn't want to have to go through all that apprenticeship again. I'd done it once and it does age you. I feel like an old man now."

By March 1985, Pete had received substantial royalty payments from *Pyromania* and was recording demos on an eight-track tape machine in his house on a farm outside Sheffield. There was talk of forming a kind of hard rock superband with former members of Iron Maiden and Gillan under the aegis of British producer-svengali Jonathan King, but nothing materialized.

The same day that Pete Willis got his fateful phone call, Phil Collen also received one from Joe Elliott. Joe told him Pete was out of the band. Would Phil mind coming down and helping out with the new album? Joe had already heard through the British hard rock grapevine that Phil's band Girl was on the verge of breaking up. And from what he knew of Phil and his guitar playing, he was perfect for the Leppard job. Indeed, Peter Mensch claims that no other candidates were seriously considered that day. Phil Collen got the one and only call.

Phil was a friend of the Leppards from way back – he'd sent them a congratulatory telegram the day of their headlining show at London's Lyceum in April, 1980 and had jammed with the band at club dates in Sheffield and London. The Sheffield jam took place following a Girl performance with Pat Travers at Sheffield City Hall. After the set, Joe and Steve went to a local club with Collen and Girl singer Phil Lewis, where they commandeered some gear from a heavy metal trio called Sledgehammer and proceeded to play delightfully sloppy renditions of *Do You Love Me* by Kiss (also covered by Girl) and the Kinks' *You Really Got Me*. In London, at the Music Machine, Joe, Steve, the two Phils and Iron Maiden singer Bruce Dickinson – then with Samson – got on stage late one night for a jam during which Joe played drums, Dickinson sang a bluesy version of *Whole Lotta Love* and Steve, playing bass, laid down on the drum riser and fell asleep.

Phil was well aware of the Pete Problem. During the Ozzy Osbourne leg of Def Leppard's *High'n'Dry* tour, Joe had called Phil to say, only half-jokingly, "Can you learn sixteen songs in four days?" He talked about Pete's drinking and the trouble it was causing within the band. But that was the end of the subject, until the World Cup Sunday in July 1982.

Phil agreed to meet with the rest of Leppard at Peter Mensch's house the next day. Things got off to an interesting start when Phil's car, a Ford Cortina, broke down right outside Peter's house. He walked in carrying the Ford's gear lever in his hand. He and Joe went outside to try and fix it. They put the gear stick in backwards, which put the car in reverse. Suddenly the Ford lurched back and nearly went through Peter's living room window.

Finally, Phil and the Leppards got down to the matter at hand. The initial plan was for Phil to hang around the studio and put down lead guitar parts on a handful of tracks, just to see if the chemistry was right. Mensch figured that since *Pyromania* was nowhere near completion, there would be plenty of time to repair any damage if Phil didn't work out.

Phil received tapes of a few unfinished *Pyromania* tracks and was asked to cook up some solo ideas for them. One of the songs, ironically, was *Stagefright,* which had already been Pete Willis' undoing. The day after his first meeting with Def Leppard, Phil arrived at Battery Studios and told producer Mutt Lange that he'd worked up a little something for *Stagefright.* Phil played the solo for Mutt, cut it in one take and dropped in a couple of extra notes on another go-round. That was it; Phil Collen was a member of Def Leppard. By the time *Pyromania* was released, it included four other Phil Collen solos on *Rock of Ages, Photograph, Foolin* and *Rock! Rock! (Till You Drop).* He also added rhythm tracks and a few feedback wails on every track except *Too Late for Love* to which he also contributed vocals.

Phil proved to be invaluable in another way. As Joe put it, "He totally brought Steve out of his shell. He was always a very shy guy. And he still is on his own to a certain extent. But he's a lot more lively now that Phil's around. He's definitely brought Steve on by leaps and bounds."

The Pete Willis situation had been particularly stressful for Steve. According to Sav, "Pete was a bad influence on Steve. At one stage, Joe was actually put off drinking because of the way Pete and sometimes Steve would be. He didn't even want to go down to the bar. It got as bad as that. But when Phil joined, there was this enthusiastic person who got on well with Steve. Everybody would have a drink, but Phil would be the guy who could say to Steve 'Come on, pull yourself together.' And Steve would say "Yeah, you're right.' He really gets on with Phil and doesn't want to fall out with him. Not that he wants to fall out with the rest of us. But basically, he'd do anything for Phil."

Phil Collen, in a way, was Steve Clark's identical twin. They were both fanatical about guitars. They also had the same twisted but essentially good-natured sense of humor, which blossomed into some memorable adventures during the *Pyromania* tour. There was also a touching brotherly quality about their relationship. On the road, Steve had always roomed with Pete Willis, an unsteady combination at best. When he started rooming with Phil, it was as if they'd been joined at the hip. They became inseparable.

"I must admit there was a time when I thought I'd lost touch with Steve because he wouldn't socialize with anybody else but Phil," notes Joe. "I think it was just my own little ego, thinking, 'Whoa, I'm being left behind here.' But I soon realized it was a good thing. And whenever we did see each other, it was more exciting anyway because we weren't getting on each other's nerves.

"The thing with Pete was unfortunate," he admits soberly. "In a perfect world, there would be nothing better than to form a band, get successful and never have a line-up change. To me, that is the ultimate, like Slade or like Led Zeppelin until Bonzo died. To be a nice family unit that really kicks ass on stage and on record. And we've always tried to work as a family. The only difference between Leppard and a family is that a family wouldn't have kicked Pete Willis out."

Phil Collen picked up his first guitar at the age of three. It was a big acoustic monster, roughly the same size as he was. He couldn't play it and he could barely hold it up in his tiny hands. But his mother Connie has a picture of young Phil with that guitar, indisputable proof that from an early age there wasn't much in Phil Collen's

ABOVE: Phil (far left) with Girl, 1980.

Collen quits Girl

DEF LEPPARD, *who've been lying low lately recording a new album called 'Pyromania' which should be released in the Autumn, are reported to have gained a new guitarist —* Phil Collen *(above) from* Girl.

Collen maintained a discreet silence on the matter when questioned by Sounds *this week, but was able to confirm that he's left Girl. However, he was sceptical of reports that Girl had split up or that singer* Phil Lewis *had left the band — he believes the band will probably resurface under a new name.*

Quite who Collen would be replacing in Def Leppard isn't clear as the band's management are also maintaining a low profile over their activity at present. All should be revealed officially shortly. 'Sounds' Aug '82

BELOW: A (very) young master Collen.

life except guitar playing.

Born December 8, 1957, the son of a truck driver, Phil grew up in London's East End, in a rough'n'tumble neighborhood called Hackney. It was, in Phil's words, "a shitty neighborhood with slummy houses, about as shitty as you can get in London." He was very good at sports in school, especially swimming and soccer, but he invested most of his extra-curricular time in music. "The only alternative to playing the guitar, something creative like that, was going out and beating the shit out of Asian immigrants. I thought playing guitar was a better way to let off steam."

As a little boy, Phil and his best friend Terry, who lived next door, would climb on top of the garden shed in Phil's backyard, don plastic Beatle wigs and pretend to play air guitars. It wasn't much, but it was a start. At 14, he went to his first rock concert, Deep Purple at the Brixton Sundown, and was completely smitten by Ritchie Blackmore's freakout fretwork. He pestered his parents for an electric guitar of his own and, on his sixteenth birthday, was given a brand new Gibson SG model. Phil immediately started taking private lessons from the masters – Blackmore, Jan Akkerman of the Dutch group Focus, jazz axemen like Larry Coryell and Al DiMeola – by listening to their albums and creating his own interpretations of their recorded solos.

Phil spent so much time studying the finer points of hard-rock guitar that his schoolwork suffered drastically. When Phil left school at 16, he got a job at a burglar alarm factory. "I used to wire up the alarms. But I'm colorblind. Certain shades of brown and green are bad for me, so I kept screwing up the wires." Not surprisingly, Phil only lasted a year at the burglar alarm factory, after which he landed a job as a delivery man for a London printing firm, Profile Typesetters. "That was great because I'd started playing in bands by then and I'd come in pretty tired in the morning from playing the night before. But the guys at the company were really sympathetic."

Phil's very first band had a rather limited repertoire, mostly early ZZ Top songs. From that, he took a quantum leap into glitter-rock with a neighborhood metal-and-mascara combo called the Dumb Blondes. Heavily influenced by the New York Dolls, the group – Phil on guitar, drummer Fred Ball, bassist Pete Webb and singer Jeff Hepting – spent hours applying their make-up for a gig. They were, however, too macho to go and buy it themselves. Phil would get his mother to purchase lipstick and eyeliner for them or they'd borrow some from their girlfriends. "We did the whole bit," Phil laughs. "Stacked heels, black lipstick. We're talking major embarrassment here."

The Dumb Blondes played standard Seventies buzzsaw-rock covers along with a few rickety originals. The height of their fame came on September 6, 1978 when the *Sun*, a London tabloid, ran a photo of the Blondes posing with European light welterweight boxing champion Colin Powers. Powers and the Blondes were handled by the same manager, Vic Andretti. Andretti didn't accomplish much else on the Blondes' behalf, though. The best he could do were a few support slots at major London clubs like the Marquee and the Music Machine

In 1978, Phil answered a classified ad in *Melody Maker* for a guitarist. The band turned out to be another rouge'n'roll band called Girl, although Phil passed the audition without wearing makeup. In fact, Girl passed their record company audition without even playing live. Instead of sweating out an apprenticeship in London clubs, Girl had the inspired idea of making a video and using that as a demonstration tape for record companies. It wasn't the first time it had been done – a British band called the Babys (featuring singer John Waite) snared a Chrysalis deal in 1976 the same way – but it worked. Before Girl had played a note on stage, they had a deal with Jet Records.

"The guy who went on to manage Wham!, Simon Napier-Bell, put up the money for the demos. We rented two video cameras and went to a heavy-duty gay porno place in Muswell Hill where we mimed to one of our songs. Later, we got a lot of stick for not paying our dues. But I'd been playing in all those shitty pubs for years before that, with no success whatsoever."

Girl caused a minor sensation in trend-happy London, although Phil says the group met with considerable hostility from greasers out in the hinterlands. "In Aberdeen, Scotland, we went out with makeup and these Scots did *not* go for it. We didn't look like Judas Priest or anything, so they thought we were a bunch of faggots. We'd finish a song and there would be complete silence. You could hear a pin drop. And there was a guy in the front row who pulled a scarf over his eyes through the whole set."

Nevertheless, Girl enjoyed a brief flurry of fame in England. They opened for Kiss at London's Wembley Arena – an inspired double bill – and their first major tour was opening for UFO. Girl's 1980 debut album, *Sheer Greed,* peaked on the British charts at Number 33, between *Kenny Rogers Singles Album* and *20 Hottest Hits* by Hot Chocolate. Singer Phil Lewis was also romantically linked for a time with actress Britt Ekland. (Because there were two Phils in the group, Phil Collen was nicknamed "Phillis.") A major highlight of Girl's career, as far as Phil Collen was concerned anyway, was the night in 1980 when his idol Ritchie Blackmore came on stage and jammed with him on Steppenwolf's *Born to be Wild.*

In the fall of 1980, Girl toured the Far East where they were pretty hot stuff with teenage females, headlining in 3000-seat concert halls. But upon their return to England, the band was almost dropped by their record label. The second album, *Wasted Youth*, sank without a trace and a planned 1981 visit to the U.S. opening for Ozzy Osbourne was scrapped when Def Leppard got the job instead. Girl played its last concert in June, 1982 at the Zigzag Club in London. "I got drunk that night, the first time I think I ever got drunk on stage. Usually, I have a bit more pride than that. But nothing was going right with Girl." Strangely enough, Joe Elliott and Steve Clark were in the audience that night. Two weeks later, Pete Willis was out of Def Leppard and Phil Collen was in.

Recruiting Phil solved only one of Leppard's three big headaches. There was still the problem of the band's increasing debt, thanks to mounting recording costs and the Burnstein-Mensch suit against Leber-Krebs. There was also the small matter of *Pyromania* itself, which was still months from completion. According to Cliff's arithmetic, Def Leppard were £750,000 in the hole. The band would have to sell over a million copies of *Pyromania* just to break even. Joe and the boys frequently arrived at Peter's house in London after recording sessions for grilled-cheese and peanut-butter sandwich dinners because there was no money for anything more extravagant.

Fortunately, in September, Cliff and Peter settled with Leber-Krebs out of court. Leber-Krebs paid Peter £300,000 for his work with AC/DC, a welcome windfall for the financially strapped Leppard. Cliff and Peter also swapped their interest in the Scorpions to Leber-Krebs for complete control of Def Leppard's affairs. "We swapped a current," Peter says, "for a future."

In the meantime, Mutt Lange slaved away over a hot console on overdubbing and mixing for *Pyromania.* Young keyboard wiz Thomas Dolby provided discreet but effective synthesizer parts on several tracks, although he was actually credited as Booker T. Boffin on the album jacket. While using a pseudonym was Dolby's idea, the end result was a Mutt Lange-Peter Mensch collaboration.

"Mutt used to call Dolby 'Book-A-Boffin,' as in rent-a-boffin. I thought he was saying 'Booker Boffin,'" explains Peter, "so I took to calling him Booker T. Boffin, as in Booker T. and the MGs. And that's how he got credited on the album."

In classic Lange fashion, Mutt mixed the album right down to the wire. The original plan was for the album to be released in time for the Christmas rush. The day before deadline, Mutt still had two tracks to go, *Stagefright* and *Rock! Rock! (Till You Drop).*

"I was really tired and pissed off," Mutt admits. "I was told that we had to send those tracks off on the Concorde to New York the next day. So I worked right through the night with Nigel Green, because Mike Shipley had passed out again."

But while they were mixing *Rock! Rock!,* Mutt and Nigel discovered that because of edits on the master tape, some of the handclaps were out of sync. They had to bring everything back into proper rhythm using digital delays. That took all night. With an hour and a half left to go, Mutt and Nigel quickly mixed *Stagefright.* At one point, Mutt had to wake up Nigel, who had dozed off at the board. They had just finished when the phone rang. It was Cliff Burnstein: "Don't worry, guys, the album's been pushed back to January."

"At least they got us to finish the thing, though."

There were a few grumbles in the Leppard camp about some of the mixes on *Pyromania.* Joe was unhappy about the way *Photograph* and *Stagefright* had turned out, considering the whole year the band had spent making the album. Burnstein, however, was so sure of *Pyromania*'s musical and commercial merits that he started the promotional buzz going before Mutt had even finished mixing. He hit the phones with a vengeance, spreading the word among key record company personnel and radio contacts in the U.S. He also took a few of Mutt's rough mixes back to New York with him after a brief visit to London in the fall.

"I was not supposed to do this, but a Mutt Lange rough mix is beyond what everybody else does with a final mix anyway. What I'd do is go out to dinner with someone from the record company and say 'I got a tape I'd like to play for you.' We'd go back to that person's house and I'd play a few tracks from the album. They'd go crazy – and then I'd take it away. But A didn't know I was playing it for B, who didn't know I was playing it for C. Meanwhile, people would go back to their offices, get on the phones and say 'I tell ya, I have it on the highest authority that this Def Leppard album is incredible.' I started this whole buzz

ABOVE: Rick and mum at Chelsea Football Club party, December '83.
BELOW: Phil and his mum, same party, after Hammersmith Odeon show.

going with everybody talking to everybody and nobody knowing where it came from."

Cliff applied a similar give-a-little-get-a-lot scheme to video promotion for the album. Def Leppard filmed promotional videos in December, 1982 for both *Photograph* and *Rock of Ages* with director David Mallet (there were two versions of the *Photograph* video, one with dancing girls and one without), but Cliff offered only *Photograph* to MTV at first.

"My theory was to give the videos to MTV sequentially, so they could only play *Photograph* for a certain period of time and then only *Rock of Ages* for a period of time. Also, I wanted to get my point across to the record company that *Photograph* should be the first single, not *Rock of Ages.*"

His strategies, backed up by *Pyromania's* undeniable pop-metal wallop and impressive hook-and-riff architecture, paid off handsomely. Released in late January of 1983, *Pyromania* went gold in five weeks and platinum five weeks after that. For most of the year, the album consistently sold 100,000 copies a week. "It was unreal," Cliff marvels, "just like clockwork."

"Def Leppard have picked a perfect title for their third effort. In fact, it's so hot the arson squad is investigating it. They're becoming the standard for Eighties heavy metal." – WMMS, Cleveland, Ohio.

"Def Leppard's *Pyromania* comes on like a three-alarm blaze. This band of young rockers had become one of Seattle's favorites in the past year. We honestly had calls since last summer asking when their new album was coming out. The delay was well worth the effort." – KZOK, Seattle, Washington.

"Def Leppard's *Photograph* is a smoker. Instant phones. . ." KWXL, Albuquerque, New Mexico.

Those were just three of many raves for *Pyromania* and its flagship single *Photograph* in the January 21, 1983 issue of *Friday Morning Quarterback.* A weekly industry tipsheet, *FMQB* monitors radio action on all the latest record releases. And from the cries of "Heavy rotation!", "Hot! Hot! Hot!" and "Great phones" (meaning listener requests) that leaped off of every *FMQB* page, the only action on FM rock airwaves that week was *Pyromania.*

To be sure, *Pyromania* was an album calculated to make program directors swoon in its wake. Mutt Lange had seen to that – refining the full-throttle fuzz of the Collen-Clark guitars to a rapier-like stab, cranking up Rick Allen's computer-drum boom until it sounded like Krakatoa blowing its stack, layering those schoolboy Leppard harmonies over the record's knifeblade guitars like marshmallow cream over a field of metallic punji sticks. Without softening the band's youthful attack, he'd heightened the seductive quality of those suckerbait harmonies and the songs' knockout hooks. *Pyromania* had a steely pop sheen that distinguished it from the glut of grunt-by-numbers heavy metal, yet it could still drill right through the namby-pamby Journey-fied thud-pop that was choking the life out of U.S. rock radio at the time. Program directors who were puzzled by punk and afraid of turning too far left or right of the middle of the road had in *Pyromania* an album they could spin to their hearts' content, and to the delight of their teenage constituency.

Of course, radio hype is like the common cold – it's catchy, but you eventually get over it. *Pyromania's* longevity was due to much more than its ability to charm PDs and DJs. It pinched a central nerve in America's mainstream rock populace. With hardcore punks and electro-pop scientists declaring rock & roll dead as a doornail, *Pyromania* was a righteous declaration of its basic powers, the unquenchable fire that had ignited worldwide teenage revolution thirty years before.

Critics who praised the complex orchestration of Leppard's melodic

Joe with ZZ Top's Billy Gibbons. . .waiting for the beard.

and metallic strengths dismissed Joe's lyrics as typical Saturday-night six-pack philosophy. The truth was that he'd made a serious effort to sidestep clichéd "let's party" scenarios with the edge-of-madness scripts for *Die Hard the Hunter* and *Billy's Got a Gun.* However, what the rock critic intellegentsia didn't take into account was that Black Leather Nation anthems like *Rock of Ages* ("Still rollin', rock'n'rollin'. . .") and *Rock!Rock! (Till You Drop)* were timely reaffirmations of rock & roll's simple joys for a generation beset by synthetic pleasure from every angle – rock videos, video games, *Star Wars* fantasia, identikit rock radio. And Def Leppard hammered home their argument with tried but true heavy metal force.

Pyromania also proved that heavy metal, good inventive metal, didn't have to be ugly. With Mutt's help, Def Leppard designed a rich dynamic sound with all the piercing highs and ominous lows of a good 19th Century symphony. Joe's screams of sexual frustration and desire in the brilliantly arranged *Foolin'* were dramatically echoed in the stuttering chorus and the thoughtful deployment of Steve and Phil's guitars (the accelerating motorcycle roar of a fuzzed-up guitar under a second guitar's window-shattering feedback shriek). Even if you didn't like heavy metal in general or Def Leppard in particular, you could not help at least admiring the ingenuity with which they made the old noise seem new on *Pyromania.*

With *Pyromania,* the Def Leppard Admiration Society increased its membership by the multi-millions. By September, 1983, *Pyromania* had sold more than four million copies, becoming the biggest-selling non-soundtrack LP in their record company's history. Notably, cassette sales of the album were outstripping record sales three-to-two. Fans were obviously buying *Pyromania* tapes to play on their car stereos, confirming that the album was great teenage cruising music.

Fans didn't just vote with their bucks. In the 1983 year-end readers poll in the hard rock monthly *Circus,* Def Leppard strolled away with top honors in eight out of seventeen categories, including best album, best group, best live act, best video (they had three out of the top five in this one) and best songwriters. Strangely enough, they came in fourth, tied with AC/DC, for comeback of the year, suggesting that Leppard fans had been deeply concerned about the band's welfare during their extended absence after *High'n'Dry.*

Amidst this snowballing euphoria, Def

Leppard prepared to take their act back out on the road. A public rehearsal of sorts was scheduled for February 9 at the Marquee in London. The idea, Joe says, was to let Phil Collen warm up with Leppard on a hometown stage, one that he'd played on plenty of times before. Besides, Joe adds, "you can play the Marquee, screw up and not that many people would see it anyway."

At the Marquee, Def Leppard raced through a set that, with a few additions and subtractions here and there, would become standard concert procedure for the coming year – a generous helping of the new album (*Photograph, Billy's Got a Gun, Rock of Ages, Stagefright*) spiked with gonzo charges through *Rock Brigade* and *Wasted* from the first album and *Let It Go* and *Another Hit and Run* from *High'n'Dry*. For encore purposes, Leppard had also jazzed up Creedence Clearwater Revival's 1970 hit *Travelin' Band*, giving the CCR number a high-octane workout that later knocked out no less than the song's composer, John Fogerty. Fogerty told *Creem* magazine in a 1984 interview that his son was a big Leppard fan and had begged his old man to take him to see the band when they passed through the neighborhood during the '83 *Pyromania* tour.

"They had just nailed the audience and they went off and the audience was applauding and all that," Fogerty recalled. "So they came back out and the drummer started 'Boom de de de,' you know, the whole thing. Then they said 'We'd like to do a song by a bloke that lives around here . . . his name is . . . JOHN FOGERTY!!' It was a great moment for a father and a son."

The Marquee show, in the meantime, was a good warm up for Phil, "not too nervewracking or overpowering," according to Joe. "It was very hot and really sweaty, but that was okay because that's what the music was all about anyway, hot and sweaty things." Leppard then ventured over to Dublin, Ireland for a second public rehearsal at a place called the TV Club. Further north, in Belfast, Def Leppard officially inaugurated the *Pyromania* tour with a show at Ulster Hall, the first time the band had ever played in trouble-torn Northern Ireland.

"It was the most amazing gig," Joe exclaims. "Those kids really loved it. They went absolutely mad. Toilet rolls were being thrown all over the place. We even ended up with a toilet seat onstage. Jackets were coming off all over the place, but there were no fights. They were just charging, all drunk, and cheering and shouting and screaming. Belfast was definitely a winner."

That turned out to be the highpoint of Leppard's February European swing. After nipping briefly through Europe, the band arrived in Manchester with Joe Elliott hacking and wheezing thanks to a nasty bout of flu picked up in a freezing Belgium dressing room. Joe barked his way through the Manchester show but was told by a doctor the next day that he had severe laryngitis. The next show in Nottingham was cancelled, but Joe's voice was only in marginal shape for the rest of the tour, which finally ended the first week of March at Hammersmith Odeon in London.

To add insult to Joe's injury, people were not exactly banging down doors to go see Def Leppard in England. Out of a dozen shows, only one came close to selling out – Sheffield City Hall. The rest of the way, Leppard played to half and two-third houses. Peter Mensch drolly called it "the most unattended tour in British rock history," a measure of how far Leppard's popularity had fallen in England over the past three years.

The tour wasn't well reviewed either. Longtime Leppard spotter Geoff Barton complained in one review that – horror of horrors – Joe Elliott moved around too much on stage. "He liked the album" Joe says, "but said I was leaping around too much. He thought I looked silly doing splits off the drum riser, climbing up the scaffolding and shining a big light down on the audience. Now if Paul Stanley or David Lee Roth had done it, he would have loved it. For some reason, he didn't like me doing it."

Two weeks after the London show, Def Leppard flew to America where they were booked on twenty-four shows as the opening act for Billy Squier. On the first night, in Atlanta, Leppard stood together nervously in the dressing room before going on stage. "Phil was saying 'I'm shitting myself,'" Joe recalls. "So Steve poured him a big stiff brandy. That was the first time any of us had ever drunk before going onstage.

"The lights went out, we went on and Phil later said that within two minutes of going on, he never felt more at home doing anything else – except sex."

The Squier tour, Cliff Burnstein claims, made good sense for Leppard. It was still too early to tell how big *Pyromania* was going to be, so why not play it safe for the first few weeks on the road? Besides, Squier was willing to pay Def Leppard good money to open his shows, a hint that Squier himself knew how hot Leppard would be and that they would help him sell out his shows. He was right.

Squier was also outclassed. Before the tour, Def Leppard had rehearsed themselves sore. Cliff says they spent six weeks alone getting their backing vocals down pat. "They were so tight and they could play anything, even running around the stage like maniacs. That was the test. Playing out there with Squier proved to them they had what it takes. And playing to almost 20,000 people a night gave the band such confidence." The nightly merchandise sales were good for their egos as well; during the course of those twenty-four shows, Leppard outstripped Squier in T-shirt and memorabilia sales (Leppard also had a better line of rockwear on sale, including sleeveless British Union Jack T-shirts and matching Union Jack shorts which became *de rigeuer* wear for style-conscious teens on the beaches that summer.)

Surprisingly, there was some resistance by concert promoters to the Squier-Leppard package, Cliff reveals. 'When the booking agency put Def Leppard out with Billy Squier for $7500 a night, a few promoters told Squier's manager that they didn't want to accept Def Leppard on the shows, that they weren't worth the money and couldn't draw flies. And that rankles me to this day because a few weeks later those same promoters were saying 'I told you Def Leppard were going to be big – can you give us some headline shows?' "

After concluding the Squier tour in Los Angeles and taking time out for an appearance on *American Bandstand*, Def Leppard rehearsed for four days in Odessa, Texas before commencing their first headlining tour of America there on April 30. In keeping with their new top o' the bill status, the band added a few snazzy new touches to the show. A tape of *Apocalypse Now*-style sound effects – sirens, gunfire, helicopters – announced their arrival on stage, which featured enormous clouds of dry ice and six columns of fire blazing eighteen feet high. Two big Roman candle wheels turned during *Rock of Ages*. Joe also had the run of the stage. During *Travelin' Band*, which had been moved back to the second encore following *Stagefright*, Joe handed his mike to a roadie and then scampered up the PA scaffolding to the cheering of the crowd below. The crew had fun with that one. Often, when Joe came back down, the roadie would hand him back a banana wrapped in black gaffer tape.

Foolin' was added to the set list and *Action! Not Words* was dropped after the first show in Odessa because "it went down like a pork pie at a Jewish wedding," laughs Joe. "It was all experimental for us for about two months. We had it great with Squier – our gear in front of his gear, forty-five minutes, bang! and we'd go down great. Now we were headlining, doing seventy, eighty minutes, and really working for it. By June, we were cooking, though. The shows were selling out and we were playing real well."

Def Leppard were playing better than well. They came out busting skulls with *Rock!Rock! (Till You Drop)* and then soaked their audience with a triple-shot of *Rock Brigade, High'n'Dry* and *Another Hit and Run,* all in the first twenty minutes. Instead of saving the big hits for last, Leppard kept the heat turned up full blast by playing *Foolin', Photograph* and *Rock of Ages* (complete with obligatory singalong) in the middle of the show, taking a slight dip in mood with *Bringin' on the Heartbreak* and then zooming back to maximum warp drive with *Switch 625, Let it Go* (prefaced by a Phil Collen guitar phreakout) and a last blast of *Wasted* (prefaced by steamin' Steve Clark solo) before nipping backstage for a breather and returning to encore with *Stagefright.*

A lot of bands would have ended the evening right there. (Most bands take their encores for granted; if encores were distributed according to merit instead of ritualistic audience frenzy, a lot of bands wouldn't get any). But *Travelin' Band* became one of the tour's biggest thrills. "This is the part of

All on this page: *Rock of Ages* video.

the show we call "We don't give a shit,'" Joe would often announce, after which he stripped off his sleeveless Union Jack T-shirt to reveal – voila! – a sleeveless Stars and Stripes T-shirt underneath. The band then came out and played "switch the instruments." Sav strummed Phil's guitar while Phil played Sav's bass, which he then traded halfway through the song for Steve's guitar. The song usually included a quote from Led Zeppelin's *Rock and Roll* and Phil would slip in a split-second quote from Mott The Hoople's *All the Young Dudes* before *Travelin' Band* climaxed with one final ignition of those eighteen-foot columns of fire. When Queen's Brian May joined the band for an encore jam of *Travelin' Band* in Los Angeles, he was nearly reduced to a pile of ashes; he was less than two feet from the fire columns when they went up at the end of the song. Joe had to yank him away at the last minute "or that would have been the end of Queen."

Music was only part of the daily routine. Thanks to *Pyromania,* they also had superstar PR responsibilities as well. Def Leppard had always been diligent about promotion, publicity and plain good manners when it came to their fans and the *Pyromania* tour gave them a chance to say thanks for everything. Charitable activities included several benefit soccer games, adopting a snow leopard at the San Francisco Zoo and making a donation to a summer camp in Rochester, New York for children with cancer.

Sometimes spreading good vibes meant travelling and playing under trying conditions. The Leppards were flying between Canadian dates in a six-seater plane one day when another plane zoomed past, missing the band's plane by mere inches. "I heard the other pilot's voice come over the intercom, going 'Hey, that was close,'" Phil says. "Then our guy replies 'Yeah, too fucking close. You scared the shit out of our passengers.'"

In Fargo, North Dakota, the lighting trusses collapsed before showtime. The crew was ready to cancel the date, but the band insisted on playing anyway. "They were convinced they had to play," Cliff insists. "What were they going to do, be the big prima donnas in front of 15,000 kids? They didn't get the biggest light show of all time, but they played."

The group tried to do a few record store autograph sessions, but those were quickly nixed when it became obvious that most record stores could not handle an invasion of several thousand Leppard fans. At the only two in-store appearance Leppard tried, in New Jersey and Denver, police were called in to break things up.

In Seattle, Joe and Steve made an encore appearance at KISW-FM where they had played DJ one night during the Blackfoot tour. The strictest security prevailed. The station could not promote Joe and Steve's arrival at the station ahead of time. They also had to provide plenty of security and make sure there was a foolproof escape plan afterwards.

When they arrived, Joe and Steve had problems just getting in the door. Word leaked out of their imminent arrival and a small army of fans had gathered outside. Joe and Steve, accompanied by Cliff, zoomed in and did a ninety-minute DJ shift on the air, during which time, the small army outside became quite a large one. With the help of a few security men, Joe and Steve went out to the KISW parking lot and signed autographs for another thirty minutes. There was no trouble and everybody, including Joe and Steve, went home happy.

"Some people are very paranoid about these things," Cliff explains "Not Leppard. They handle it very well. I went with Joe into a 7-Eleven in Los Angeles once. We were buying some milk and cupcakes when a kid walked up to Joe and said 'Hey, Joe Elliott, how ya doin?' Joe said 'Okay.' And that was it. As long as you handle the thing naturally, nothing bad ever develops."

With Leppard's new mega-popularity, though, came girl trouble. Groupies are as old as rock & roll itself, but with the success of *Pyromania* the band was also attracting new young female fans who craved nothing more than an autograph and a smile. To distinguish between the two, the band created "Boiler Passes" about halfway through the Billy Squier tour. "We wanted something that was so blatant only a groupie would wear it because everybody else in their right mind would be disgusted by it." Imagine their surprise when the Leppards actually saw a guy wearing one.

The boiler passes were actually the brainchild of Phelim "Phay" MacMahon, the band's mad Irish lighting engineer. Instead of saying "Def Leppard" in the band's trademark angular script, the boiler passes said "Dik Likker." It was juvenile macho humour to be sure, but Joe insists "it would have been unfair for a girl that's done half the crew in forty-five minutes to be wearing the same pass as the wife of the promoter. It was, in a way, for the protection of our real guests."

The crush of femme fatales backstage (and frequently lying in wait back at the hotel) put serious pressure on Leppard members with serious romantic attachments, like Rick Savage whose relationship with Joy Major back home in Sheffield almost predated Def Leppard itself. "When we first started in America, we were nobodies going out for twelve weeks. This time, we had an album in the Top Twenty and we were going to be away six months." There were touching moments, like the girl in Houston who gave Sav a notebook which she'd carefully written "I Love Sav" 20,000 times.

"But there were times when I'd find myself leading girls on when I didn't realize I was doing it. I try to distinguish between groupies and a genuine fan that just wants to get to know you better. But sometimes I'd really fuck up. I'd think I was on to a fan that just wanted to talk. Then I'd find out she's trying to ring me up in the next city and writing letters.

"If you have no worries and no responsibilities, having all those girls around is brilliant. And it's still brilliant if you have responsibilities and you can keep them. But it becomes difficult if you start doubting the responsibilities. That's when you can spoil it."

Most of the women crowding the backstage dressing room and hotel lobbies along the *Pyromania* tour receded into the basic scenery. After a few weeks of touring, Def Leppard settled into a 9-to-5 routine that was almost like having a day job, except this was a rock & roll band specializing in night work. Soundchecks at the hall usually started at four or five o'clock. Band members could either partake of the dinner provided by the promoter or dash back to the hotel for room service and forty winks. Most of the time, Joe ate at the hall with the road crew and did ten miles on an exercise bicycle. To keep his voice in shape, he sang in the locker-room showers before the show, turning each shower up to ultra-hot to steam up the room.

Leppard were always on stage by 9.15 at the latest and off by 11 pm. A minute or two past that and union stagehands would qualify for overtime. "But most of the time, we couldn't get out of the building before midnight," explains Joe. "It would take me at least an hour to stop sweating, even if I had a cold shower as soon as I came off. And we'd spend an hour meeting people, having a drink with the radio station people, meeting the press, saying hi to the promoter's daughter. Then once we got outside, we'd sign autographs for the kids. If we were lucky, we'd get back to the hotel by one and maybe – just maybe– the bar would still be open."

If it wasn't, the band and crew would arrange to cart any leftover backstage booze back to the hotel. Then a discussion would follow as to whose room the party would be held in. And even if the bar was open when Leppard returned from the gig, that was no consolation to Rick Allen. At nineteen, he was still too young to legally drink in most states, but the other band members would sneak a few beers up to his room to keep him happy.

Def Leppard were unusually kind to their opening acts, which included Seventies heavy metal vets Uriah Heep (then on the comeback trail), ex-Thin Lizzy guitarist Gary Moore, Jon Butcher Axis (a hot trio fronted by Butcher, a superb black guitarist) and Swiss metal hacks Krokus. Leppard always tried to soundcheck as early as possible to give the opening acts time to get their audio balances right. The band also made a point of socializing with the opening acts, making them feel every bit at home on the road as Ozzy Osbourne had done for them two years before.

Even so, there were problems. Backstage at Alpine Valley, an outdoor amphitheater outside

Milwaukee, Gary Moore – a temperamental Irishman at the best of times – got pissed off about some small matter and threw an empty Heineken bottle on to the floor. Unfortunately for Sav, who happened to be standing nearby, a few pieces of the broken bottle bounced up off the floor and into his leg. He received eight stitches in that leg after the show.

Def Leppard didn't get along particularly well with Krokus. Leppard were actually quite generous to Krokus, allowing them full use of the stage and giving them more lighting than Leppard had ever been allowed as an opening act. When Krokus asked to be allowed to use a mirrored ball during their set, the Leppards consented. "We said go for it," Joe laughs. "You want to go back to 1969, fine. We actually insisted that they get a mirrored ball." But when Krokus demanded use of flash pots and dry ice, Leppard drew the line. There are some privileges that go with being the headliner.

That wasn't the end of it. One night, Jon Butcher told Joe to watch Krokus' set. Singer Marc Storace was lifting Joe's stage raps word for word as well as climbing atop the PA and the lighting scaffolds, which he'd been asked not to do – that was part of Joe's act. After that, it was war the rest of the way. One night while Krokus manager Butch Stone was exchanging angry words with Peter Mensch, Joe Elliott popped his head out of the dressing room and told him to "shut your festering mouth." Rick Allen, quite a dynamo with his fists despite his size, pushed Stone up against a wall while a Krokus bodyguard looked on helplessly. If there is one unforgivable breach of opening act etiquette, it's punching out the headline band's drummer. Besides, says Joe, "Rick would have torn him limb from limb."

The Leppards did not let the Krokus hassles go unavenged. As part of their set, Krokus had one of their roadies, a real mountain of a man, come out on stage in a black executioner's hood holding a big medieval axe, which one of the guitarists used to demolish his guitar in a big end-of-set climax. To celebrate Krokus' last night of the tour, Def Leppard decided it would be fun to sabotage the executioner bit by locking the Krokus roadie in a room so he could not get out to the stage. Peter Mensch paid the Leppard crew extra money to lock the guy up tight, after which the roadie started using his axe to hack his way out.

"It was like Jack Nicholson chopping at the door in *The Shining*," Joe laughs. "We had two tons of flight cases stacked up against the door and they moved six or seven inches every time he hit the door."

Krokus was a minor bummer compared to the highs that continually lifted Def Leppard's spirits along the *Pyromania* tour route. Tennis superstars John McEnroe and Vitas Guralitas stopped by at the Meadowlands in New Jersey. Geddy Lee of Rush brought his wife and a few friends along to the show in Toronto. Nancy Wilson of Heart, David Lee Roth and Alex Van Halen came to the September 10 and 11 shows at the Los Angeles Forum. Joe remembers soaking up some rays poolside at the Le Parc hotel in L.A. when a phone next to him rang. "I picked it up and a real deep voice on the other end goes 'Is this Joe Elliott? This is Frank Zappa. I got two kids, Moon Unit and Dweezil, they dig the band, they want to come to your show. Can you make sure they get in?' I'm thinking, wow, I am really hip today. Frank Zappa is ringing *me* up!"

Def Leppard's hipness quotient shot up dramatically when Brian May came on stage at the end of one of the Forum shows to play *Travelin' Band*.

"That was great for us," exults Joe. "We had all been Queen fans for ten years. I bought *Sheer Heart Attack* when it came out in 1974. So to have him on our stage was a real buzz."

Capping a great stand was the presence in the audience of five sets of Leppard parents, specially imported from England for the evening to watch their sons in action. "When we saw their show in Sheffield last February, we thought they could do no more," Sav's mum told a reporter from the *Sheffield Star* that night. "But tonight they pulled something more out of the bag and the vast crowd really made it."

The mainland portion of the tour climaxed September 17 with an outdoor blowout at Jack Murphy Stadium in front of 55,000 fans. Leppard topped a bill featuring Motley Crue, Uriah Heep and Eddie Money. Leppard's entire set was captured for posterity on videotape by Joe's girlfriend at the time, Denise, who filmed the show from the mixing desk with Joe's video camera. It was the perfect ending to a nearly perfect tour. The only serious blemishes had been the theft of one of Sav's black Fender basses at the Barton Coliseum in Little Rock, Arkansas and a claim for $15,000 in damages by a thirty-two year old Denver man, Michael Townes, allegedly hit in the left eye with one of Rick Allen's drumsticks during an April 13 show at McNichols Arena. (In one letter, Townes' lawyer referred to the show as the "Billy Squire/Death Leopard Concert.")

A little more frightening was Joe's sudden loss of voice in August. A week's worth of shows was rescheduled and Joe was promptly shipped off to see a New York throat specialist who told him that he had something called "a shelf" in the middle of his vocal chords which had become inflamed and consequently swelled up from all that screaming. Eight days off and the right medication remedied the problem, but two key shows in Detroit had to be postponed at the last minute. Steve and Phil hit the Detroit airwaves to explain the situation and one Detroit radio station opened up a special telephone line so fans could leave taped get-well messages for Joe. Joe still has those tapes.

"There were some really funny ones. Most of them were real short – 'Hi, Joe, my name's Lori. I just wanna say get well soon.' Then someone would call and say 'Hi, my name's Candy and I'm going to chain myself to the backdoor at the gig and I'm not going to leave until Joe Elliott fucks me.' There were also guys who would say things like 'Hey, Joe Elliott, uh, get well soon, make sure you get your voice back, but don't forget, Van Halen's Number One, you dickhead.'"

Despite Joe's croaking and the Krokus nuisance, the U.S. *Pyromania* tour was a roaring success. The album was second only to Michael Jackson's *Thriller* on the *Billboard* charts throughout most of the summer, still selling 100,000 copies weekly. After two final shows in Hawaii (and getting beat 5-3 by a team of barefoot natives in a charity soccer game), Def Leppard, their management and crew settled back for a well-deserved week's vacation, understandably pleased with themselves. On September 26, Joe, Phil and Cliff Burnstein touched down in Japan for a few days of press and promotion in anticipation of a forthcoming Far East visit. Everything was hunky dory – doing sixteen interviews a day, partying at night with John and Roger Taylor of Duran Duran who happened to be staying in the same hotel – until Cliff received a phone call from America at 6:30 one morning. It was George Knemeyer, his assistant.

"They're burning Def Leppard records," he told Cliff, "and breaking them over the air in El Paso."

It had been a passing remark. During the September 16 show in Tucson, Arizona, while exhorting the audience to clap along during *Rock of Ages*, Joe tried to whip up a little competitive enthusiasm. "Last night we played in El Paso, that place with all the greasy Mexicans," he yelled, "and they made a lot more noise than that."

Steve, Phil and Sav were backstage during the drums-and-chanting part of the song. They didn't find out about the remark until later when all hell broke loose. But Rick Allen cringed when he heard the words "greasy Mexicans." "I tried to crouch lower into my drum kit, looking over the tops of the drums, thinking 'No you didn't say that. You couldn't have.' Fortunately, nobody in the audience seemed to notice it."

Nobody, that is, except a journalist who reported the incident in the Arizona *Daily Star*. When word of the racial slur reached KLAQ, an El Paso radio station which had promoted the band's appearance there, Def Leppard's records were quickly yanked off the playist and local Hispanic leaders called for an immediate apology and a nationwide boycott against Leppard. KLAQ program director Arin Michaels was pictured in the El Paso *Herald-Post* holding a *Pyromania* cover ripped in half in protest.

Joe came to greatly regret the "greasy Mexicans" remark; for several weeks during October and November, those two words eclipsed the euphoria of Def Leppard's sell-out tour and threatened to destroy the goodwill the band had built up in America during the past three years. The slur, Joe insists, was the result of trouble in the front rows at the El Paso Coliseum during Leppard's September 6 show there. "That comment, I swear, was aimed at five Hispanic kids who were spitting at us, throwing Jack Daniels and kung fu stars at the band. It was aimed at those five kids, not at anybody else in El Paso or at El Paso itself. I was slagging off those five bastards." The "greasy Mexicans" reference sprang to mind "purely because I'm a Cheech and Chong fan and they use it all the time."

According to Joe, the El Paso show had been a nightmare from start to finish. The troublemakers were harassing other fans as well as the band, trying to steal T-shirts. Half a dozen Jack Daniels bottles had landed on stage and after the show the road crew found a five-point metal star imbedded in one of the amplifiers. Someone was spinning them across the stage "and I instantly linked it to these five kids."

That might have been the end of it, except that the Tucson show was also marked by unnecessary violence. A security guard at the foot of the stage punched a teenage girl in the face, which angered Joe so much that he picked up his mike stand, poked it in the bouncer's back and threatened to go one-to-one with him if he tried it again. Joe says he later received a letter from the head of security of the Tucson facility apologizing for the guard's behavior. But the cumulative effect of the aggressive tension in both El Paso and Tucson was too much. "Greasy Mexicans" was the result.

The same day George called Cliff with the bad news, Joe dialled KLAQ from Japan and apologized for the remark on the air. "It wasn't intended as a harmful thing," he told Arin Michaels. "It was the same way as we get called Limey tea bags . . . Being an English person I really didn't

understand that was such an insult . . . if I've offended anybody, then I'm very, very sorry about it." He offered to send albums and T-shirts to the station for giveaways and promised to fly two KLAQ listeners to an upcoming European show, all expenses paid.

Joe Loya, El Paso district director of the League of United Latin American Citizens, called the offer an insult, "a pay-off," and pressed for the boycott. When Joe offered to come to El Paso and apologize in person for the incident, Loya refused the offer. "LULAC basically told us we should never show our faces there again," Cliff says.

At the same time, civic leaders in Southern California informed Cliff that Hispanics there were also riled up about the slur. It was particularly frustrating, he claims, "because a lot of our biggest fans are Mexican-Americans, and that's no bullshit. I didn't want to ruin our relationship with Mexican-Americans and I didn't want the band not to be able to play Southern California any more." Together with California state senator Joseph Montoya, Cliff scheduled a press conference for November 23 in El Monte, California. Joe flew in from France, where the band was touring, and apologized again. He also contributed $15,000 of his own money to local charities and posed for photos with representatives of Latin youth groups. "The last thing Mexican-Americans need as they try to rid themselves of the stereotype is for me or anyone else to make such statements," he told the assembled reporters. "It was stupid of me to make such a false accusation."

"We did our best to right a wrong," Cliff says in retrospect. "And Joe knew what he said was wrong. I always felt the passage of time would help people forget. But I know it will come up again when we play the Southwest on the next tour. There will be reporters who have been saving their questions for two years."

The El Paso incident, in a way, prepared Def Leppard for the next blow to their ego – a second swing through England and Europe. After wowing crowds of 20,000 and 50,000 at a time, the band was reduced to playing in small theatres and, in some European cities, clubs. In Hamburg, Steve and Phil had their Marshall amps set up on beer bottle crates.

A show in San Sebastian, Spain was disrupted by a full-scale brawl when a gang of rowdies at the foot of the stage started spitting at the band. Then, during the audience participation break in *Rock of Ages,* Joe was leading the singalong when he was knocked unconscious by a

large coin thrown by one of the spitters, which hit him about an eighth of an inch from his eye. When he came to with blood splattered all over his shirt, and peering from under his badly swollen eyelid Joe saw the kid being congratulated by his pals, put two and two together and jumped into the audience to "do him a bit of injury."

"But then his mates joined in and beat the shit out of me," Joe says. "Some of our road crew jumped in and within minutes there were fifteen people at the foot of the stage fighting, ten of us and five of them." Joe nearly punched roadie Malvin Mortimer in the face by mistake. "We didn't finish the song. The rest of the band came out, whipped through *Travelin' Band* and left. I had a headache for three days after that." Joe still bears a scar from that coin.

The three English shows were all sellouts and the December 5 clincher at London's Hammersmith Odeon was followed by an end-of-tour party at the Chelsea Football Club. Revellers included Billy Gibbons of ZZ Top, members of Motorhead and Iron Maiden and, of course, the Leppard moms and dads.

The only shows left on Leppard's *Pyromania* itinerary were a December 19 performance with Iron Maiden, Ozzy, Scorpions, Quiet Riot and old rivals Krokus on *Rockpalast* – a German rock & roll TV mega-broadcast beamed all over Eastern and Western Europe – and brief New Year visits to Australia and the Far East, their first performances there. The Japanese shows in Tokyo and Osaka recalled the recent frenzy Stateside, but the Down Under gigs in Sydney and Melbourne were quite a comedown. At the Narara Festival outside Sydney, Leppard played in the pouring rain for 30,000 people who, for the most part, had no idea who or what a Def Leppard was.

There were probably only six or seven people in all of Thailand who'd ever bought a Def Leppard record, at least a legal one anyway (cheap pirate cassette copies of the top albums are the big-sellers in the Far East). Nevertheless, 6000 folks turned up for the grand end-of-tour finale in Bangkok February 7, an impressive turnout made sweeter by the fact that Hall and Oates were also playing in town.

"Bangkok was very strange for me," says Joe. "We were in this nice hotel, like *Fantasy Island,* with fifteen-foot-high walls around it. And on the other side was this severe poverty. Sav and I went out for a walk and all these fifteen and sixteen-year-old kids came up to us, going 'Hey, you want my sister?' We said no thanks, mate, kept on walking and all of a sudden these kids started throwing stones at us. One kid threw a housebrick right between us. I guess they didn't like the fact that we had nice clothes, obviously had money and had turned down their sisters.

"I did get to see a guy riding an elephant in downtown Bangkok, though. I was eating in this restaurant and spotted this fellow on top of an elephant through the window. I had to run out and take a picture of him. I thought 'I'm never gonna see anything like that again in my entire life.' And the actual gig was good too."

Delighted with the show, amazed by the elephants and unscathed by the bricks, Def Leppard finally said goodbye to the road and boarded a plane to Dublin on February 8 – almost a year to the day since they'd walked on to the stage of the Marquee.

Gibson

CHAPTER 7

THE TERROR TWINS

"I ain't goin' out with you two, the terror twins."

A Def Leppard roadie

Someone, somewhere far back in the big black hole of rock history, started a rumor that life on the road was fun. Well, it is – up to a point. At best, maybe three or four hours out of every working musician's day could be described as pleasure. That includes an hour or two of actually performing on stage. Any road warrior with both oars in the water will tell you that being on a stage, playing your music for a cheering audience, makes everything worthwhile. Coming in a close second is the backstage action after the gig – towelling down after a particularly hot set; sucking down an ice cold beer or Gatorade; the congratulations from femmes and fans; the increased sensation of being the center of attention, not just in a big hockey arena, but in a tiny dressing room full of hot legs, figure 8 frames, and warm (if often insincere) smiles. Not far behind that is the *aprés*-gig party, which is essentially more of the same but without the lingering smell of old sweat sox that usually stinks up a rock band's dressing room. A distant fourth is the obligatory record company schmoozing – posing for trade magazine photos, maybe getting a gold or platinum album in a modest little champagne ceremony if your record is red hot on the charts.

But that's about it. The other fourteen hours are taken up with long bus rides along America's asphalt ribbons, Howard Johnson's cuisine, and the same old goddam movies on the bus VCR. There are some bands who come off six months' worth of touring with nothing to show for it but total retention of every line of dialogue in Cheech and Chong's *Up in Smoke*. Join a rock band and see the world? Most musicians only see the sights through half-mast hangover eyes and tinted bus windows. Sleep, when you get it, is either in a cramped bunk on the bus or in a lumpy hotel bed. We're talking frolic with a capital F.

To stave off boredom and counteract the oppressive idiocy of the perfumed bimbos and music biz leeches who often attach themselves to a nationwide rock tour, musicians get up to all sorts of mischief. The members of Def Leppard are no exception. Indeed, given their tender ages and the world of wonder laid at their feet as soon as they stepped on Yankee soil in 1980, the Leppards are a fascinating study in manic road behavior.

Half the time Peter Mensch and Cliff Burnstein weren't acting as managers; they were camp counsellors, combination nannies and drill sergeants. Remember the nun who had to keep an eye on her schoolgirl charges in the film *The Trouble With Angels*? Mensch and Burnstein had their own movie going, except it was called *The Trouble With Little English Bastards in Spandex*. Backstage at the Palladium in New York on the '81 Blackfoot tour, Burnstein could be overheard scolding one of the Leppards: "If any of you guys are caught screwing around with the fire extinguishers in a hotel, you're going to be fined!"

Actually, the Leppard brand of tour jollies was pretty mild compared to the Visigothic antics of television-out-the-window, groupie-tied-to-the-bedpost legends like Led Zeppelin. Yet during the 1980, '81 and '83 tours, the Leppards were practical jokers to be reckoned with. One particularly memorable stunt during the Pete Willis era was the night that Steve Clark and lighting director Phay MacMahon surreptitiously moved a snoring Willis out of his hotel room in the middle of the night and out on to the roof of the hotel's patio restaurant. The funny part about it was that Willis was still in his bed. Steve, who was rooming with Willis, and Phay had actually moved Pete's mattress, with him snoring contentedly on it, onto the patio roof along with all of his room furniture and luggage. Steve and Phay just stood on the roof "pissing ourselves with laughter" as Willis started shivering in his sleep, mumbling "Steve, isn't it a little cold in here?"

Phay, a longtime road veteran, lent an experienced hand to the band's tour follies. On previous tours with other bands, MacMahon had developed a worldwide reputation for his famous mattress trick. He would take a bed mattress and lean it up against the door in an elevator. Then he'd send the elevator down to the reception area where, nine times out of ten, a room service waiter with a breakfast tray was waiting for it. When the elevator door opened, the mattress fell right on top of the waiter – and his overloaded breakfast tray.

Steve and Phay quickly formed a prankster partnership. One of their finest moments was the night they invaded an amusement park in Calgary, Canada. "One of the local record company guys had taken us out for a meal," Phay explains, "and before you know it me and Steve are completely obliterated. We were taking a cab back to the hotel when we passed this fairground, the Calgary Stampede. So Steve says 'Fairground, let's go!' I said 'It's 11:30 at night!' He says 'So what? Let's go.'"

So in they went. Steve and Phay stopped the cab in the middle of the adjacent freeway and jumped out, leaving the record company guy gasping with amazement.

"We climbed this fence to get in," Phay continues. "We couldn't get around the entrance. The fairground staff were waiting to take the rides apart for closing time, so of course, we start promising people tickets to our show the next night if they let us go on them. So we go on the rollercoaster. When we were done, we had to climb over the side to get off because all the stairs had been packed away.

"Then we get on this Helter Skelter thing with mats. The fairground guy says 'Okay, sit on the mat and ride down the chute.' Well, the guy nearly has a heart attack. Steve comes down on the mat head first.

"That's fine, we finish that. Then there was a forklift parked there. So we said 'Great, transport back to the hotel.' We jump on the back of this forklift to get a ride and the driver goes 'Get off, you two.' We get off and the next thing we knew there were two policemen following us around the park. That's when we decided we'd better be good and get the fuck out of there. The policemen escorted us out of the park and back to the hotel."

The original Def Leppard line-up was always good for road laughs. But when Phil Collen joined the band, he ushered in a glorious new era of tour chuckles. Phil Wilkie, the stage monitor engineer on the *Pyromania* tour, is credited with dubbing Steve and Phil the Terror Twins. When the deadly duo invited him out for an evening of alcoholic hi-jinx on one of the band's off-nights, Wilkie replied "I ain't goin' out with you two, the Terror Twins."

They worked hard to earn that title. "It all started because we were sharing rooms on tour," Phil says. "When we were an opening act, we didn't make enough money for each member to have his own room. Actually, those dates were more fun because we did share. We had a real laugh.

"It started in Amsterdam on the first European leg of the *Pyromania* tour. Joe and Sav roomed together, Rick shared a room with his brother Robert who was road managing and that left me and Steve. We had such a laugh we just went on from there. We'd hang out all the time." A great comic team was born.

Since a lot of these stunts were done in an alcoholic haze, that is usually where they are best appreciated. You really should be sitting on a bar stool, nursing a tall cool one and munching pretzel sticks, to appreciate the full ludicrous glory of the following rundown of the Terror Twins' greatest hits. This should not be misconstrued as an endorsement of excessive drinking. These comic vignettes are just a good example of the lengths to which touring musicians will go to keep from drowning in road *ennui*.

And, please, don't try these stunts at home.

"THE FRENCH CONNECTION"

Phil: "We actually had a fight with each other one night. Really! It started in Hamburg on the European tour. We'd gone out with this guy Tony Z of the lighting crew and he got blind-drunk. Fell off the barstool and made a complete twat of himself. The next day we were all saying to him 'Oh, you were so pissed last night.'

"Anyway, we had a few days off in France after that and we met up with him on the beach. I told him 'Ah, forget about the other night. Come and have a drink with us.' We drank two bottles of frozen vodka between the three of us in half an hour – after we'd had a few beers.

"We got completely bollocksed. I fainted. I'd pulled my trousers down in this bar and then passed out with my trousers down around my ankles, holding a camera and a Walkman. I managed to get up, walked outside and passed out again. One of our truck drivers found me and brought me back into the bar. Then he fell asleep as well."

Steve: "Tony, meanwhile, was also lying on the floor of this bar asleep.

"Then, one of the guys in the bar rang up the hotel and said 'You'd better take these guys out of here.' So they picked us up and brought us back to the hotel. But by the time we got back, I decided it was time for another drink. Phil decides he's had enough and he bags it. So we had an argument in the elevator about it. We started this fight, but we were so pissed out of our minds that we both fell down and somehow jammed the mechanism on the elevator door so it kept opening and closing, over and over again, while we were in there lying on the floor, sound asleep."

"THE CINCINNATI INCIDENT," co-starring Phay MacMahon

Phay: "We were on the first half of the *Pyromania* tour, supporting Billy Squier, and Phil, Steve, Robert Allen the road manager and myself decided to go out to this Malibu Grand Prix track because we were all fans of Malibu Grand Prix mini-car racing. We went out there and had a grand old time. After that, we were hungry so we decided to get something to eat and we went to a Mexican restaurant next door. There's a happy hour on, so we sat at the bar and they gave us margarita drinks in these big goldfish bowls. Time passes and after awhile, nobody's interested in food.

"We went back to the hotel with Robert driving. And we're all a total shambles. As soon as we arrive at the door, we jumped out and yelled to the porter 'We need the other car!' Out comes the other rental car. Phil and Robert stayed in the first car, Steve and I got into the other one and we all took off to see a local Golden Earring gig. Just as Robert pulled up at a traffic light in front of me and Steve, Steve said 'Go on, Phay, give 'em one.' Without any hesitation, I put my foot on the gas pedal and go right up the back of Robert's car, pushing him into the intersection. Robert screamed 'Stop!' and put his car in reverse, with his foot on the gas. I was pushing him, he was pushing me and here are these two cars screaming in the middle of the road, spinning their wheels!

"We got to the club, somehow. But we eventually got slung out of the place as undesirables. The problem was we couldn't remember where we parked the cars. We ended up getting a cab back to the hotel. I ended up giving the keys to my rental car to Joe and Joe had to go out at some ridiculous hour of the morning, walking the streets of Cincinnati looking for it."

"A BICYCLE BUILT FOR TWO"

Steve: "There was the day we went to the gig on a bicycle. It was in America on the last tour. Some bands get really uptight about security, travelling in limos and stuff. Phil and I were on the bus coming into town – I don't remember which one – and we passed this bicycle shop. And there in the window was this great two-seater bicycle. We decided to go back there in an hour and rent it.

"So we went back. Now as the Terror Twins, we used to dress identical, just for a laugh. We'd have different-colored flip-flop sandals on, except I'd have green on the left foot and red on the right foot and Phil would wear red on his left foot and green on his right. We'd also wear identical shorts, cut-off T-shirts and silly hats with glasses. We'd look like identical silly twits.

"Anyway, we got this bike and rode it over to the hall in time for the soundcheck. Here we come on this bike, pedalling furiously, and the fans standing outside are looking incredulous – 'No, it can't be them!' Finally, they realized it was and suddenly there are 200 kids chasing us. We pedalled faster while the kids ran up to us trying to get us to sign autographs. We managed to get into the tunnel leading into the arena, but then I started to panic. The garage door was closed! I yelled to the woman security officer at the bottom

Joe demonstrates his outrage at the antics of the Terror Twins. . .

of the tunnel 'Lift up the fucking gate!' They managed to get it up and we raced right into the arena. After the soundcheck, we rode the bike back to the hotel. There were all these cars full of kids chasing us too.

"The best part, though, was when we got to the hotel, we rode the bike right into the reception area, got off, leaned it up against the desk and asked 'Do you have valet parking?' "

"FUN WITH FLOORS"

Steve: "We were in this hotel once and the management was redecorating some of the floors. So they pulled the numbers off the doors and just wrote the numbers on tape. So we figured that was good for a laugh.

"We took all the seventh floor numbers off the doors and stuck them on the doors on the sixth floor. We also took the sixth floor numbers and stuck them on the doors on the seventh floor. To make the job complete, we also changed the elevator signs.

"Everybody got totally screwed up by it. You would ride up to the seventh floor and all the signs would say you were on the sixth. So people would think 'Oh, I'm on the wrong floor.' They'd go up one more floor and come out on 8."

"SWEDISH MEATBALLS"

Phil: "This is a real embarrassing one. After the U.S. tour, I went to Japan to do radio and press interviews with Joe before doing another European tour. We got back and the first gig was in Stockholm. We still had our summer tans from the States, so Steve and I decided to go down to the hotel bar in our shorts and our flip-flops. The crew were already there drinking beer when we got there, so we ordered champagne, just to wind everybody up. But this Swedish guy in the bar got really offended by us. Steve and I started drinking and dancing on the dancefloor. He spilled some, which made the floor real slippery. So everybody started slipping and sliding on the dancefloor.

"After a while, we decided to leave. As we went out, this Swedish guy said something nasty to Steve. So we gobbed beer on him. The guy threw a punch and decked me. We deserved to get it really. But one of the crew guys, Brooksie, who was 6'4", flattened the Swedish guy. All of a sudden, it was like a big saloon brawl in one of those old western movies. Glasses and chairs flying, everybody hitting everybody else. I went to kick the guy who'd decked me, but my flip-flop came off and my foot went sliding on the dancefloor into this broken glass and ripped the skin off the sole. The brawl was going full-steam, my foot was bleeding, Steve was dragging me off, I was yelling at the guy who hit me – and then the police showed up.

"Brooksie had been thrown through a plate glass window which Steve and I had to pay for. (At about $75, we got off pretty cheap, I guess.) Steve rubbed vodka on my foot to help the pain. Still, we had gigs to play and I did 'em, but I couldn't walk on that foot for two weeks. I'm used to being pretty lively on stage, but I couldn't manage much

more than a hop. The rest of the band were taking the piss out of me the whole time, although I certainly deserved it. It was frustrating and real embarrassing. I felt a real dork, hopping around."

"KNUCKLE SANDWICH"

Phil: "You might think we're a right brawling band, but we're not really. It usually just happens to us, although we ask for it sometimes. Like the time I went out to dinner in London with my mother, a girlfriend and a friend of mine, Fred, who was a drummer in some of my earlier bands.

"We went to this Mexican restaurant and there was a guy there who was a real asshole. He and his mate were drunk and barged right into my mom. I though that was pretty uncool, but I ignored it, especially after what happened in Stockholm. And we were going to be playing the Hammersmith Odeon in London the week after, so I didn't want any extra injuries.

"So Fred and I went outside to get our car and there was this same guy

standing in the middle of the road talking to his mate. I tooted the horn at him and he said 'Fuck off, you wanker.' I jumped out and said 'What did you say?' Then Fred got out of the car and this guy's mate went straight for him. We ended up brawling right there in the street. After it was over, I didn't think any more of it until one of my hands started swelling up when I got home. My mum was freaking out and I felt really bad about the whole thing, her watching me fight in the street.

"I went to a hospital to have the hand looked at. The nurse took one of the fingers, bent it over backwards and put this kind of metal splint on it and said 'You can't move it for two weeks.' I said 'No, you don't understand, I have to play guitar next week.' After a while, though, the doctor said I could take it off – in time for the show – and the finger ended up sort of healing itself. But the top part of the knuckle is still a little farther back than it should be."

"THE ROLEX WATCH ADVENTURE"

Phil: "This was one of the dumbest things I have ever done in my life. When we first went to Ireland to work on the songs for the fourth album, Steve and I went to a pub in Dublin called the Punch Bowl to have a drink. And we ended up getting *really* pissed. I still don't remember exactly what I did. But the way I understand it, we left the pub and, for some reason, went into a jewelry store that must have been nearby. And I said 'Give me the most expensive Rolex watch you've got.' The people behind the counter brought one out, but it had a funny color and I said 'I don't like that one. What else have you got?' They brought another one out and I said 'I'll have it.'

"Now Steve and I had borrowed Joe's car to go to the pub in. We drove it back, but we were so out of it, we left the car running with the keys in it and the radio on. And we went up to bed. Joe came up and said 'What are you trying to do to my car?' I said 'Oh, fuck off.'

"The next day, Joe came up to me, real hurt, and said 'You know, you told me to fuck off last night.' I honestly didn't remember saying it. On top of that, I woke up with this incredibly expensive watch on my wrist. I went into Steve's room and he had a Cartier watch on, an earring and a gold necklace that he'd bought as well. We spent a fortune in that store – and it was *pathetic*. After that, the next day, I stopped drinking totally for three months solid. I did a lot of sit-ups, a lot of push-ups and I felt a lot better for it."

CHAPTER 8

BAND ON THE RUN

After the final *Pyromania* show in Bangkok, Def Leppard had every right to return home in triumph. Over the past twelve months, they had sold over six million records and played to standing room only crowds in America, Canada, Europe and the Far East. Given the depressed state of Sheffield's steel industry, Leppard were probably the city's most valuable export commodity for the year 1983.

Def Leppard, in fact, didn't return home at all. The plan was for the band – energized by twelve months of solid touring and musically as tight as a miser's purse – to set up shop in Ireland and plunge straight into songwriting and pre-production for the next album. The first week, though, was spent looking for lodgings. The band found a six-bedroom house in a quiet Dublin suburb, but the place was totally unfurnished. To make the place habitable, the group marched down to a nearby discount furniture shop and bought just about anything that had four legs and no sizeable cracks.

"The guy who ran the place couldn't believe it," Joe laughs. "We went straight into the place and said 'We want five beds.' The thing was, we had to buy a lot of stuff. The house was completely empty. So we told the guy we were going to buy a lot, could he give us a decent discount? He said yeah.

"So we picked out five beds, five bedside cabinets, five wardrobe closets, a dining room table, six chairs, a TV table, a coffee table and a video cabinet. The whole lot cost us less than a thousand pounds, but we practically cleaned the guy out. When it was all delivered the next day, we went out and carted it all into the house ourselves.

"It was all very funny. We were carrying this furniture up the driveway, saying 'Can you imagine David Coverdale doing this sort of thing?' Sure, it would have been nice to walk into a hotel again, or get a house that was already fixed up. But we wanted to do something normal. We'd been on the road for so long, living in this overprotective shell, and although the place was no palace, it didn't do us any harm. So the white walls had all gone yellow – big deal. We just covered them up with posters."

But Def Leppard weren't in Dublin just to play happy homemaker and write rock ditties. Def Leppard were in Dublin principally for tax reasons. Nineteen eighty-three had been a banner year for the band's accountants. The band had gone from making $1000 a night in 1980, opening act peanuts, to commanding hefty

The young guitarists

A FOLK dance festival was held yesterday at the City School, Stradbroke Road, Sheffield. Picture shows musicians (from left) Glenn Ward, Thomas Winks and Stephen Clark, all from Wisewood Comprehensive School, who took part.

Steve's first press cutting! (*Sheffield Star* 7 July 197

percentages of six-figure concert grosses. *Pyromania* royalties were still coming in, along with money from increased sales on *On Through the Night* and *High'n'Dry*. Leppard had also been setting arena records on merchandise sales across America. There was going to be money and plenty of it. And Mother England wanted a big chunk of it.

It's only fair that the more money you make, the more you should pay in taxes, but the British government has a system that can make you liable for a large portion of it. Which can leave you with precious little rock star moolah. So it has become traditional for British pop stars to live abroad for at least a year or two, if not more, to avoid getting socked for all that tax, which probably goes to feed the country's lumbering bureaucracy and water the Queen's rose garden anyway. The Rolling Stones, Rod Stewart, David Bowie and the Police have all done their time in tax exile.

Now it was Def Leppard's turn. The group had already invested a good deal of their profits in a money market fund where it could quietly gather interest instead of going down the toilet, wasted on Rolls-Royces and palatial country mansions. Nevertheless, Mother England was already getting its chunk of the *Pyromania* money. "We paid sixty per cent of the money we earned on *Pyromania* to the government," Joe grumbles. "For every £10 in net profit that we made on that album, we only ended up with four. And that was on world sales, because the album had been recorded in England." By living in Dublin and subsequently recording the next album in Dublin and Holland, Def Leppard would not be taxed so severely. They would not, in fact, be taxed at all. The catch was that they could not stay in England more then 60 days out of the full 365 a year. The other big drawback was living abroad and the attendant image of big time rock stars swanning around the globe while the fans at home greased the wheels of government with their own hard-earned wages.

"I can understand people thinking that," Joe admits. "I used to think like that myself. But it's not really true. To a certain extent, the reason you go into tax exile is the money, obviously. There's no point in lying about it. But these are our earning years. We have to look out for our future."

Living in Ireland was the next best thing to being in England itself. You could get fish and chips and all the latest English soccer scores with no problem. People drive on the same side of the road and you could watch English television programs. And if you didn't mind the low-key nightlife, at least compared to London, you were all set. Which was fine by Joe. It was fine for Sav too, even though he'd already bought a house in Sheffield. They both eventually rented their own apartments in Dublin. Steve and Phil, on the other hand, were bored stiff. Eventually, they bought their own apartments too – in Paris.

"Touring had its advantages," Sav explains. "You're actually working, doing a different gig every night. You're into a routine and being on stage is the icing on the cake. There's always that to keep you going.

"But in Ireland, we didn't have the excitement, the changing cities and atmosphere, the day-to-day experience. We were stuck in the same house, knowing we had to write songs and get them together. That was pretty depressing, although we'd periodically be cheered up when we knew we had a good song together. That would keep us going to the next one."

The songwriting was quite productive. Each member of the band bought little drum machines so they could work out song ideas on their own. Group sessions were held in a special music room set up in the Dublin house. Steve and Phil played their guitars through tiny Rockmans (the guitar player's equivalent of a Walkman headset, invented by Boston's hard rock Einstein, Tom Scholz) and everything was laid down on a small portable Fostex cassette recorder with Joe singing through chorus and echo effects.

That was it. Whenever they felt a pretty good tune coming on, Leppard adjourned to a rehearsal room they had rented in central Dublin where they thrashed the song out at proper volume with Rick playing a full drum kit. By the time Mutt Lange arrived in Dublin to help the group with pre-production, Leppard had accumulated twenty-three backing tracks with formidable potential.

The problem was that pre-production was about as far as Mutt was willing to go with Def Leppard's fourth album. The recording and mixing of *Pyromania* had already sent him to the brink of insanity. On top of that, Mutt had just finished working on the Cars' *Heartbeat City* album, a project that ran over deadline, resulting in serious friction with the Cars' principal driver, guitarist-songwriter Ric Ocasek. Mutt could commit to Leppard's fourth album only at his peril.

"I'm always on the verge of cracking after every album," Mutt confesses. "It's my own fault. I never take a break between records. But I had to say no at some point. And after the Cars album, I was really knackered. Also, the band was going into tax exile. So I couldn't even be tired in England. I'd be tired in Ireland or Holland. So I said no."

That created a major crisis. Mutt was the principal architect of Def Leppard's studio work and had been active in criticizing and editing the band's songwriting. They were hardly his puppets, but they owed a great deal of their success to him. Without

Mutt, Leppard would practically have to start from scratch.

The search for a producer began in earnest. Ted Templeman, best known for his work with Van Halen, and Asia/Journey producer Mike Stone were considered, but both Leppard and their management were concerned about ending up with some other band's "hit" sound. Templeman and Stone were archetypal hard rock producers and Def Leppard had already made the archetypal hard rock record of 1983 with *Pyromania*. They wanted the new and exotic. That was easier said than done.

Trevor Horn, the brains and ears behind Frankie Goes To Hollywood, refused to leave England and because of their tax exile status, Leppard could not record there. Chris Thomas, who had worked with Roxy Music, the Pretenders and the Sex Pistols, was approached. Another name that came up was Steve Lillywhite, the young buck of British post-punk who had produced smash albums for U2 and Siouxsie and the Banshees. Leppard even approached renaissance man Phil Collins, popular solo artist, songwriter, producer, singer and Genesis drummer. Joe says Collins was up for the job but was already committed to several hundred other projects. Then Cliff Burnstein came up with Jim Steinman.

Steinman was a strange choice, but not totally inappropriate. He first hit the big time writing pseudo-Wagnerian pop operas for that round mound of sound, Meatloaf. The Loaf's 1977 platter *Bat Out of Hell* went platinum several times over, but the duo never got around to recording a follow-up. Steinman and the great fatsby split up before they could finish the projected second album, which eventually became a rather anticlimactic Steinman solo outing called *Bad for Good*. Steinman recovered nicely though, later producing hits for songstress Bonnie Tyler and Australian MOR wimps Air Supply. His taste in clients wasn't too great, but he was producing hits and *Bat Out of Hell*, for all of its bloated lyric pretentiousness, was a real heavy metal rollercoaster.

There was one other thing in Steinman's favour too. He thought *Pyromania* was one of the best rock albums he'd ever heard. "He said *Stagefright* was the song that really got him going when he was in a driving mood," comments Joe. "God knows how. That's hardly the song I'd want to hear if I was out for a drive. It's too aggressive for that. Maybe he likes to drive when he's angry."

In any case, Steinman was interested. The band sent the Dublin demos to Steinman in America. He liked them; all systems were go.

Mutt, in the meantime, had lived in Leppard House for a month, listening to the new songs, criticizing them and in some instances rewriting hooks and bridges. A lot of time was also spent trying to convince the band they could do the next record without him.

"It was a big shock to us, to think that he wouldn't do it," Joe recalls. "But he kept saying it was no big deal. We had to believe in ourselves, that we could do it without him." Subsequent events would prove Mutt wrong, but his power-of-positive-thinking rap sounded good at the time.

After treating themselves to a ten day vacation, Leppard knuckled down in August to serious recording with Jim Steinman at Wisseloord Studios in Holland. Within a month, Steve and Phil were conspiring to dump Steinman.

"It was over guitar sounds," Phil claims. "He wanted us to play live, with the entire band in the studio. We didn't want to do that. We wanted to overdub, the way we'd done *Pyromania*. And he would accept a lot of things that Mutt wouldn't – guitar sounds, sloppy timing. He would get a terrible guitar sound and we'd think 'Oh, it must be the amps.' "

"He didn't have any ideas guitar-wise," adds Steve. "We thought then that maybe he could give Joe some ideas for his vocals, maybe draw something different out of him. But when Joe started doing vocals and they weren't happening, we knew something was wrong."

Sav aged eight: dreaming of soccer boots and megawatt mayhem.

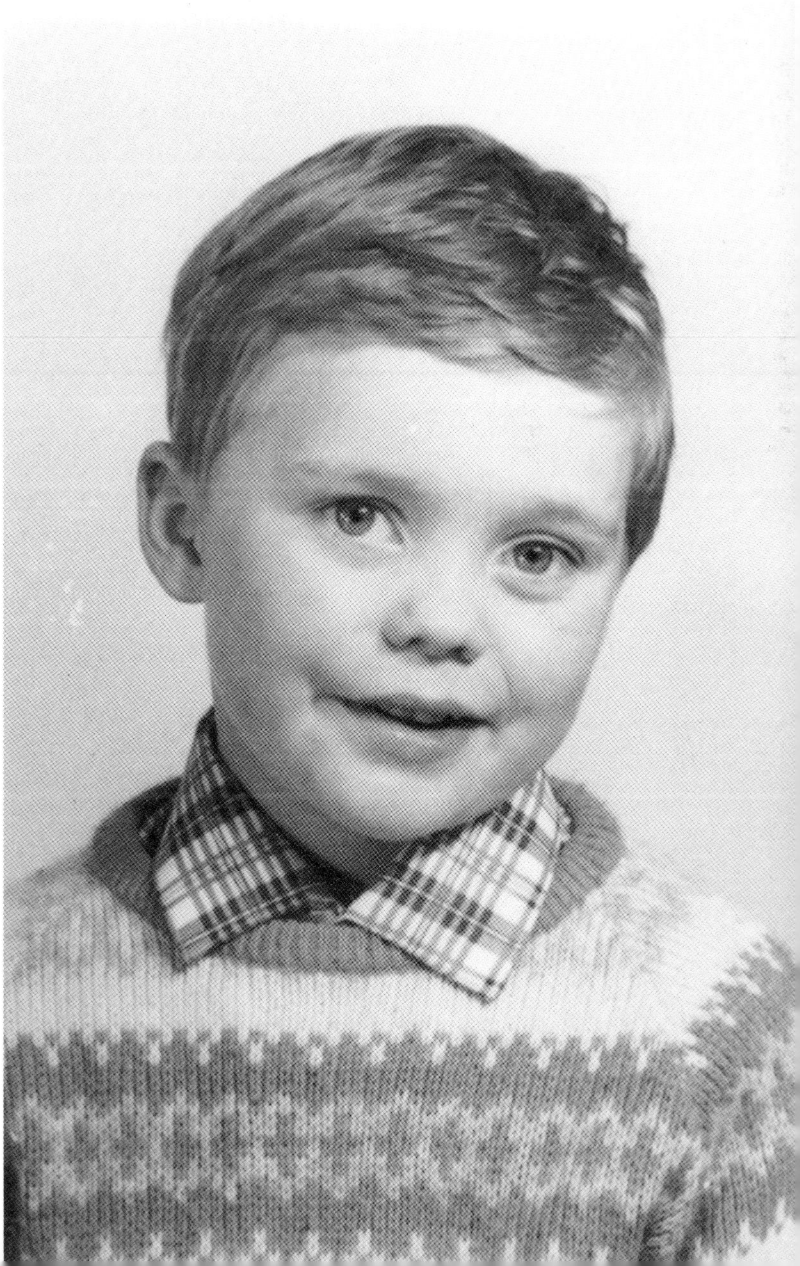

"He was a nice enough guy," Phil says with a shrug. "But it seemed like we were banging our heads up against a wall." And it began to hurt after a while.

Steinman, according to Joe Elliott, "was a 'vibe' producer. He wasn't a producer of sounds. He wanted to put this echo over everything and have these big backing 'answer' vocals, like you could see angels with wings on their backs, holding harps. He'd tell Steve to play his guitar with more grease and Steve would think 'What does he want to do, cover it with oil?' "

Joe says Sav was usually in the control booth with Steinman during vocal and guitar takes. After a while, Sav began overruling Steinman on recording decisions. Finally, in November, Steinman was informed that Def Leppard would be finishing the record without him. Leppard subsequently scrapped the eight backing tracks they had managed to complete under his supervision.

It was a messy divorce. Peter Mensch and Cliff Burnstein decided it was best if Leppard's lawyers initially contacted Steinman's lawyers to clear up any contract entanglements. By the time the legal beagles were done haggling over "the party of the first part," Steinman already knew from his manager Stateside that he was out of the picture. Joe called Steinman's hotel room for three days after that, hoping to clear the air and at least part amicably. Steinman never returned Joe's messages.

Unfortunately, along with Steinman went his engineer, the highly regarded Neil Dorfsman. At the same time Steinman got his pink slip, Dorfsman had to return to the States to start work on a new Dire Straits album. Another engineer, Dave Thoener, who had worked with John Waite, filled in for two weeks. Leppard tried to get *Pyromania* engineer Mike Shipley, but he was already committed to a new Loverboy project. Mutt Lange then suggested Nigel Green. He'd done time as an assistant engineer on *High'n'Dry*. He knew the band, he knew Mutt's style of recording and he could start immediately. So with Green behind the console and the band essentially producing themselves, the laborious process of recording the new Def Leppard album began anew.

Leppard were back in overdub city. Steve and Phil did the bulk of the initial work, laying down their parts riff by riff, chord by chord, note by note. Whoever wasn't working behind the studio glass had to be content with enjoying the fresh smell of cow manure wafting over the Dutch farmland around Hilversum, where Wisseloord was located. Phil says Steve had trouble killing time while his Terror Twin was cutting tracks at the studio. "It was really hard for him because while I was doing my guitar parts, there was nothing for him to do."

Sav made a point of going to Wisseloord every day to act as a combination advisor-and-cheerleader, even though his bass parts would be the last things recorded. Joe amused himself back at the hotel in Ood Loosdrecht with his Led Zeppelin bootlegs, his impressive collection of rare Ian Hunter and Mott The Hoople cassettes and a portable Fostex cassette recorder. With a guitar and a portable synthesizer, he made tapes of song ideas and recorded solo versions of some of his favourite hits – David Bowie's *The Man Who Sold the World*, the Mick Ronson version of *Slaughter on 10th Avenue*, the Troggs' *Wild Thing* and *House of the King* by Dutch art-rockers Focus.

Joe also had plenty of time to think about Def Leppard's recent accomplishments and their small but hard-fought-for place in the rock continuum. "You know, I used to listen to a lot of punk rock, believe it or not," he laughed one afternoon in his room, as a stiff wind rattled the windows of the Hotel Loosdrecht and the masts of the boats in the hotel's lakeside harbor. "I bought all those records by the Sex Pistols, Slaughter and the Dogs and the Drones when they came out. I liked them for the wrong reasons. As much as I still listen to *Crime of the Century* by Supertramp, it was nice to put on something that was completely out of tune.

"But the New Wave of those days isn't the same as the New Wave today. Then, it was the Clash, *White Riot*. Today, it's Simple Minds. And Simple Minds are basically a rock band that

The producer that almost was: Jim Steinman (second from left).

One for the (family) album – with parents backstage at LA Forum, 10 September, 1983.

doesn't have a heavy guitar sound. They're tight, they sing well and they write good songs. How would you describe Billy Idol? His guitarist Steve Stevens is brilliant. He's not punk or heavy metal. It's all just rock."

The lines, he admitted, had blurred. In 1979, there was practically an iron curtain between heavy metal kids like Def Leppard and the punk-rock competition, even though both factions had created thriving parallel undergrounds with their independently released EPs and separate club circuits. Now, the same people who liked Eurythmics could easily take a shine to *Photograph* with little ideological distress.

"The lines are not as definitive as they once were. I can't believe that anyone who bought our first album wouldn't like *Pyromania.* It's just more melodic – and more powerful. The songs on the first album were badly mixed, badly produced, badly played and badly sung. Apart from that, of course, they were pretty good. But it's a matter of broadening your horizons. Some bands stay the same. Black Sabbath will never change. Metallica will never change. And that's okay for them.

"But we always wanted to be different. We wanted to progress. And I hate calling our stuff heavy metal now. It's a silly term. It's just music to me. I just wish you didn't have to keep putting things into all these separate bags. I know this sounds weird, but it would be nice to be like the Rolling Stones. They never get bagged into anything other than the fact that they are the Rolling Stones. They're a rock band. They can sound pretty heavy metal at times, they can play like punks, they can sound funky, they can even play disco. But they're still the Rolling Stones.

"The problem with bands now is that they're just a part of a continual history. People don't look at you as being founders of something. That doesn't bother me about Def Leppard, though. There will never be another Beatles no matter how good a song you can write. They were first and that's it. You can't change that, even in the year 2050 when nobody's playing their songs anymore. It will never start again the same way.

"The only way you can even attempt to carve anything in stone is just to stay around for a long time and be successful. In your own little world, you've got to try and take steps that you think are a progression, or at least a little different. You can't go around just copying yourself all the time."

From their isolation chamber at Wisseloord, Def Leppard earnestly believed they were about to step into the New Year, 1985, with their best foot forward. Their next record might not be a giant step for rock & roll, but it would at least be a giant step for Leppard themselves. The band adjourned for the Christmas holidays with smiles and grins all round – until Rick Allen's black corvette Stingray had a head-on argument with a brick wall on the A57 outside Sheffield.

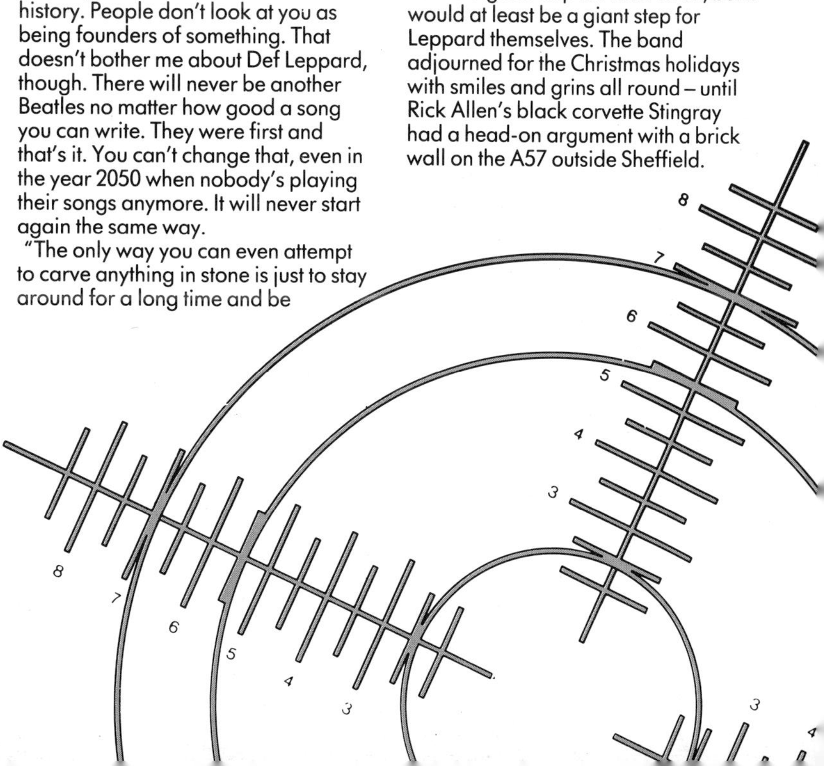

CHAPTER 9

THE HEALING

In the living room of the Allen residence in Green Lane, Dronfield, near Sheffield, there is a little wooden curio shelf just to the right of the fireplace. It is pockmarked all over with dozens of small indentations, as if someone had been compelled to beat the shelf into submission for some terrible breach of furniture etiquette. The avenger, of course, was young master Richard, then just a toddler but even at that age a tough customer with a pair of drumsticks.

"Yes, it's still here," he exclaimed with glee on a gloomy March afternoon only three months after the New Year's Eve auto accident that claimed his left arm. "Can you see the marks there?," he chuckled elfishly, running his right hand over the roadmap of welts with delight. "There was always a pair of sticks knocking around the house. So I'd be listening to records, banging away on the shelf there. And dear me, when I realized what I'd done . . ."

These were definitely not the smiles and giggles of a young man, barely out of his teens, whose body was now minus one essential limb and whose career as a drummer was clouded with doubt. This was just normal old Rick, the same mischievous, trouble-making, often irritating imp who for the past twenty years had been driving his parents and, more recently, bandmates to distraction. The other members of Def Leppard had marvelled at the speed of Rick's recovery from the accident, both physically and emotionally. But it was truly remarkable to sit with Rick in his parents' living room and listen to him speak calmly, thoughtfully, about his ordeal and its future consequences. One minute, he spoke hopefully about his new drumkit, a customized electronic marvel with special footpedals to trigger the bang-boom-crash sounds he used to make with his left arm. The next minute, Rick talked of designing special one-armed Rick Allen tour T-shirts, or "L-shirts" as he called them.

"We'll get people sending them back though," he smirked, "because we're gonna sew the left arm up!

"Actually, I'd love to get something together for merchandising on the next tour," he added, a bit more seriously. "It would be quite novel and, really, I don't mind. People can laugh their bloody heads off. At least I'll be up there on stage playing."

Allen's recovery was no breeze. He'd suffered occasional bouts of doubt and depression since the accident and they would continue to plague him now and then during the coming year. Yet he'd benefited not only from the support of his family and fellow Leppards, but from the visible example of other handicapped people who had made do with less, just as Rick was now forced to do. Earlier that day, he'd been sipping lunchtime pints of bitter at a pub down the road, Chaplin's, with two middle-aged men whose respective left arms had also been amputated. One of them was a co-owner of the bar. The other, Graham, was a well-known local sportsman whose specialities despite his handicap, were race car driving and skeet shooting.

And there they were, laughing it up, cracking jokes, not actually making light of their plight, but seeing the humor in it while drawing strength from each other's courage and achievement. It was as if the three of them had formed an exclusive little club. "Now everybody's going to want one arm," Rick cracked at one point.

"I think I feel more complete now than I ever did," he remarked later back at the house. "It puts all your priorities into perspective. It has for me, anyway. All those stupid thoughts that come into your mind – they don't anymore. I seem to be able to command a situation better. That's the one good thing that's come out of it.

"No," he added quickly "there's a lot of good things that have come out of it. A hell of a lot."

"I remember waking up in intensive care, one time. I saw the nurse and I didn't know what had happened – I really didn't. I was trying to get out of bed, shouting for brother Robert, 'I want my brother, I want my brother.' I told Robert to take me home. I wanted to go home, although obviously I couldn't. I was in a right old state, with pipes and bloody needles and all kinds of stuff stuck into me.

"Since then, I've seen the whole accident in my head. But it's difficult to explain. There really wasn't any sensation. It was like my whole body was numb, tensed. There was no pain, no nothing. Just emptiness.

"Later, though, I had this strange sensation about the arm. It still changes from day to day. Sometimes you can feel that there's nothing there. But most of the time I can feel everything. I can even move my fingers, really. If I concentrate, I can move my first finger and thumb and sometimes I can move the rest of them, too, as if it was evolution, like those starfish that can grow their arms back. It's as if my brain is still telling me that the arm is there, or supposed to be there.

"The biggest shock was when I actually came around and realized what had happened. Sitting there, looking out the bloody window,

looking at myself, listening to my music. That's the thing that upset me most at first, listening to music. I had my usual supply of tapes in the hospital – Billy Idol, Journey. My favourite was *Joe Cocker's Greatest Hits*, because he was from Sheffield.

"But I'd hear the drums and couldn't help but think, 'Yeah, I used to be able to do that.' I didn't want to listen to any Def Leppard stuff at first though. Eventually, I got back into it. I had a tape of the 1983 show at the Forum in Los Angeles. That kind of got to me a bit, the frustration of not knowing what I was going to do. There I was, with my right arm all strapped up and (pointing to his left shoulder) now knowing what was going on over here.

"I was never aware that they tried to put the arm back on. They kept me under the anaesthetic the whole time. Actually, I was pretty surprised that they tried. Mr. Page, the doctor that did it, is a very well-respected microsurgeon. He was heartbroken that it didn't work.

"I'm glad I didn't find out about it until later, though. That would have started me thinking, about drumming again, about being normal. I don't even remember Joe or Sav being there that first day. I don't remember there being any pain of any sort, just a helpless sort of feeling. I still get that feeling now, asking people to do things for me. Because I can't do them myself.

"The last thing I wanted, though, was a lot of sympathy – 'Oh, I'm sorry this, we're sorry that.' And I certainly didn't get it from the band! When Phil and Steve came, and Phil said I was an 'inconsiderate bastard,' you have no idea how great it was to hear that. It was a real boost for me. I left the room for a while to get a glass of milk and Phil turned to my mum and whispered 'He's so normal!' which I thought was quite funny. I think they thought I wouldn't be mentally very coherent. That would have been the worst, not being able to communicate. I was very lucky in that respect.

"There was never any need for psychological therapy either. Right from the word 'go,' I was right in there, my old self again. I complained about this. I complained about that. The food was bloody awful. After a while, I ended up getting these Hare Krishna people – Mutt Lange had made some contribution to their temple in Watford – who actually came all the way up from Watford, stayed with friends and cooked food for me everyday. Great vegetarian grub. They'd bring it to the hospital every single day. I put on about fifteen pounds while I was in the hospital, just eating all that great Krishna food.

"Boy, I got countless cards and

telegrams, too. I got telegrams from the guys in Scorpions, from Billy Idol and Steve Stevens, even Phil Collins, who I'd never met. All just saying 'Get better.' Doug Clifford, the drummer from Creedence Clearwater Revival, sent me a double album of Creedence's greatest hits with a note that said 'Drummers are a different breed from everybody else. Keep the faith.' He knew that I'd pull through.

"Drummers are different, I guess. It's like this fighting sort of spirit, always trying to get out. It probably comes from hitting things. Who in their right mind would spend their whole life sitting there, hitting bits of plastic with pieces of wood? There's gotta be something wrong with you – or at least something different. And all the musicians and drummers who sent me cards and telegrams, they knew I'd be alright. I told myself that. I had to.

"I heard from a lot of people in America, too, fans, admirers of the band. They sent all kinds of T-shirts. I got a hat that said 'Pittsburgh loves Def Leppard.' There was a T-shirt that said 'Somebody in Arizona loves me' with my picture on the back. Cuddly toys galore, too. Lots of stuffed Garfield toys.

"It was amazing to me to think of the amount of people who were concerned about me. And it was worldwide, not just England and America. Japan. Australia. I got things from Hungary and East Germany, places where we hadn't even played.

"That did me a hell of a lot of good. I could feel myself improving day to day. It also had a lot to do with my own determination. All I ever wanted to do was get out of that hospital. It was like a prison for me. They said I was going to be in that hospital for six months. I was out in less than a month. I got out January 29."

"After I got out of the hospital, I came back here to my parents' house. There was a district nurse who would come around and check up on me. They didn't send a young pretty one either. This one was a big, big woman. 'You will eat your chicken soup!' Actually, I think she was taking her orders from Mensch.

"I couldn't go anywhere until my arm had cleared up. When I went skittering along the road, I scraped my arm almost down to the bone. So I had to wait for that to clear up. But as soon as that was pretty well healed, I was straight off to Holland. I left on February 22, less than a month after I'd gotten out of that hospital.

"The doctors weren't too sure about letting me go. But I said I needed to do this for my own satisfaction. I was going mad at home, sitting around all bloody day watching the TV screen and listening to records. Going to Holland was going to be like hanging out with my mates.

"It was weird going over there, being on the plane by myself with all these people looking at me. But it's great because now I can use this to my advantage. When I was coming back from Holland the last time, there were these two chaps on the plane and they wanted to sit together. So I said, 'But I'm disabled, I've got to sit on the end seat.' Of course, I don't *have* to sit there at all. I was just putting the guy on, saying 'I've lost my arm,' and he bolted out of the seat, *vroom!*, 'Here, sit down, no problem, 'all embarrassed. It was pretty funny.

"You get lots of sympathy from the girls too. Like I say, once you've been with a man with one arm, you can't go back to anything else!

"Miriam, my girlfriend, has been great, though. It's good, in a way, that she was there at the accident. She saw it all. And that gave me a hell of a lot of strength in turn. She would say 'Come on, you've got to do this, you've got to pull yourself together.' Not that I wasn't doing it on my own, but it was nice having somebody else there. And she helped me a lot with the day-to-day stuff.

"Still, it's good that I've been put into a situation where I've got to do things on my own. I've got to tie my shoelaces, I've got to put my sweatpants on, my shirt, the whole bit, It's different, but that's all it is. I think I can go as far as to say I can do basically anything – it just takes a little bit longer.

"That's been good, too. Ever since the accident, I don't want to be in a rush anymore. I don't want to have to get from point A to point B in two minutes all the time. I'm at a stage now where the world can wait. I want to enjoy what I've got now.

"When I first got out of the hospital, that was an amazing feeling. When I was in there, just to look out the window, to see the world, that was incredible by itself. When I woke up from the anaesthetic, that hospital room seemed so BIG, absolutely huge. Towards the time I got out, the room seemed to get smaller and smaller. Then I got out and I was totally overwhelmed – 'Wow, there's people walking around!' It was actually a little frightening.

"Then I had to get on a plane to go to Holland. And that seemed overwhelming. But now I feel I can deal with virtually anything. The hardest thing was being here, in Sheffield, seeing schoolfriends, people who hadn't seen me since I'd joined the band. There have been a few awkward moments, mostly in pubs. Mostly people just staring. But you get

used to it. The thing that really embarrasses people more than anything is when you stare back. It bothers them a hell of a lot more than it does me.
"The thing is that you're always trying to hide the fact, make it *look* normal. That's the worst thing, trying to look inconspicuous. Like you always make sure your empty sleeve is tucked in your pocket. At one point, I was going to stuff it with tissue paper.
"It's not so bad with people you don't know. I don't really mind being in public places. I was in a pub yesterday and there was this older chap and his wife. He'd been in the same hospital I was and he was so easy to talk to. He'd had some kind of bowel operation and I found it so easy to talk to him, much more so than with younger people. They tend to be a bit strange about it.
"For some reason, though, people in general seem to have more respect for you. Not making me out to be a hero or anything, but they definitely approach you in a different way. Before, because I was the youngest guy in the band, if I said anything or had an opinion about something, people might turn around and go 'Aw, what's he on about?' Now I open my mouth and they all pay attention – 'Yes? What's that?'
"The car? Right now, it's at my cousin's place. He runs a towing business and he towed it in after the accident. I never got any insurance money on it. I found out after the accident that I wasn't covered. And I have to sell it out of the country because it was never registered in England.
"It's still in fairly decent shape. It's actually driveable. You know anybody that wants to buy a broken Corvette Stingray? Real cheap?"

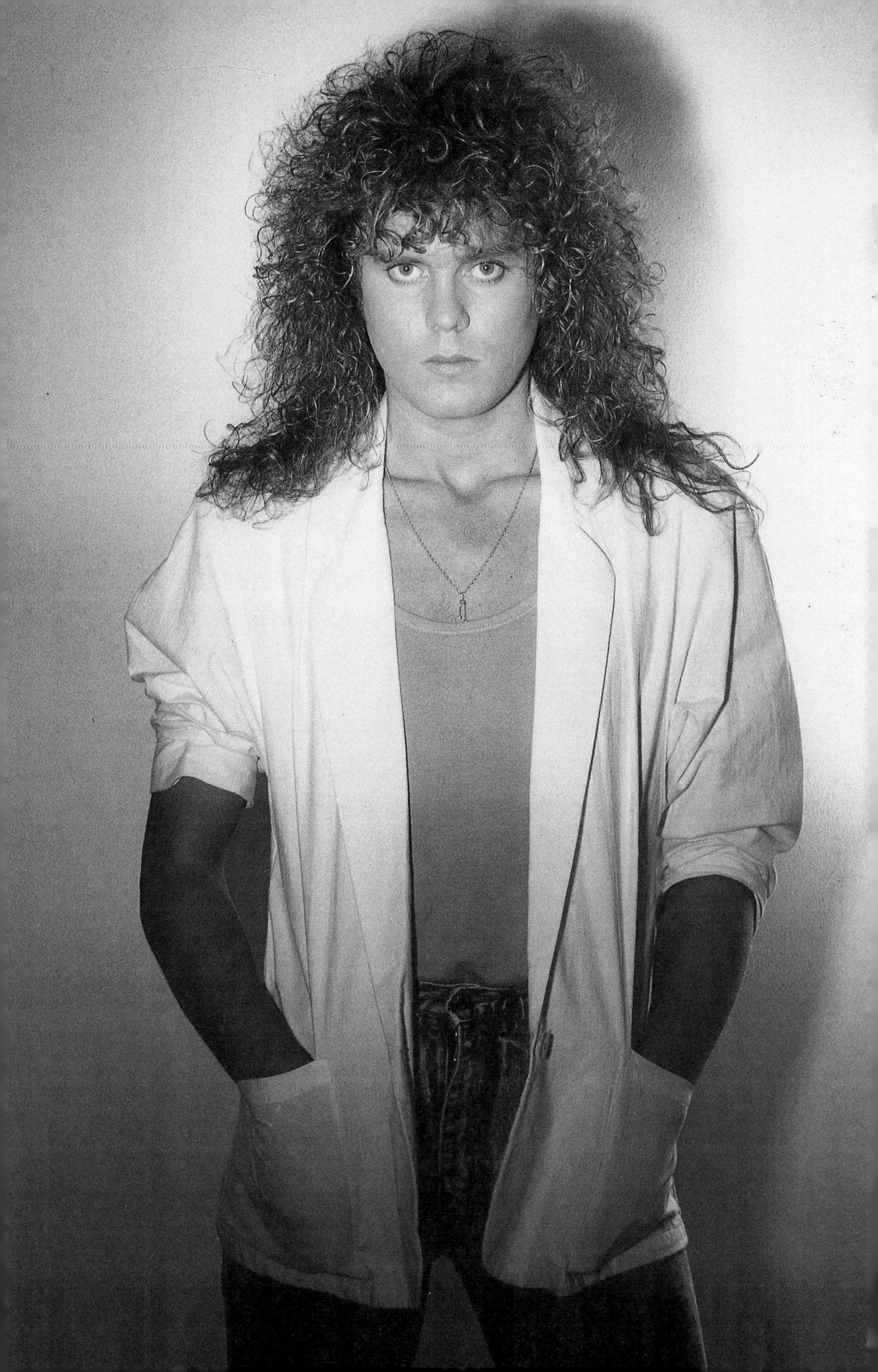

CHAPTER 10

CRISIS? WHAT CRISIS?

"I was having a rare weekend back in Sheffield in my local pub and somebody asked me what we were going to call the new album. I said I wasn't sure yet. Somebody turned round and said 'Why don't you call it *Halley's Comet*? It comes around about as often.' In fact, Halley's Comet has already been out and we're still recording."

Rick Savage
December, 1986

In the living room of his small apartment on the lake front in Ood Loosdrecht, Holland, only twenty minutes from Wisseloord Studios, Joe Elliott sat on a couch holding his head gently in the cup of his hands. Every once in a while, he would make a low but audible groaning noise, obviously in great pain. The night before, he'd embarked on a booze-a-thon with some folks from the studio, a spree that lasted well into the wee hours and included knocking back a few exotic poisons with Mick Jagger, who was in town cutting basic tracks for his second solo album at Wisseloord two doors down the hall from Leppard. Joe had been trying to drink up enough courage to ask Jagger if he'd be so kind as to make a special vocal appearance on one of Leppard's songs. The only thing he got for his trouble was a monster hangover.

But his head wasn't the only thing killing him. His pride was also taking a nasty beating as he tried to explain how hard Def Leppard had been working on its fourth album in the almost two years since the interviews for this book first began. That was in March, 1985; Christmas '86 was now only three weeks away and, as far as the outside world was concerned, the band had accomplished absolutely nothing.

"It's not the recording," Joe sighed quietly, trying not to aggravate the little men kickboxing inside his skull. "The thing that's taken so long is *thinking* about it. We spent so much time sitting around, saying to each other, 'What is this album lacking?' And we'd always talk in song titles. Somebody might say 'It's lacking a *Satisfaction*, a *Free Bird* or a *Stairway to Heaven*.' Then we'd try and come up with a song that would measure up to that.

"We were also very paranoid, something I thought we'd never suffer from – the Follow-Up Album Blues. How do you follow six million albums sold? And I realize now that you can't think about it. But it's too late now. Because once you've thought about it, you can't be naive and just say 'Oh, fuck it, let's just make an album,' We didn't want to become another REO Speedwagon – eight million sold and then a crappy follow-up album.

"Why is it taking so long?" he asked almost hopelessly. "I don't know. Maybe we're not as good as we thought we were. Maybe we can't play as well as we thought we could. I don't know. I can't give you a nice tight reason for what happened."

If, as Tom Petty once sang, the waiting is the hardest part, it was actually the fans, not the band, that got the Follow-Up Album Blues. At least the Leppards had a gruelling work schedule to take their minds off the pain. Sav estimates that at least one member of the band was in the studio every day recording *something* between the winter of 1985 and the group's Monsters of Rock mini-tour in August, 1986.

Yet Leppard lovers had nothing to show for it but broken deadlines and broken promises. The few microscopic news snippets that appeared in the press made, for the most part, pretty depressing reading. At the dawn of '86, manager Peter Mensch fearlessly predicted in *People* magazine that Def Leppard's soon-to-be-released fourth album "will be the biggest record by a white rock band since Bruce Springsteen." Not in our lifetime, it seemed. By the dawn of '87, Springsteen was back at the top of the charts with a live five-record set, while Rick Allen was only halfway through knocking out computer drum programs for the new album, Joe had at least another month's worth of vocals to do and Sav hadn't even laid down bass parts for nine of the LP's twelve songs.

As time passed, the faithful no doubt wondered whether Def Leppard, having made history with *Pyromania*, were now just part of it. While they were busy recording their fourth album three times with as many producers, whole pop music fads passed before their very eyes. The Sixties psychedelic revival came around two or three times. British groups like Culture Club and Frankie Goes To Hollywood shotgunned to fame, racked up fistfuls of hits and faded into oblivion in the time it took Phil Collen and Steve Clark to inchworm through a single guitar track. London dreamboats George Michael and Andrew Ridgely formed Wham!, signed a record deal, repeatedly went to Number One in Britain, conquered America, toured China, broke up and gave a farewell concert in the three years it took Leppard to make one album. In America, heavy-melody bands like Bon Jovi and Cinderella were practically minting money with the stadium rock mix of Top Forty hooks and glam-metal crunch that sold six million copies of *Pyromania*. They hadn't just copped Leppard's action, they'd Xeroxed the sound.

There was also the small matter of Live Aid. On July 13, 1985, nearly every mega-act of rock's first thirty years donated twenty minutes of its time to benefit starving millions in Africa, whipping through hit after hit for sold-out crowds in London's Wembley Stadium and Philadelphia's John F. Kennedy Stadium, not to mention the two billion folks glued to their TV sets around the globe. Instead of being on one of those two stages, the members of Def Leppard saw rock's finest moment on TV in Paris, where Mutt Lange was putting Joe through his vocal paces in the studio. Live Aid organizer Bob Geldof had called Peter Mensch earlier that spring to ask if Leppard would join the Live Aid superbill. Mensch barely had time to explain the finer points of Rick Allen's condition before Geldof barked "Thank you" and hung up.

Phil Collen felt miserable watching the show on television. "Not because of the cause. At the time, I felt terrible every time I saw a live audience." At that point, it had been eighteen months since Def Leppard had been on a concert stage. And there was no guarantee that they would stand on one before the year was out.

"We went through a phase at one point," grumbles Steve Clark, "where we didn't even want to go to see a group play live, because we wanted to do it so badly. It was too painful."

But Steve wasn't feeling any pain as he sat in the studio manager's office at Wisseloord one sunny afternoon in March, 1985 listening to rough tapes of the new songs. With sunlight streaming through the window, music blaring out of the office stereo at nuclear volume, Steve rocked back and forth in his chair, gulping Heineken between shit-eating grins. These were only demo tapes of the new songs, recorded during pre-production in Ireland the previous year. The versions cut at Wisseloord at the end of '84 with Jim Steinman as

producer were a total write-off. The message, however, was written clear across Clark's face. Def Leppard had plenty of confidence, not only in these songs, but in themselves to produce them on their own with Nigel Green.

Green had been Mutt Lange's assistant engineer on *High'n'Dry* and was familiar with Mutt's preferred method of piecemeal recording. While Rick Allen recovered from his accident and worked to develop coordination between his three working limbs, Green and the other members of Leppard set about recording the fourth album at Wisseloord in exactly the same manner – note by note, chord by chord, scream by scream. Another *Pyromania* was in the offing; the platinum was sure to follow.

The songs Clark played in the Wisseloord office that day were an uncanny marriage of Def Leppard's old spoon-factory instincts and the platinum pop lessons Mutt Lange had drilled into them on the last two albums. As a package of roaring arena metal and pop accessibility, the album-to-be seemed to be at least equal to *Pyromania*, if not better.

Run Riot was a hot bodyslam rocker with an unmistakable Aerosmith bite. Steve got to show off his best Jimmy Page *Kashmir* drone in the intro to *Gods of War* while *Women*, a hard stomp taken at Black Sabbath tempo, was the perfect showcase for Phil Collen's zigzag solo fourishes. There was a classy pop flair to the chorus in *Animal*, although that hadn't stopped the band from tagging no less than three false endings to the track. "We did that," said Steve with a playful leer, "to fuck up the DJs."

But they would be more than forgiving because the band had also tagged

two surefire hits to the album line-up, perfect for spinning on any radio frequency. One was *Love Bites*, a song quite different from the original Irish demo of the same name. Together with Mutt Lange, at the time acting as a kind of executive advisor on the album, Phil and Steve had written a strong rousing ballad combining the minor-key glow of *Bringin' on the Heartbreak* with the Top Forty shimmer of *Photograph*. The other song was a little one-riff number called *Excitable* that had been cooked up after a modest bout of carousing in Dublin during pre-production there.

According to Sav, every Thursday evening he, Phil, Steve and Mutt would take a break from songwriting and treat themselves to an evening on the town – a nice meal, a few drinks and a few laughs in a local Dublin disco. On one particular Thursday, Sav recalls, "there were a lot of good songs coming over the disco. One of them was the Michael Jackson – Mick Jagger song *State of Shock*. It just had a great groove from start to finish, no real musical changes, and we all got to thinking how neat it would be to have a good dance number like that on the album.

"The next morning, I got up and started messing around with my guitar. Within ten minutes, I had this groove. I asked Mutt what he thought – the actual riff only lasted about six seconds – and he said 'Let's tape it.' We made a ten-minute tape of the riff, played it back and Mutt started singing melodies over it. That was it."

That, literally, was it. A fourth album with hard rock clout, whistle-while-you-work tunes and the unmistakable ring of record store cash registers. By the time Def Leppard broke camp at Wisseloord in mid-June of '85 and moved to Paris, Phil and Steve had recorded nearly all of the guitars with Nigel Green and Joe had laid down a guide vocal on another new song, *Fractured Love*, that was deemed hot enough to keep.

Mutt Lange deemed otherwise when he joined the band in Paris. Indeed, he eventually deemed the entire album to be worth redoing. Although he didn't want to commit to producing the entire album, Mutt had previously agreed to work with the band on key "radio" tracks and to produce Joe's vocals. But after he heard what the band had recorded in Holland with Nigel Green, he put Joe's vocals way back on Leppard's docket. "A lot of the stuff had been completed musically," Phil says. "Then Mutt came along and said 'The standard's not that hot, boys.' We didn't know. We couldn't tell, because we'd been in there doing it for so long. We'd lost the plot a bit."

Essentially, Mutt was sentencing Def Leppard – already out of the public eye for almost two years – to another eighteen months in the studio. There were guitar parts to be recut and, in some cases, totally rearranged. All that was left of *Animal* after he, Steve and Phil were done restructuring it were the basic chord changes. Mutt also commissioned the band to write some new songs to replace the *Pyromania*-by-numbers tracks that dominated the album. *Ring of Fire*, a spirited rocker that had nothing to do with the old Johnny Cash song (it was actually about the digestive after-effects of a red-hot Mexican dinner) was one of the first songs to be dropped from the album.

"It's a real fast song and it always sounded better as an instrumental," Joe says. "We weren't sure what to do with it, so Mutt said leave it and come up with something else that wasn't so metal."

Mutt's vocal disapproval of the new album – which had the tentative title of *Animal Instincts* – came as a blow to the band. "We already had three or four potential singles on it and the rest were good album tracks," explains Sav. "At the time, I don't think any of the guys agreed with him. But we were happy he was there at all and starting to take a big interest in the whole thing."

"We had to learn through our mistakes," Steve admits. "We tried to make a record by formula, exactly the way *Pyromania* was done."

"The problem with that," Phil adds, "was that we'd done that record with Mutt. He was part of the formula."

To make matters more frustrating, recording in Paris turned out not to be such a great idea. "We were there for six weeks, in a place called Studio Des Dames" Joe says. "It was an okay studio, but it was so bloody expensive." Leppard were paying about £120 an hour for the studio and hardly getting their money's worth. "It was so hot in that studio," Joe grumbles, "that Mutt and I had to get out every twenty minutes just to get some air." Joe only managed to

complete vocals on *Animal* and *Run Riot*.

Housing the band in Paris also proved to be costly. Steve and Phil already had their apartments there, but the rest of the band and crew rented rooms on the historic Champs-Elysées. You pay dearly for that kind of history.

Rehearsing was the only thing that made the whole Paris residency worthwhile. While Joe was sweating it out in the studio with Mutt, Steve, Phil, Sav and Rick set up their gear in a little rehearsal studio on the outskirts of central Paris to rediscover the joys of playing together. It was the first time they had played live in over a year and for Rick, now counting time behind his specially designed electronic drum kit, it was his first opportunity to slam out the jams with his bandmates since the accident.

He had help. When the possibility of using a second drummer for touring was brought up after his accident, Rick immediately suggested a friend of his named Jeff Rich, a Londoner who had previously worked with British singer Judie Tzuke. Rick didn't consider any other names, no auditions were held and no one else in the Leppard organization questioned Rick's decision.

Rick and Jeff practiced together for several weeks in Holland before the Paris rehearsals. While the rest of the band was busy at Wisseloord, they went over old Leppard songs in a small rehearsal space (conveniently located next to a bar) in the town of Hilversum. "We went over the obvious songs, "Rick explains. "We'd go in there every day for three or four hours and run through the numbers, the ones we thought we'd be playing live. It took us about three weeks to get them to the stage where we felt good about them. It was different playing with another drummer. I didn't have to play as much. Also, there are certain flicks and feels that no two drummers play alike.

"It felt a bit strange at first. I told Jeff, 'You know, I do feel a little uncomfortable.' There he was, with his two arms, doing all the stuff I used to be able to do. I felt a bit left out.

"But I'm glad I did it. It gave me a chance to experiment a bit. I could sit back on his meter and start to experiment with things myself, rather than just keep the beat rock solid."

Rick and Jeff, then, were ready for anything Steve, Phil and Sav threw at them on the first day of the band rehearsals in Paris. First up was *Another Hit and Run*, the song with which they used to open soundchecks on the *Pyromania* tour. The band tested a couple of the new songs during rehearsal, including *Excitable* and *Love Bites*, but concentrated on the old numbers. These rehearsals were supposed to be a prelude to more extensive workouts with Joe in anticipation of a major winter tour. In theory, anyway.

"It was as if the last gig we'd played was only a week ago." Sav remembers. "We plugged in, got a proper balance and then took off. Nobody sang, which was a good way to do it. You learn not to take your cues off of Joe. You concentrate on the sound. I surprised myself because I didn't think we'd be so together. It had been such a long time, but we clicked right in."

"It was fun," echoes Rick, "a novelty to play with two drummers. It was so powerful, so loud. It actually changed the sound of the band *too* much. Def Leppard drums have always been sparse. And it got a little too busy here and there, Jeff trying to compete with me, me trying to compete with Jeff. It was under control, but that little bit of rivalry was always there, like two lead guitarists on stage."

Before rehearsals were over, though, it became apparent that touring was out of the question. "It was a strange time," says Rick. "We were getting all keyed up, ready to go out and play and it was such a disappointment when it didn't happen. We were in there playing hard, preparing for a tour that we knew was never going to happen. When Mutt started ripping the record apart, any kind of schedule or deadline went out the window."

After Paris, Leppard morale took a nosedive. The band returned to Dublin – where they had done pre-production for the album over a year ago – and set up shop in less expensive quarters, Windmill Lane Studios. "Actually, we were in Windmill 2," Joe notes. "Windmill 1 is the good studio, where U2 record. Windmill 2 is the shitty one, where everybody does jingles for

radio ads. But Mutt said it didn't matter as long as we mixed the album on a good desk. He didn't mind at all."

Neither did Joe and Sav, both of whom had rented apartments in Dublin as part of the Leppard tax exile program. For Sav, it was the next best thing to being back in Sheffield; he had easy access to English newspapers and the daily soccer results. But the combination of Ireland's relentlessly grey, rainy weather and watching six months' work being dissected and eventually discarded by Mutt Lange sent the band into a terrible funk. For a few hours one night, Sav considered leaving the band.

"It was just a depressing evening and I started to think it was all too stupid. I could see time elapsing. I was twenty-two when we last toured America and I was getting old. But the feeling only lasted a couple of hours. And I never got as far as thinking about what I'd do if I ever did leave."

Joe suffered emotional blackouts as well. "When I was singing in the studio, my voice would pack in now and then. I'd go through a lot of mental anguish. I remember a lot of pain, worrying about it." Every once in a while, he would also come down with a bad case of the Fourth Album Blues.

"I'd think 'This is stupid. Somebody ought to stand up and say something.' But when I sat down and thought about it, I realized there was fuck all we could do about it. All we could do was make sure it never happened again."

Steve, Phil and Rick had bigger problems. The first accommodation they shared in the Milltown section of Dublin lacked basic amenities. "This apartment was really funny," Phil laughs, adding that it wasn't such a giggle at the time.

"The place was heated by gas, but the gas had been cut off before we got there. It takes a long time to get anything done in Ireland, so we waited

six weeks for the gas to get turned back on. And the day after they finally turned it on, they came back and turned it off again. they were switching to another type of gas.

"So you have three so-called rock stars in this place. Anytime we wanted to have a shower, we had to put kettles on the stove, heat up the water and throw it in the bath. With three guys in the place, can you imagine how long that takes?"

Not only that, the electricity was turned off at one point and the phone was disconnected. The last straw came when Phil's Porsche was stolen from right outside the building. After that the three so-called rock stars moved to nearby Donnybrook where they rented a cottage whose previous tenants had included members of Spandau Ballet.

"It was bigger," admits Steve, "but it was difficult living together like that for so long. You had to compromise on everything, even what television shows you wanted to watch."

"It was pretty good," Rick insists, "apart from when the Fun Police showed up (the Fun Police being the trio's respective girlfriends). Occasionally there was a little bit of niggling going on between the girls, but we were fine on our own."

Rick developed a talent for cooking tasty Indian curries. Phil, a vegetarian, dabbled in stir-fry dishes and ordered a lot of Indian and Japanese take-outs. Steve would periodically whip up a real mean beans-on-toast. And two or three times a week, they would get together and jam in the dining room, where they had set up a little heavy metal workshop with Phil's stack of Marshall amps and Rick's drum kit.

"When we first moved into the house," Phil explains, "it was beautifully decorated. It had a brand new dining table. Well, we moved it all out and put all this other shit in there – speakers, amps, drums."

The jams would usually start with a stab at some Joe Walsh or Led Zeppelin ditties. Then, Rick says, "we'd start playing anything that came into our heads. Phil would play something and I'd set up a rhythm. We'd even do original stuff that he was messing around with, putting down a few demos live. I actually heard a few songs, like *Love and Affection*, go from one of those demos to being a multi-track recording, about to be mixed and put on the album."

If his roomies were busy in the studio, Rick would often work out in a Donnybrook gym, lifting weights with his right arm to strengthen the muscles in his shoulder, which had been badly bruised in the car accident. He built up his stamina by pedalling all over Dublin on a bicycle equipped with a special handbrake and gear arrangement. He also practiced the drums on his own, regularly putting in eight-hour days. Phil says Rick

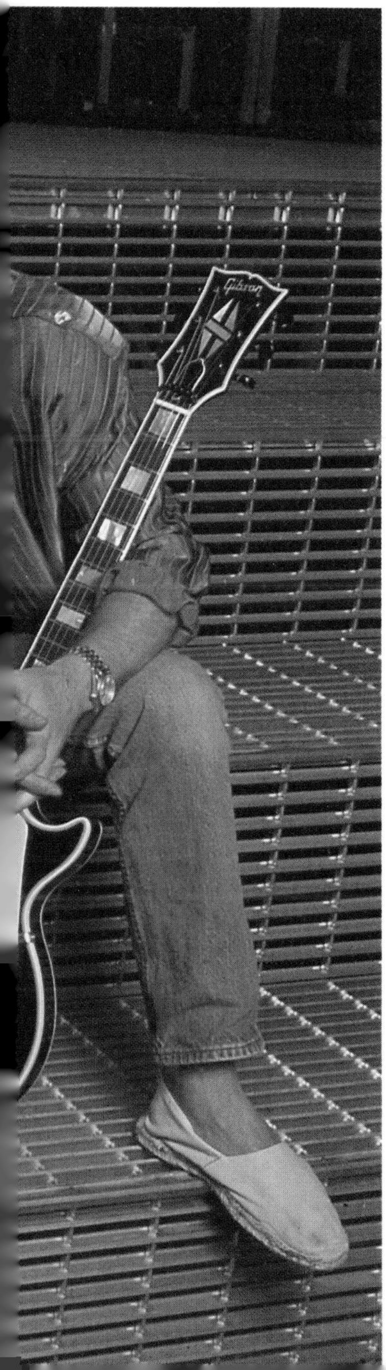

"resigned himself to the fact that he would have to rehearse his ass off. And it was a real pain for us sometimes, living there. He was waking me and Steve up in the morning – boom-boom-*brrrrrump!* But we figured 'Fuckin' A, peace, man, go for it.' And it made a difference. When we got ready to tour later on, it was obvious he could play on his own."

By now, Rick's kit was in good working order, with most of the bugs worked out. It was basically a standard Simmons electronic kit, with six hexagonal pads where cymbals, snares and tom-toms would be, plus a large bass "drum" pad. The actual sound of the pads was controlled by a patchboard with pre-sets for whatever arrangement of tones, timbres and special effects were required for a certain song. The notable difference between this and other Simmons kits was the array of footpads under Rick's feet.

The pedals had, indirectly, been Mutt Lange's idea. Mutt believed that Rick could easily compensate for the loss of his arm by utilizing his feet more. In the hospital, Rick tested his foot coordination by tapping on a piece of foam at the end of the bed. When he got into a wheelchair, he tapped on the metal footplates in time to his favorite records, trying to mimic the drum parts. Instead of playing the parts with his left arm, he "played" them with his left foot.

Rick then worked on a design for a special footpedal with a Sheffield engineer named Peter Hartley, who had also built Sav's bass gear. After experimenting with a couple of prototypes, because of problems with controlling the speed at which the pedal would trigger the sound, Rick eventually settled on a version made by Californian Arnt Anderson. By the time Def Leppard finally hit the road, Rick had as many as six pedals under his feet. Several major two-armed drummers, like Mel Gaynor of Simple Minds, expressed interest in using the pedals in their own kits.

But for Rick, practicing was not just a matter of mastering the kit and tightening his time. It was more like psychotherapy, coming to terms with his disability and confronting a difficult future as a working musician. The frustration would mount as he missed a beat here and screwed up a lick there. He'd think "Fuck it" and break for a beer. After a half hour or so of brooding, he would take a deep breath and have another go at it. A few of those eight hour days were actually four hours of playing and four hours of paralyzing anxiety.

The rest of the band, in a wisely understated way, continued to provide support and encouragement. At this point, Rick did not want or need sympathy for his condition. It was more important that Def Leppard shared the confidence he was starting to develop himself.

"Joe came up with a lot of good things in the early days, just pushing me to practice," he remembers.

" 'Never mind the way you look,' he'd say. 'You're the same guy you were before. Get up to that practice room, sit there and play until you are blue in the face, until you can't stand it anymore. You will do it. I know you will.'

"He had real confidence in me, so I felt it was my duty to show the band that I *could* do it. To say that the way I looked, the way I was now, didn't effect what he thought of me – that was the nicest thing anybody could say."

The second nicest thing anybody could say to Rick Allen or anyone else in Def Leppard was "Okay, boys, showtime!" Phil and Steve had done the odd guest shot on stage during the Dublin winter of Leppard's discontent. They plugged in with a local pub band, No Sweat, one night for a couple of numbers, the first time the Terror Twins had played together on stage since the Far East *Pyromania* shows. In Paris, Phil hopped on stage with pals Motley Crue for a tear through *Jailhouse Rock*.

Joe Elliott celebrated Christmas, 1985 by joining Elton John on stage at Wembley Arena in London with a few other minor pop deities like Rod Stewart, George Michael of Wham!, Nik Kershaw and Gary Kemp and John Keeble of Spandau Ballet. Joe and the other Leppards had met Elton in a TV studio two years before, at which time Ol' Four Eyes told the band he loved the *Pyromania* album. When he passed through Dublin on his '85 tour, Elton extended an invitation to Joe to come down to Wembley and take part in an encore singalong. Joe accepted, only to discover when he arrived for soundcheck that he didn't know the song Elton had picked for the grand

finale, Marvin Gaye's *Can I Get a Witness*. He spent a couple of hours before the show sitting in a car in the backstage area, trying to learn the words from a tape of Elton's show the previous evening.

"He put this daft wig on for the encore and then he introduced everybody as we came out. It was nice that he introduced me first, because there was no real way I was going to follow Rod Stewart and George Michael. He said 'Please welcome Joe Elliott from Def Leppard' and I got a pretty good reception, although there was probably a lot of people wondering 'What the hell is *he* doing here?' "

At the end Joe and Rod Stewart took their bows together and headed backstage for a celebratory drink. "Rod had this brilliant black-and-white checked suit on, and when he got up to get a drink, he lifted his arm up and the suit still had the price tag on it. No one else was around, so I reached up, pulled off the tag, threw it in the trash and said 'I won't say anything about it if you don't.' "

Those occasional guest appearances did wonders for Def Leppard's mounting depressions, but they were no substitute for real roadwork. Relief finally came in the summer of 1986 when Peter Mensch booked four shows for Leppard as part of a Monsters of Rock heavy metal package tour of Europe. In addition to playing the major Monsters of Rock all-day bash at Castle Donington in England, the band would also do shows in Sweden and Germany, third on the bill between speed-metal kings Motorhead and alternating headliners Ozzy Osbourne and the Scorpions.

It wasn't exactly the big world tour they wanted so badly, but as Phil says, "if we hadn't done those Monsters of Rock dates, we'd have been in serious psychiatric trouble." Rick was as ready as he'd ever be for the fateful roadtest and the new album was so far behind schedule that another three or four weeks wouldn't make any difference. Mensch booked an additional week's worth of warm-up shows in Ireland, mostly in small clubs to let the band iron out any wrinkles before they started doing the festival shows.

Although second drummer Jeff Rich had by this time joined Status Quo full-time and had a tour diary of his own to worry about, he agreed to work the Leppard shows into his schedule. While Jeff finished off a few Quo dates in July, the band – minus Joe, who was in the studio with Mutt – rehearsed in an old Dublin factory for five days with Rick on his own. They did another four days with Jeff when he returned and then went over the proposed set list for one more week with Joe.

The set list, according to Joe, pretty much wrote itself. "Obviously, we were going to play *Rock of Ages, Photograph, Rock! Rock! (Till You Drop)*. It was a one hour set and seventy-five percent of the set picked itself." The plan was to open with *Stagefright* and do the first two songs with Rick drumming on his own, as proof that he really was playing and not using tapes or other duplicitous gear. Then Jeff would come up behind the second kit and the band would rip through the bulk of the old *Pyromania* tour set. They added *Too Late for Love*, which the band had never played live, and decided to use *Love and Affection* and *Run Riot* (Joe: "downright blitz-a-rama") as a preview of the new album. *Photograph, Bringin' on the Heartbreak, Switch 625*, and *Wasted* would be the big finish with *Travelin' Band* as the encore, provided they got one.

Four days before the first show, the band got totally blotto at a bar called the Pink Elephant in honor of Joe Elliott's twenty-seventh birthday. Joe got so ploughed he couldn't sing at rehearsal the next day. By the next Tuesday, August 5, he was suitably recovered as Def Leppard boarded a mini-bus and set out on the five-hour drive from Dublin to Cork, the first stop on what would turn out to be a memorable adventure.

CHAPTER 11

Hi Ho! Hi Ho! It's Off to Work We Go!

For Def Leppard, the drive to Cork was like a school picnic, all yucks and giggles despite the ominous weather and unspoken fears about the evening ahead. "It was lashing down with rain," recalls Joe, "but we didn't care. It was the first time we'd even been out to play in ages."

Like most of the other venues on the Irish tour, Connolly Hall in Cork was small – capacity 1000, practically microscopic compared to the hockey arenas and outdoor baseball stadiums Leppard had played in America. But these little clubs and theaters were the perfect laboratories for Leppard to test their long-dormant road mettle. "If we made a mistake, it didn't matter," argues Joe. "And in the places where we played, if we made a mistake, they'd probably clap anyway. Because nobody ever plays in Ireland."

The Cork gig was far from sold out, a couple of hundred bodies at best, although the band was impressed anybody had shown up at all. For a half hour before showtime, everyone rummaged through their road cases trying to find something snazzy to wear. They ended up going on in just T-shirts and jeans, each Leppard downing a shot of brandy to calm their collective nerves. Even Rick, who was used to performing in just gym shorts, agreed to wear a T-shirt. "I didn't want to look like a freak up there. And I still had a lot of scars on my shoulder. Besides, I couldn't be up there wiggling my stump around with all these little girls at the front of the stage."

Of all the Leppards, Sav had the worst case of stage fright. "I was more nervous for that first gig than any other we've ever done. I don't know what it was. Maybe it was just the strange feeling, after all that time in the studio, of performing for people that had paid to get in. There was no stopping halfway through a song and doing it again."

The backstage atmosphere, according to Sav, "was like a football team before a match." Most of the dressing room pep talk was for Rick's benefit. "I felt for him," Sav admits. "It wasn't just doing it that was important for him. It was doing it so other people could *see* him doing it."

"Then we all went out on this tiny stage," Phil recalls, "hit those first few chords and, suddenly, we all remembered." It was, Joe echoes, "like we'd never been away."

Rick's timing was a little shakey during the set opener, *Stagefright*,

although even without Jeff up there to cover for him on the first few songs, nobody seemed to spot the screwups. "I was messing up all the time, but I covered my mistakes pretty well. I'd miss the odd beat here and there. Or sometimes I'd hit the wrong preset and the kit's sounds would be all set up for a different song. I'd hit the drum and get the wrong sounds. Also, it would get so sweaty on stage. When it got damp, the patchboard had a tendency to change the presets on its own. It was all a bit hairy for me at times." Phil and Steve were having too much fun to notice, revelling in their stock guitar-hero poses and getting up to all the old mischief – kicking each other in the ass, doing silly walks across the stage, flicking switches on each other's guitars as they passed. Incredibly, on that tiny stage, they never once bumped into each other.

Joe refused to milk the occasion with any glad-to-be-back stage raps. He did not want to spoil the band's first show in two and a half years with any "stupid cabaret crap." But when the band retired to the Victoria Hotel for a little *aprés-gig* celebration, it was plain that a very heavy burden had been lifted from Leppard's shoulders. In order to preserve his voice for the next show, Joe kept his mouth shut for most of the party, opening it only to let the liquor in.

After raising the roof of Leisureland in Galway the next evening – same set, a shot of courage from the same bottle of brandy – Def Leppard headed for the town of Limerick. They were booked into a 1400-seat venue called the Savoy. Unfortunately, the promoter, Dennis Desmond, had sold less than two hundred tickets in advance. The band was enjoying a little pre-show beverage at a pub next to the Savoy when Desmond informed the band that if ticket sales didn't improve by showtime, he was just going to give the damn things away. At least it would make the place look a little fuller (and probably improve the evening's take at the bar).

By 8.30, one of Desmond's assistants was stopping into every pub in Limerick handing out Def Leppard tickets. The idea of giving the tickets away was hardly a blow to the band's ego. They thought it was hysterical – "Can you believe this? In America in '83, what people would have done for these tickets! Here, we can't even give them away."

When Leppard hit the stage at nine, there were less than three hundred people in the audience, at least a third of them there out of curiosity since they hadn't paid to get in. "We went out there," Joe says, "thinking 'There's nobody here, just a few kids down in front. But they deserve a good one.' " They got it. Leppard consensus is that Limerick was one of the hottest shows on the whole tour.

The next stop was a small holiday resort on the west coast of Ireland with the rather comic name of Ballybunion. With two days off before the show – Jeff Rich was booked to play three Status Quo gigs in between – the band hit the beach fully equipped with flip-flop sandals and silly hats, spending the evenings in local pubs where they were occasionally approached by visiting American teens who could not believe (a) that a superstar band like Def Leppard would even be in a place like Ballybunion or (b) they would actually play there. "They'd see these posters for the gig in a fish'n'chip shop window," Joe laughs, "and go 'What? Def Leppard playing *here*?'"

"Here" turned out to be a shoebox-sized venue called the Atlantic Hotel. The stage was barely large enough to fit Rick and Jeff's drum riser, much less the band itself. Nevertheless, in an attempt at setting some kind of Guinness World Record for most-gear-on-smallest stage, the crew piled every piece of Leppard equipment they could on the stage, including enough PA speakers to blow Ballybunion right off the Irish map.

Trouble loomed again at 6pm when Jeff didn't show up for the soundcheck. He'd missed a connecting flight from Stockholm, where he had played a midnight show with Status Quo the night before. There was a taxi waiting for Jeff at nine when he arrived at Shannon Airport near Dublin, an hour and a half's drive from Limerick. By 11:25, though, there was still no sign of Jeff at the hall. His taxi had broken down two miles outside of town.

Backstage, Joe says, Peter Mensch was whipping up the troops. "Mensch was screaming at us, 'This is your one chance to try Rick out on his own.' Sav is saying 'No' and I'm saying 'Oh, fuck, why not? It's only Ballybunion.' Besides we had to go on. We couldn't wait any longer. So we went for it."

Halfway through the sixth song, Jeff arrived at the hall and snuck up behind his drum kit. But the first five songs had already sealed his fate. "We were going mad" raves Joe, "the kids were going mad (Joe had his T-shirt ripped off by the crazed Yanks in the crowd). And it wasn't until a couple of songs into the show that I turned around and realized Jeff wasn't there. I'd forgotten all about him. It convinced me and everybody else, especially Mensch, that we could play as a five-piece again. We always thought that we could, but we figured it would take about a year to get it together."

At a meeting the next morning, Peter and the five Leppards decided that Rick would play the next show in Waterford completely by himself. The stage at the club wasn't big enough for two drum kits anyway. Jeff took the news very well. He was suffering from exhaustion, the result of doing shifts with Leppard and Quo; unbeknown to Leppard, he'd collapsed on stage in Stockholm after playing four shows in three days. He agreed to hang around for the Waterford show in case Rick had any serious problems.

Rick didn't have any. At the end of the show, Jeff – who watched the entire set from the sound desk – told the band backstage "He's great. You don't need me." When Def Leppard pulled in to Dublin for the last show of the Irish tour, Jeff Rich was already back in London.

Dublin was almost like a hometown gig for the band. They had spent nearly half of the last three years there, doing pre-production and recording. Indeed, at the S.F.X. Hall on August 13, the freebies practically outnumbered the paying customers. Among the more than three hundred guests were Windmill Lane Studio staff, lawyers, accountants and their families as well as members of U2 and top Irish folk band Clannad. U2 drummer Larry Mullen raved about Rick's drumming after the show and at the post-show party people kept going up to Joe Elliott and saying "God, I can't believe it's really you up there." "That's because they'd never seen us as a band, actually playing," Joe explains. "As far as they were concerned, we were studio musicians."

As far as a lot of the metal fans at Castle Donington were concerned, Def Leppard were a bunch of studio pansies. Leppard's fame in England had peaked during the New Wave of British Heavy Metal scene of six years earlier. Since then, they were scorned by hardcore heavy metallurgists as teenybopper posterboys and puppets of America's FM radio Hitlers. Their extended absence since *Pyromania* hadn't helped. There was also the memory of their 1980 Reading Festival appearance where it rained cans and bottles.

Fortunately, at Donington the trash deluge was over before Def Leppard took the stage. The August 16 Monsters of Rock festival opened with Bad News, a heavy metal parody band formed by a group of popular British Monty Pythonesque comedians called The Young Ones. As they were filming their short raucous set for a future TV show, Bad News encouraged the assembled mob to hurl beer cans as well as verbal abuse at them. The gimmick worked too well. By the time Motorhead roared on to centre stage, the shower of garbage had reached monsoon proportions. Joe Elliott was backstage waiting to go on when he suddenly heard the music stop.

"I thought Motorhead's gear had broken down. But it was Lemmy; he'd stopped the show. Some kid had thrown something really heavy at him and he just stood there going 'I've been in this business for too fucking long to have you cunts throw things at me. If you're going to throw things, get it all over and done with. Throw it now! And anybody who throws it, have the guts to come up here so I can kick the shit out of you.' " Lemmy, a fearsome presence at the best of times with chiselled caveman features and long greasy hair, just stood there and waited. No talking, no music. And, as it turned out, no cans.

"Nobody threw anything after that. Which did us a big favor because we were up next."

Leppard didn't bother with a formal introduction. As Steve Clark explains, "we were playing in broad daylight. We didn't have any big lights or effects. We hadn't dressed up for it either. We just went out there and rocked and rolled for each other. If anybody else liked it, great." Joe went into his familiar repertoire of Mick Jagger-Gary Glitter poses while Phil and Steve turned on the guitar-heat Aerosmith style, jagged zigzag riffs punctuated by fireball bursts of feedback. At one point in the set, Steve slipped around the back line of amplifiers, snuck up behind Phil and gave him a wicked boot in the caboose.

The crowd's response was better than Leppard had ever expected. During the encore, while Rick was taking a brief drum break, Phil suggested to Joe that he give Rick a special introduction, something he hadn't done on any of the Irish shows. "So I went out after he was done and said 'Ladies and gentlemen, Rick Allen on the drums.' You could have knocked me over with a feather. The cheering was so loud they practically blew us off stage. I mean, they were louder than we were. I could barely hear Rick because of the big waves of 'YEAH!' which rolled over the stage."

It was an especially poignant victory for Rick. Before the tour, Ozzy Osbourne had told Peter Mensch that putting Rick Allen on display for fifty thousand headbangers amounted to nothing more than a freak show. At the end of the Monsters of Rock tour, Ozzy paid a vist to Rick's hotel room and took back every word he said.

Rick was the center of attention backstage as well as on stage. Drummers Herman Rarebell of the Scorpions and Lars Ulrich of Metallica both came over and paid their respects while a small army of photographers dogged Rick's every move before and after the set. "The lads would huddle together around me, so my condition wasn't so noticeable in the pictures. But it didn't bug me much." He was just happy to be playing on English soil again through a big PA. "Just doing the soundcheck the day before was great, being the Thunder God again!"

Reviews of Def Leppard's Donington triumph in the weekly English rock comics ranged from derisive ("Americanized monotony-merchants": *Melody Maker*) to ecstatic ("Their sound was pristine . . . and the clean cut razor-edged hooks which line their classy and almost sophisticated metal took the place by storm.": *Sounds*). The band had a week to let the compliments and complaints sink in before the next Monsters of Rock show in Stockholm. Joe was packed off to Wisseloord to cut some more vocals with Mutt Lange while Sav and Rick used up a couple of precious tax exile days in Sheffield visiting friends and family. Phil and Steve decided to recharge their batteries back in Paris.

They reconvened in Stockholm the day before the show, just in time to catch a local performance by Prince. Pop goddess Frida of the Swedish multi-billionaire quartet Abba was also there, which sent Steve Clark, an ardent admirer, into a state of near-paralysis. Already a bit tipsy anyway, he summoned up the courage to introduce himself by downing a fast brandy, blurting out "Hi, I'm a guitarist in a heavy metal band and I just want to say I think you're brilliant" and dashing off in mortal embarrassment without actually mentioning who he was or what band he was in.

He had good reason to be embarrassed at Stockholm's Rasunda Fotbollstadion the next day when, at one point during Leppard's set, he decided to pull a fast one on Phil Collen by racing across stage left and switching Phil's guitar off in mid-song. Too bad for Steve that it rained earlier in the day. As he zoomed past Phil, his foot hit the wet plastic covering at the side of the stage and he went down ass-first on the floor, knocking all the tuning heads off his guitar.

After Stockholm, Phil and Steve bopped back to Paris for two quick days of frolic, where they had another fateful encounter with His Purple Mini-Majesty, Prince. The Terror Twins attended Prince's Paris gig and, after getting a tip from someone in the lighting gang (Leppard had used the same crew on the *Pyromania* tour), talked their way into a secret post-show blowout at a Parisian jazz club called New Morning. When they were introduced to Prince, Phil boldly asked him why he wasn't playing as much lead guitar on this tour as he had in the past.

He got his answer when Prince and his band the Revolution, with Prince's father John Nelson on piano, took the New Morning stage for a surprise jam session. To Phil's astonishment, Prince donned a Les Paul guitar and kicked off a sizzling version of the Jimi Hendrix blues *Red House*, complete with a heartstopping guitar solo. "Here's Prince, in this little club," gulps Steve in awe, "playing guitar like Jimi Hendrix, just for Phil!"

Compared to that, the next Leppard show was a bit anti-climactic. The next-to-last stop on the tour, the Zeppelinfeld in Nuremberg, West Germany where Adolf Hitler once held huge outdoor Nazi rallies, was standard Leppard procedure – an hour out in the afternoon sun, knock

All on this page: Donington '86.
ABOVE: Joe with Bad News and Marillion's Fish .

'em dead with the hits. Sav and Joe were in less than peak physical condition – Sav with food poisoning, Joe with a sore throat – but Joe was excellently attended by Ozzy Osbourne, who gave Joe some honey in a hot lemon drink half an hour before showtime.

Mother Nature had big plans for Leppard's August 31 Monsters of Rock finale in Mannheim. When the band arrived at the Maimarktgelaende stadium, the sky was a bright iridescent blue and the sun smiled down on the thousands of boozed-up metalheads below. When Leppard took the stage promptly at 4.30, however, the skies turned pitch-black and, as if triggered by Phil Collen's first opening kerrang! in *Stagefright*, a rain of hurricane intensity exploded over Mannheim. Panicked roadies scurried across the stage trying to cover the electrical equipment with plastic sheets. Even Rick, who was 22 feet back from the front of the stage, got drenched in the storm. Soaking wet even before they'd finished *Stagefright*, the band decided to play out the set in defiance of the weather.

"With all the speakers covered up with plastic, the guitars sounded like banjos," Joe cracks up. "The rain was coming down so hard it was bouncing off the carpet on the stage. And all you could see for miles were umbrellas." Iron Maiden singer Bruce Dickinson, who was watching the show at the side of the stage, ran out in the middle of *Love and Affection* and opened up a giant umbrella over Elliott's head. Joe introduced him at the end of the song as "Bruce Dickinson on lead umbrella."

The rain stopped just as Leppard finished the last song of the set. Not about to be upstaged by the weather, Phil and Steve had something extra-special planned for the encore. Unbeknown to the rest of the band, the two guitarists had hatched a plot with Peter Mensch to go on for the encore wearing Scottish kilts – with nothing underneath, of course. Joe recalls hearing Mensch say to Steve before the Mannheim show, "Are you going to do it? Remember, this is your last chance to do it this year."

"I couldn't figure it out," Joe continues. "I knew they were going to do something daft, but I had no idea it would be that." Well, out they went looking like the Brothers MacLeppard, cutting their heavy guitar hero poses in two traditional plaid Scottish kilts. Joe literally almost died laughing. He couldn't even finish singing the song. He just got down on his hands and knees, banging on the floor in hysterics. Even funnier was the Scottish

He was quarantined in London for a couple of weeks. But that queer Leppard karma returned with a vengeance on the day Joe arrived back in Holland. Mutt Lange was making his daily morning commute to Wisseloord when his car hit an icy patch of asphalt and ploughed into an oncoming van. Sav, fifteen minutes behind Mutt in a taxi with Leppard aide d'camp Malvin, was speechless when he saw the gruesome sculpture of crumpled metal ahead.

"Mutt had already been taken to the hospital. We saw the crash and the police cleaning things up. We knew Mutt was okay because we were told the driver got out and tried to free the other guy. But we weren't sure about the other guy."

A policeman told Sav and Malvin that the driver of the van had lost both his legs in the accident, which fortunately turned out not to be true. But it was all the scare Sav could take. "I was thinking, there are more important things in life than getting this stupid record done. Rick had lost his arm, we thought this innocent guy had lost his legs. It just wasn't worth it."

Rick had other thoughts racing through his mind when he got the news. He had arrived at Wisseloord that morning expecting to see Mutt already at the studio console. "Everything that happened to me came rushing back. As soon as I heard about it, I rushed straight over to the hospital. But it was the only time I went. Because I knew he didn't want me over there bothering him," Rick laughs. "He wanted me to be in the studio working." In fact, Mutt had sustained serious, but not critical, leg injuries. Within three weeks, he was back behind the mixing desk.

kid who managed to scam his way backstage. Joe asked him what he thought of the kilts and the kid replied "What kilts? I couldn't even see the stage from where I was standing."

"Forty thousand Germans think Phil and Steve are up there wearing dresses and the one Scottish kid in the entire crowd couldn't even see the kilts."

Before returning to the drudgery of making Album Number Four, Def Leppard bussed over to Hamburg to take part in a charity soccer match with members of Iron Maiden and Bon Jovi, pitted against a team of local German ex-footballers and radio jocks. But after that, it was back to work, mostly for Joe, still singing under Mutt's watchful eye, and Rick, now in the process of working out Fairlight drum programs for the record. Joe and Mutt also came up with another new song, a hot minimalist getdown called *Pour Some Sugar on Me* created in the image of the glitter-funk hit *New York Groove* from ex-Kiss guitarist Ace Frehley's 1978 solo album.

By now, the album at least had a title – *Hysteria*. "We used to have two name columns," notes Sav. "There wasn't much in the 'serious' column. *Animal Instincts* is the only one I can remember. Then there was the 'joke' column. Most of the titles in that one were takeoffs on *Pyromania*, like *Paranoia*. One of those was *Hysteria*. As I remember it, Rick came up with that one. He meant it as a joke, but it caught us all in a serious moment and, for some reason, it stuck. Mensch liked it, Joe said 'Well, it's alright,' and I said 'I don't mind.' So it stuck. Nobody objected to it, anyway."

Subsequent events made the title particularly ironic. In late November, Joe Elliott came down with the mumps.

It was a screwy way to end the year. A successful mini-tour, mumps and a potentially fatal auto accident. And still no album. In response to increasingly tiresome queries about the record, Peter Mensch had printed up sets of three T-shirts apiece. One said, on the front, "Yes", and on the back, "Mutt Lange Does Exist, Rick Allen Is Playing Drums And We Are Recording a New Album." Another said "No" and, on the reverse, "We Haven't Split Up." The last one said "Not Yet" and, on the flipside, "Listen, If It Was Ready, You Would Have Heard It." It was a funny idea, but with a grim air of desperation about it.

The best Def Leppard could do was carry on and pray that 1987 would bring a major reversal of fortune. Mutt swore he'd finish recording in January and mixing in March. That would mean an album by July. Maybe. All the band could do was soldier on in the hope that the past three years, in spite of all the cockups, false starts and one-in-a-million disasters, would ultimately be worth it. At least that's what Rick Savage, his still boyish face pale with exhaustion and etched with small but visible lines of worry, said one night over a beer at the pinball machine in the Wisseloord lounge.

"When we started this band, we always concentrated on the songs. If we had five good songs together, we wouldn't just slap four more 'okay' ones together just so we could go out and play. That's why we spent so much time in that spoon factory in Sheffield before we went out to play. We did that first gig only because Steve was so pissed off and threatening to quit if we didn't go out and play a gig.

"But there was always that feeling there – that we have to do it right. Or we don't do it at all."

CHAPTER 12

EPILOGUE

You figure it out. Def Leppard spent over three years writing, arranging, recording, re-recording and re-re-recording their fourth album, *Hysteria*. Then they turned right around and in only ten days at Wisseloord during February, 1987, the band cut almost an entire album's worth of tracks – live, for the most part, in the studio with Rick behind his special Simmons kit, with five of the eight songs mixed by Joe and Steve – for use as B-sides with the projected *Hysteria* singles.

"We came out after doing all those B-sides," says Joe, "thinking 'Why did the album take so damn long?' Because those B-sides sounded alright. It felt very odd. But we had a certain standard that we'd developed, one that had been battered into us by Mutt to a great degree. And when we sat down and actually listened to the tracks, there was a vast difference between recordings on *Hysteria* and the B-sides we did. But still, those B-sides weren't too bad."

"Indeed, they were B-sides that any lesser band would have been proud to include on a full-length LP. What's more, they sounded like the work of a band itching to get into a recording studio after a long layoff, not vice versa. The actual completion of *Hysteria* at the end of January, 1987, was an occasion marked not by celebration but almost utter exhaustion. Mutt had moved shop back to the Windmill Two studio in Dublin, where he spent eight days cutting vocal tracks with Joe for *Pour Some Sugar on Me* and *Armageddon It*.

"*Armageddon It* was the last one," according to Joe. "Mutt and I were the only ones in the studio. And as soon as I finished doing the last bit of that song, it wasn't so much a feeling of anti-climax as it was an inner sense of being totally relieved. I didn't jump up and down. We didn't hug each other and drink tons of champagne. It was more like 'Oh, we're finished, man. This is great.' We shook hands, sat down, looked at each other and we both let out a big sigh."

Mutt still had the mixdowns to do, a process that was scheduled to take at least two months. Aware that they were now looking at, at the very least, a full year of non-stop press interviews, radio promotion and world touring, the Leppards decided to leave Mutt to his mixing for a while and spend what little free time they had left to them visiting their families and psyching themselves up for the grind ahead.

Monsters of Rock tour 1986: Castle Donington, England.

"For the first half of Mutt's mixes, we didn't do anything," explains Joe, "other than mentally prepare ourselves for what we had ahead of us. Also, we spent time individually learning our parts, so that when we did get together for tour rehearsals, we wouldn't turn up not knowing them. We had to be ready to get in there and basically do a live version of an album that had been recorded piecemeal."

The way Leppard whipped through those B-sides at Wisseloord, then, wasn't just a revolution. It was proof that they were ready to take on all comers. Resurrected from the *Hysteria* Dead Dogs File were *Ring of Fire* and *Fractured Love*, both given a new coat of heavy metal paint. Two *Love Bites* prototypes, retitled *I Wanna Be Your Hero* and *Tonight* respectively, were also cut anew. A brand new rocker, *Tear it Down*, had actually been written in rehearsal shortly before recording.

The Leppards also worked up new arrangements of their own mouldy oldies *Switch 625* (now played in 3/4 time and rechristened *Swing 625*) and *Ride Into the Sun*, the leadoff track on the nine-year-old Bludgeon Riffola EP. Joe thinks it was Steve who suggested exhuming *Ride Into the Sun*. It made sense, at least as a B-side anyway. Rick and Phil had not played on the original recording and Sav told Joe that he'd always wanted to give the song another shot on record. Phil suggested changing the meter of the song a little and Joe asked for a chance to overhaul the lyrics before overdubbing his vocal.

"The original ones," he admits, "were pretty embarrassing. But after we cut it, the song didn't sound ten years old at all. The actual attitude when we did it was that it would be a nice collector's item for people who buy the singles. But it was such a vibe recording it because it was so spontaneous. It didn't matter the words were ten years out of date."

During the sessions, Def Leppard also cut a riotous version of the old Englebert Humperdink saloon song *Release Me* with a special guest vocalist – roadie Malvin Mortimer. Malvin's talents, it turned out, were not limited to merely moving gear. His brother had been the singer with a classy Welsh pub-rock band called Racing Cars in the mid-Seventies and Malvin was a pretty smooth singer himself. In fact, he could prove it anyday, at anytime, by stepping into impromptu performances of *Release Me* at a moment's notice. "He always sings it," says Joe. "He does it when he walks around on stage, in the studio, in the bath, in the middle of a shopping center. I made a video of him singing *Release Me* in an airport once."

So the Leppards hatched a plan whereby they coaxed Malvin into the studio under the pretense of cutting a guide vocal for another song. "We didn't tell him we were going to play *Release Me*, Joe cackles. "We had already cooked up an arrangement, so we went right into the song, he sang it and we recorded it first take." The result was, literally, hysterical. Malvin ripped into the song with a fervor that quickly turned into vengeance. His veins bulged, his face turned beet-red and, at one point when the band suddenly went into a higher key, he burst into expletives while the Leppards burst into laughter.

We had to re-record the last twenty seconds of the song because we were laughing so hard," Joe raves. "Steve fell down and nearly broke his guitar. Rick's drum stool almost collapsed. Everybody was in tears from laughing so much. I was in the control room scraping myself off the carpet. And Malvin's face was so red it looked like something out of *Scanners*, ready to explode.

"Afterwards, he went back and redid the first two verses, to camp it up so he would sound more like a workingmen's club singer. But all the stuff at the end, when he's going for it, that was all first take. It was hilarious we thought so, anyway.

"The funny thing about the B-sides," Joe adds, rather proudly, "is that when we played them for Mutt, he said they were too good to be B-sides. He said they were wasted as B-sides, that it would be nice to save them for the next album. We told him we didn't want to constantly be putting stuff out that had three-year-old songs on them."

The irony was that for Def Leppard,

ABOVE: Vegetarian rock & rollers enjoy a little light reading.

the bulk of *Hysteria* was exactly that. On radio, in the press, on the road, they would now have to live with an album of songs that had practically been branded into their brains, a longplayer that had to measure up to three years' worth of expectations, not to mention *Pyromania's* mega-million sales. More importantly, *Hysteria* represented a kind of rite of passage for Def Leppard. In the four years since the release of *Pyromania*, throughout the tragedy of Rick's accident and the trauma of cutting a follow-up record, the members of Def Leppard had gone from the euphoria of adolescence to the often harsh realities of adulthood. They had done a lot of growing up during that time. It was now a question, once they hit the stage again, if they had also grown old.

For Joe, it was as if all that time had never passed. "As far as I'm concerned, I'm a twenty-four-year-old in a twenty-seven-year-old body," he insisted during a break in tour rehearsals that spring. "I'm just picking up where I left off. I *definitely* don't feel it. The only difference is the actual four years during which we experienced all that stuff. That's got to help. But at the same time, the adrenalin, the atmosphere within the band, that slight amount of immaturity that you have to have – it's all still there.

Look at Ozzy Osbourne. Ozzy is old enough to be a bank manager. But he's still got enough immaturity to jump around in silly trousers screaming 'Let's go fucking crazy.' Most forty-year-old people don't do that. He must still have a certain amount of boyhood in him and I think that's something I'll always have. I'm not the type who's going to fall gracefully asleep smoking a pipe in a rocking chair when I'm sixty. It's not my style.

Oh, I've had four years of experience dealing with regular things like not being ripped off by car mechanics. I'm wise to a lot of things, like picking the right kitchen company. But when it comes to being in the band, I'll be the first one out there doing splits from the drum riser, charging around like a bull elephant. I don't feel any older other than the wisdom that comes with age. But the youthful zest is still there, if not more. After four years of not seeing an audience, we're itching to do it again."

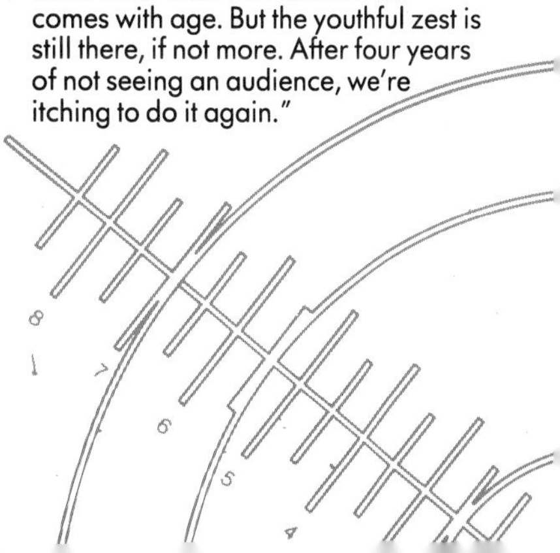

DUNLOP

DISCOGRAPHY

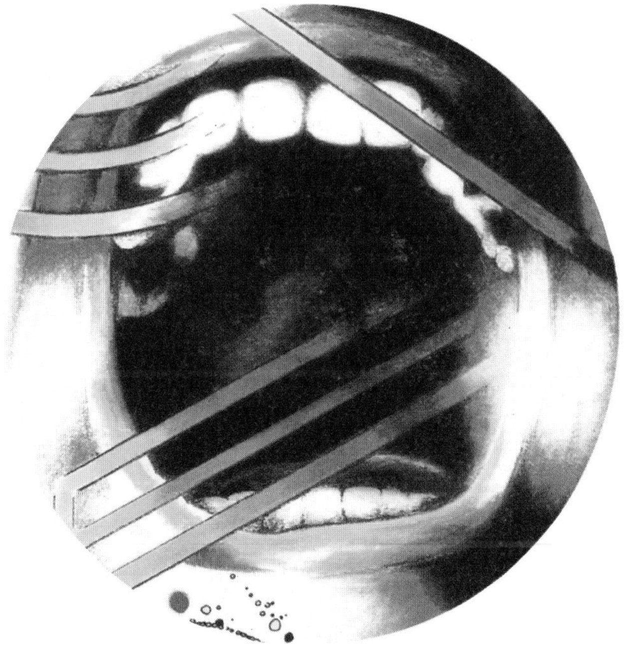

Thanks to Kathleen Kay Clark for compiling the bulk of this discography and to the legion of Def Leppard fans who helped her. If it isn't listed here, it probably doesn't exist.

EP's

The Def Leppard EP –
Bludgeon Riffola SRTS/78/CUS 232
JANUARY, 1979
Side I – *Ride Into the Sun/Getcha Rocks Off*
Side II – *The Overture*
The first pressing of *The Def Leppard EP*, a seven-inch disk playing at 33 1/3, was 1000 copies. The label was red and the cover was an illustration by Dave Jeffrey of a leopard and an old Victrola in the style of "His Master's Voice."

The Def Leppard EP –
Bludgeon Riffola MSB 001
1979
Side I – *Ride Into the Sun/Getcha Rocks Off*
Side II – *The Overture*
The second pressing of *The Def Leppard EP* was done after the band signed with Pete Martin and Frank Stuart-Brown for MSB management (note the new catalog number with their initials). This pressing was 15,000 copies, this time in a plain white sleeve and a yellow label.

The Def Leppard EP –
Vertigo 6059 240
SEPTEMBER, 1979
Side I – *Getcha Rocks Off/Ride Into the Sun*
Side II – *The Overture*
Immediately after signing Def Leppard, Phonogram Records U.K. rush-released a new version of the EP on their Vertigo label. There was no picture sleeve and they reversed the order of the tracks on Side I.

7" SINGLES

U.K.

Wasted/Hello America –
Vertigo 6059 247
1979
These are the Nick Tauber-produced versions (the credit reads "Produced by Nick Tauber with Def Leppard"). The front cover of the picture sleeve is a series of 1979 color photos of the individual band members in concert. The back was a photo of a bejeweled white boot against a black background.

Hello America/Good Morning Freedom – Vertigo LEPP 1
1980
Good Morning Freedom, recorded during the sessions for *On Through the Night*, is available only on this single. The picture sleeve is a pen-and-ink illustration of a hand waving an American flag from the side of a boat

towards what looks like the New York City skyline.

Let It Go/Switch 625 –
Vertigo LEPP 2
1981
With picture sleeve.

Bringin' on the Heartbreak/Me and My Wine – Vertigo LEPP 3
1982
With picture sleeve.

Photograph/Bringin' on the Heartbreak –
Vertigo VER 5
1983
With picture sleeve.

Photograph/Bringin' on the Heartbreak – Vertigo VERQ5
1983
This special edition of the English *Photograph* single came in a deluxe picture sleeve which folded out into a 3-D cardboard camera with an insert photograph of Marilyn Monroe. One side of the box had slots to hold the record.

Rock of Ages/Action! Not Words –
Vertigo VER 6
1983
With picture sleeve.

Rock of Ages/Action Not Words –
Vertigo VERQ 6
1983
More 3-D picture sleeve fun. This time, the sleeve folded out into a grey and black cardboard "rock box". One side of the box had slots to hold your copy of plain old VER 6.

Rock of Ages/Action! Not Words
Vertigo VERP 6
1983
Cut-out picture disc of Phil's guitar.

Too Late For Love/Foolin' –
Vertigo VER 8
1983
With picture sleeve. There are two versions, both with identical picture sleeve front. Version A for the retail trade featured the band on stage, and Version B– sent only to DJs – had the band dressed in soccer stripes.

Photograph/Bringin' on the Heartbreak – Vertigo VER 9
1984
Bringin' on the Heartbreak is the original 1982 version, not the '84 Mutt Lange remix.

U.S.

Rock Brigade –
Mercury DJ-659
1980
This seven-inch, 33 1/3 release was a promo-only EP featuring Def Leppard with two other Mercury acts, German heavy metal band Scorpions (*Falling in Love*) and a hip New Wave act from Atlanta, Georgia called the Brains (*Money Changes Everything*). Both acts, by the way, were signed to the label by Def Leppard's A&R guardian-turned-manager, Cliff Burnstein. The record came in a picture sleeve featuring a photo of the *On Through the Night* album.

Photograph/Action! Not Words –
Mercury 811 215-7
1983

Rock of Ages/Billy's Got a Gun –
Mercury 812 604-7
1983

Foolin'/Comin' Under Fire –
Mercury 814 178-7
1983

Bringin' on the Heartbreak (Remix)/ *Me and My Wine* (Remix)
Mercury 818 779-7
1984
The February '84 Mutt Lange remixes. With picture sleeve.

JAPAN

Photograph/Bringin' on the Heartbreak – Vertigo 7PP-99
1983
This Japanese release is a classy package with a photo sleeve insert. Notes are printed on the back of the insert in Japanese. The photo is a color shot of the band against the *Pyromania* rifle sight graphic.

Foolin'/Comin' Under Fire –
Vertigo 7PP-177
1983
This photo sleeve insert is notable for its shot, against a Union Jack background, of Rick Savage playing keyboards. Also pictured are Joe (in Union Jack T-shirt), Steve and Phil (in performance).

12" SINGLES

Bringin' on the Heartbreak/Me and My Wine, You Got Me Runnin' –
Vertigo LEEP 312
1982
With picture sleeve.

Photograph/Bringin' on the Heartbreak, Mirror, Mirror –
Vertigo VERX5
1983
With picture sleeve.

Rock of Ages/Action! Not Words –
Vertigo VERX6
1983
With picture sleeve.

Too Late for Love/Foolin', High'n'Dry – Vertigo VERX8
1983
With picture sleeve.

Photograph/Bringin' on the Heartbreak, Mirror, Mirror –
Vertigo VERX9
1984
With picture sleeve. (*Mirror, Mirror* is not listed on the cover.)

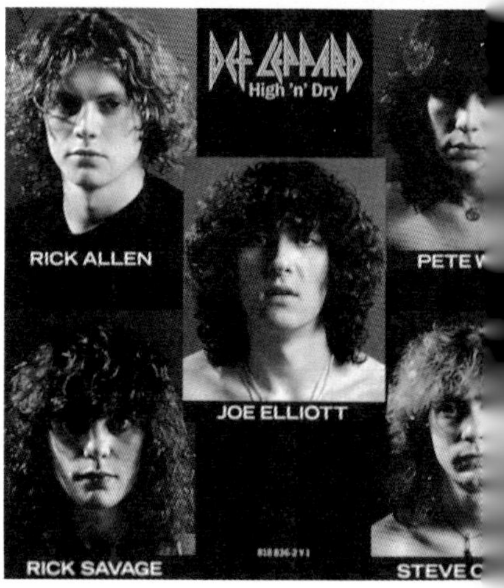

Photograph/Bringin' on the Heartbreak, No No No – Vertigo VERX9
1984
With picture sleeve. (*No No No* is not listed on the cover.)

Bringin' on the Heartbreak (Remix)/ *Me and My Wine* (Remix) – Vertigo VERX10
1984
Of the band's seven commercial twelve-inch singles in the U.K. to date, five of them include *Bringin' on the Heartbreak* and three feature *Photograph*.

U.S.

Rock Brigade – Mercury 2-55922
1980
A promo-only release with a picture sleeve featuring an illustration of a deaf leopard with a hearing horn.

Bringin' on the Heartbreak/Me and My Wine – Mercury MK 182
1981
A promo-only release in a plain white sleeve.

LPs

On Through the Night – Mercury SRM 1-3828 (U.S.)/ Vertigo 9102 040 (U.K.)
1980
Side I – *Rock Brigade/Hello America/ Sorrow Is a Woman/It Could Be You/ Satellite/When the Walls Came Tumblin' Down*
Side II – *Wasted/Rocks Off/It Don't Matter/Answer to the Master/ Overture*
Comes with a black and white lyric sheet.

High'n'Dry – Mercury SRM 1-4021 (U.S.)/ Vertigo 6359 045 (U.K.)
1981
Side I – *Let It Go/Another Hit and Run/High'n'Dry (Saturday Night)/ Bringin' on the Heartbreak/Switch 625*
Side II – *You Got Me Runnin'/Lady Strange/On Through the Night/ Mirror, Mirror (Look Into My Eyes)/No No No*

Pyromania – Mercury 810 308-1 (U.S.)/Vertigo VERS2 (U.K.)
1983
Side I – *Rock! Rock! (Till You Drop)/ Photograph/Stagefright/Too Late for Love/Die Hard the Hunter*
Side II – *Foolin'/Rock of Ages/Comin' Under Fire/Action! Not Words/Billy's Got a Gun*
Subsequently issued on compact disk, as were *On Through the Night* and *High'n'Dry* later on. (All three LPs available on cassette.)

Joe bought a pirate cassette copy of *Pyromania* in Bangkok during the band's 1984 visit to Thailand. The tape included *Let It Go* from *High'n'Dry* as well as *Photograph*, although the latter wasn't listed on the cover. *Billy's Got a Gun* was slightly amended to read *Bill's Got a Gun*. At least he didn't get ripped off. It cost him the Thai equivalent of $1.00.

High'n'Dry –
Mercury 818 836-1 (U.S.)
1984
This re-release includes the Mutt Lange remixes of *Bringin' on the Heartbreak* and *Me and My Wine*. Worth noting is the version of the updated *High'n'Dry* in, of all places, Saudi Arabia. *Me and My Wine* is actually printed as *Me and My* on the cover and label. The word *Wine* has been censored. Also, the diver in swim trunks on the cover was deemed too scandalous. Instead, he's wearing a full rubber wet suit.

First Strike –
Flash Records, 843 007 (Belgium)
1985
Side I – *Heat Street/Answer to the Master/See the Lights/When The Walls Came Tumblin' Down*
Side II – *Wasted/Sorrow Is a Woman/Glad I'm Alive*
A nasty piece of business, this one. This album consists of demo tapes produced by Pete Martin and Frank Stuart-Brown in Hull, England in 1979. Stuart-Brown had the tapes remixed in Germany in 1984 and then released the album while the band was recording their fourth record. The band's performances, considering when they were recorded, are nothing to be ashamed of, but the echo effects on Joe's vocals are annoying and the LP's total time barely clocks in at 25 minutes. Not surprisingly, Def Leppard secured a high court injunction to prevent manufacture and distribution of the LP. All existing copies were recalled. This album, for what it's worth, features the only "available" versions of the otherwise unreleased Leppard originals *Heat Street, See the Lights* and *Glad I'm Alive*. Joe Elliott would also like to point out that he is not included in the songwriting credits for *Answer to the Master* and *Sorrow is a Woman*. He wrote the lyrics to both songs.

Hysteria
Mercury HYSLP 1 (830 675-1)
August 1987
Side I – *Women/Rocket/Animal/Love Bites/Pour Some Sugar On Me/Armageddon It*
Side II – *Gods of War/Don't Shoot Shot Gun/Run Riot/Hysteria/Excitable/Love and Affection*

GUEST APPEARANCES

Tonni Wille – *Every Beat of My Heart*
A Dutch female singer. This song was included on her first album. Joe sang harmony vocals on the chorus.

Ricky and the Frog – *Lonely Road*
Joe sang all the chorus harmonies. The song was never released.

Lori Spree – *Those Faces*
A Dutch-American thrush. The song is a ballad and Joe did the backing vocals with Phil Collen.

Curtie and the Boom Box – *Black Kisses*
Phil played guitar. Went Top Ten in Holland.

Mink DeVille – *Italian Shoes (Sportin' Life*, German Polydor, 1985).
Joe, Phil and Steve Clark, with a classy assist from Mike Rogers and Malvin Mortimer from the Leppard crew, shouted the phrase "Italian shoes" everytime it popped up in the song.
All of these "guest appearances" were done in 1984-85 at Wisseloord Studios in Holland while the band was doing basic tracks and overdubs for the fourth album.

MISCELLANEOUS

Living Legends –
Vertigo 6498-072 (U.K.)
A Vertigo sampler featuring the label's heavy metal acts, including Status Quo, Rush, Black Sabbath and Thin Lizzy. Def Leppard tracks are *Rocks Off* (the version from *On Through the Night*) and *Satellite*.

Rock Gems – Polygram SA-048
A promotional collection released to hype the label's latest hard rock releases. Leppard's *Mirror, Mirror* is included.

Phil Collen Interview –
Ibanez BM 85007
1985
This is a twelve-inch picture disk featuring an interview with Phil Collen to promote Ibanez Guitars. (It was only available through musical instrument stores selling Ibanez gear.) The interview on this double-sided disk, which plays at 33 1/3, was conducted by Leppard co-manager Peter Mensch and recorded December 8th, 1984 at Wisseloord Studios.

LEPPARD ON THE AIR: Radio Sessions, etc.

1978

Radio session for BBC Radio Leeds

Session for Radio Hallam, a local Sheffield station. This session was recorded for a rock show hosted by DJ Colin Slade and included an unreleased Leppard original, *Beyond the Temple*.

Session for Radio Piccadilly, Manchester. These songs were recorded in an old church in Oldham

and were done without Pete Willis because he couldn't get off from work.

1979

Live radio broadcast of Def Leppard at the 1979 "Sheffield Show" in Hillsborough Park, Sheffield. The band was supporting a popular MOR vocal group called the Nolans.

BBC Radio One, "In Concert." Recorded in front of a live audience at the Paris Theater, London.

Studio session for Andy Peebles Show on BBC Radio One. Songs featured were *Glad I'm Alive, Wasted, Rock Brigade* and *Answer to the Master.*

1980

Live at the Reading Festival, August 26, Reading, England. This was broadcast on the Tommy Vance Rock Show on BBC Radio One.

Live in France, recorded and broadcast by Radio Luxembourg.

1983

Def Leppard live in Dortmund, West Germany as part of the *Rockpalast* TV-radio simulcast throughout Europe. The show was a heavy metal spectacular featuring Def Leppard, Iron Maiden, Scorpions, Judas Priest, Quiet Riot, Krokus and the Michael Schenker Group.

BOOTLEGS

Heavy Metal Battle VII
Side I – *Rock Rock! Till You Drop/ Billy's Got a Gun/Foolin'/Rock of Ages*
Side II –*Rock of Ages* (cont.)/*Let It Go/Wasted*
From the 1983 German *Rockpalast* television broadcast. The record is a ten-inch disk on green vinyl. Quality is decent, although the disk was mastered a bit fast. Credits are a little misleading, though: the label credits read "All songs played and composed by the Pages." Who?

Hit and Run
Side I – *Rock! Rock! Till You Drop/ Rock Brigade/Photograph/(Another) Hit and Run*
Side II –*Lady Strange/Billy's Got a Gun/High and Dry/Rock Of Ages*
Side III –*Overture/Bringin' on the Heartbreak/Switch 625*
Side IV –*Let It Go/Rocks Off/Wasted/ Travelin' Band*
This is an audience recording from Lyons, France on March 14, 1983. Sound quality is good stereo. This double album comes in a deluxe color cover.

Heavy Metal From Rockpalast '83
A compilation album from the same marathon metal German TV broadcast as *Heavy Metal Battle.* This features two tracks each from Ozzy Osbourne, Iron Maiden, Judas Priest and Def Leppard (*Rock of Ages, Wasted*).

Heavy Rock Brigade
Side I – *Rock Brigade/Photograph/ Another Hit and Run/Billy's Got a Gun/Rock of Ages*
Side II –*Travelin' Band/Let It Go/ Getcha Rocks Off/Wasted*
A decent audience recording, slightly marred by surface noise on Side II, of the band's first show with Phil Collen. It was recorded at London's Marquee Club on February 9, 1983 and comes on red vinyl in a black and white cover. The credits read "Produced by LIFE Records, 121 Great Avenue, New York." Yeah, sure.

There are no doubt other bootleg recordings of Def Leppard concerts and early radio broadcasts in circulation, most of them on cassette. Some of the recordings available include the complete set at the Marquee in '83 and a show at the Hammersmith Odeon, London. During the group's second European tour in 1983, Joe strolled into a clothing store and saw, much to his surprise a box of live bootleg cassettes, including tapes of Def Leppard's show from the night before. The tapes were selling for the equivalent of about five dollars.

DEF LEPPARD BOOK LIST-O-Mania

or Everything You Wanted to Know About Def Leppard That Didn't Fit Up Front

JOE ELLIOTT'S TOP FIVE

ALBUMS

Mott The Hoople – All of their albums, but especially *Wildlife* and *Mott*
David Bowie – *The Rise and Fall of Ziggy Stardust and the Spiders From Mars*
T. Rex – *Electric Warrior*
Queen – *Sheer Heart Attack*
Ian Hunter – *Ian Hunter's Overnight Angels*

SINGLES

Mott The Hoople – *All the Young Dudes*
The Babys – *Isn't It Time*
Rolling Stones – *Start Me Up*
T. Rex – *Get It On*
Alice Cooper – *Elected*

FAVORITE ALBUM TRACKS

Mick Ronson – *Angle No. 9 (Play Don't Worry)*
Mott The Hoople – *Thru' the Looking Glass (The Hoople)*
Alice Cooper – *My Stars (School's Out)*
Clannad – *Scarlet Inside (Legend)*
Psychedelic Furs – *Pretty in Pink (Talk Talk Talk)*
Punishment of Luxury – *Puppet Life (Laughing Academy)*
Doctors of Madness – *Out! (Figments of Emancipation)*
Montrose – *Rock Candy (Montrose)*
The Sensational Alex Harvey Band – *The Tale of the Giant Stone Eater (Tomorrow Belongs to Me)*
Kiss – *Detroit Rock City (Destroyer)*

STEVE CLARK'S TOP TEN

ALBUMS

Queen – *A Night at the Opera*
Led Zeppelin – *Physical Graffiti*
Led Zeppelin – *Houses of the Holy*
David Bowie – *Cat People* Soundtrack
The Who – *Who's Next*
Police – *Synchronicity*
Blondie – *The Best of Blondie*
David Bowie – *Let's Dance*
Queen – *Live Magic*
Led Zeppelin – *In Through The Out Door*

SINGLES

Queen/David Bowie – *Under Pressure*
Patti Smith Group – *Because the Night*
Police – *Every Breath You Take*
The Kinks – *Where Have All the Good Times Gone*
Rolling Stones – *Start Me Up*
Big Country – *Wonderland*
Simple Minds – *(Don't You) Forget About Me*
David Bowie – *Heroes*
Peter Sellers and Sophia Loren – *Goodness Gracious Me!*
Sting – *Russians*

PHIL COLLEN'S TOP TEN ALBUMS

Queen – *Sheer Heart Attack*
AC/DC – *Highway to Hell*
Billy Idol – *Rebel Yell*
ZZ Top – *Eliminator*
Prince – *Purple Rain*
Montrose– *Montrose*
Journey – *Escape*
Aerosmith– *Rocks*
Police – *Synchronicity*
Van Halen – *Van Halen*

SINGLES

Billy Idol – *Eyes Without A Face*
Police – *Don't Stand So Close (86)*
Queen – *Now I'm Here*
AC/DC – *Touch Too Much*
Montrose– *Bad Motor Scooter*
Prince – *Let's go Crazy*
Prince – *Little Red Corvette*
Rolling Stones – *Start Me Up*
Robert Palmer – *Addicted To Love*
Bon Jovi – *Livin' On A Prayer*

RICK SAVAGE'S TOP TEN ALBUMS

Queen – *Sheer Heart Attack*
Rick Springfield – *Living in Oz*
Queen – *A Day at the Races*
The Tubes – *The Completion Backwards Principle*
Boston – *Boston*
Mott – *Drive on*
Billy Idol – *Rebel Yell*
Kate Bush – *The Dreaming*
Ian Hunter – *Ian Hunter's Overnight Angels*
AC/DC – *Highway to Hell*

MOST MEMORABLE CONCERTS

Led Zeppelin, *Knebworth Festival, England, 1979*
Judas Priest, *Sheffield Top Rank, England, 1977*
Uriah Heep, *Sheffield City Hall, England, 1975*
AC/DC, *Glasgow Apollo, Scotland, 1980*
Journey, *Lexington, Kentucky, 1983*

RICK ALLEN'S FAVORITE DRUMMERS

IAN PAICE – (Deep Purple)
ROGER TAYLOR – (Queen)
DENNY CARMASSI – (Montrose/Heart)
STEVE SMITH – (ex Journey)
JOHN BONHAM – (Led Zeppelin)

"These drummers and a lot of others that I like and respect – Joe Vitale when he was with Joe Walsh, Phil Rudd from AC/DC – are people who were very important to me in the past. Now, I obviously have to look forward a little, look to the future. For example, I like Phil Collins a lot, particularly his use of electronic sounds. He's a very melodic drummer, the way he uses all those sounds. Mel Gaynor of Simple Minds is another. He's the most powerful drummer I've ever seen in a pop band."

ROLL OF HONOR ... THE LEPPARD LINE-UP

(November 1977 – January 29, 1978)

Joe Elliott	Vocals
Pete Willis	Guitar
Rick Savage	Bass
Tony Kenning	Drums

(January 29, 1978 – November 18, 1978)

Joe Elliott	Vocals
Pete Willis	Guitar
Steve Clark	Guitar
Rick Savage	Bass
Tony Kenning	Drums

(November 20, 1978 – November 26, 1978)

Joe Elliott	Vocals
Pete Willis	Guitar
Steve Clark	Guitar
Rick Savage	Bass
Frank Noon	Drums

(Borrowed from Next Band for EP)

(November 27, 1978 – July 11, 1982)

Joe Elliott	Vocals
Pete Willis	Guitar
Steve Clark	Guitar
Rick Savage	Bass
Rick Allen	Drums

(July 12, 1982 to present)

Joe Elliott	Vocals
Steve Clark	Guitar
Phil Collen	Guitar
Rick Savage	Bass
Rick Allen	Drums

WITH GUESTS
DEF LEPPARD
MAYFAIR
NEWGATE ST., NEWCASTLE
THURSDAY 13th SEPTEM
TICKETS £3·00 (INC VAT) ADVANCE MAYFAIR BOX OFFICE, 10·00 a.m. 5·00
TEL: NEWCASTLE 23109 OR H.M.V. RECORDS
Sounds
Geoff Barton
RIDE INTO THE SUN, Def Leppard
DIAMOND HEAD, Diamond Head,
A MILLION VACATIONS, Max Webster
From Sounds
GETCHA ROCKS OFF, Def Leppard, from 'Def Leppard' EP
Rose' (Vertigo)
(Bludgeon Riffola)
9 13 WATCH ME FLY, Ironhorse, from 'Ironhorse' (Scotti Bros.)
10 12 LONG LEGGED LINDA, Status Quo, from 'If You Can't
11 6 Stand The Heat (Vertigo)
(Force It (Chrysalis)
12 7
6059 247
DEF LEPPARD
"WASTED"
(Clark/Elliott)
"HELLO AMERICA"
(Savage/Clark/Elliott)
Produced by Nick Tauber with Def Leppard
of their niggling 'sameness'.
Deaf Leopard were HM as HM always was and always will be. Crosses, macho poses, bludgeon riffola that even the Sabs abandoned years ago, and — ironically, methought — the only band to screw the audience for an encore.
Monitors sounded very
we'd never
In her red satin
well, she took us
and when she asked
well, she said it
JUST GETCHA ROCKS OFF
Well when we finally
but she wasn't on her
because she'd brought
yeah, she must have been
and when they started
well we couldn't believe
because they'd got the
and they'd got us paralysed
JUST GETCHA ROCKS OFF !

TAKE ME TO the LIMIT
TEL
SHEFFIELD
TONIGHT
THE YOUNG KINGS OF ROCK
DEF LEPPARD
(Support Band: ANNIVERSARY)
DEF LEPPARD's EP, which has been getting played on Radio One and has resulted in hundreds of inquiries, has almost sold out of its original pressing. There are a few copies still available for £1.00 plus a 12½ stamp from Revolution Records, The Gallery, Sheffield. It's likely that a further pressing of the EP will be undertaken shortly and may receive widespread distribution through one of the independents.
Leppard
chance t
the music
IT'S hard to knock spots off Def Leppard, who are emerging from Sheffield's music jungle as a young band quite likely to
For such ten
ist
track
h 1979
mer
THE DEF LEPPARD E.P.
Joe "Zeff" Elliott
Steve Clark
Side One
RIDE INTO THE SUN
Savage/E
GETCHA ROCKS OFF
Savage/
Clark/W
guita
HELLO AMERI
Listen here with Def
PROMISING Sheffield rock outfit Def Leppard have gone on record with their debut EP cut at Hull's Fairview Studios.
Side 1 of the record — economically titled The Def Leppard EP — reveals the band in heavier mood, featuring Ride into the Sun, by bassist Rick Savage and singer Joe Elliott, and Getcha Rocks Off, with lead guitarist Steve Clark and Pete Willis joining the other pair on composing credits.
Flip over for the four-some's The Overture which includes flashes of their more melodic side.
Copies of the EP, produced by the lads themselves, are on sale in Sheffield record shops and at their concerts. Last night they were at Sheffield's Dial House SC with Bitter Suite, boasting a new PA.
Drums on Leppard's recording were played by session man Frank Noon, better-known for his work with The Next Band, who had a debut EP, also cut at Fairview, out last year.
ge/Elliott/Clark/Wil
t the other night
m door
le girl
gh heeled shoes
d to do
ere she was
e five or si
around
ce rockin
"I said, 'ODD NAME FOR A ROCK BAND, AIN'T IT?
RECORD WORLD SEPTEMBER 26,